The God Who May Be

INDIANA SERIES IN THE PHILOSOPHY OF RELIGION
MEROLD WESTPHAL, GENERAL EDITOR

The God Who May Be: A Hermeneutics of Religion

Richard Kearney

INDIANA UNIVERSITY PRESS
BLOOMINGTON AND INDIANAPOLIS

This book is a publication of

Indiana University Press
601 North Morton Street
Bloomington, IN 47404-3797 USA

http://iupress.indiana.edu

Telephone orders   800-842-6796
Fax orders   812-855-7931
Orders by e-mail   iuporder@indiana.edu

The paper used in this publication meets the minimum require-
ments of American National Standard for Information Sciences—
Permanence of Paper for Printed Library Materials, ANSI
Z39.48-1984.

MANUFACTURED IN THE UNITED STATES OF AMERICA

Library of Congress Cataloging-in-Publication Data

Kearney, Richard.
The God who may be : a hermeneutics of religion / Richard Kearney.
p. cm. — (Indiana series in the philosophy of religion)
Includes bibliographical references and index.
ISBN 0-253-33998-7 (cloth : alk. paper) — ISBN 0-253-21489-0 (pbk. :
alk. paper)
1. God. 2. Philosophical theology. 3. Possibility—Religious
aspects—Christianity. I. Title. II. Series.
BT103 .K43 2001
211—dc21
                                                        2001002818

3   4   5   06

For my late father, Kevin, and my mother, Ann

Contents

ACKNOWLEDGMENTS

I wish to acknowledge the indispensable support and encouragement of John Manoussakis, my assistant at Boston College; Merold Westphal, my general editor; and Dee Mortensen, my sponsoring editor at Indiana. Thanks are also due to Jack Caputo, my sparring partner and inspirational colleague, and to my wife, Anne, and daughters, Simone and Sarah, whose affectionate forbearance seemed endless, especially when they had heard the phrase "I'll be down when I've finished this paragraph" for the thousandth time.

The God Who May Be

Introduction

God neither is nor is not but may be. That is my thesis in this volume. What I mean by this is that God, who is traditionally thought of as act or actuality, might better be rethought as possibility. To this end I am proposing here a new hermeneutics of religion which explores and evaluates two rival ways of interpreting the divine—the *eschatological* and the *onto-theological*. The former, which I endorse, privileges a God who possibilizes our world from out of the future, from the hoped-for eschaton which several religious traditions have promised will one day come.

Taking four biblical texts—the burning bush, the transfiguration on Mount Thabor, the Shulamite's Song, and God's pledge in Matthew 10 to make the impossible possible—I will endeavor to retrieve their latent eschatological meaning in the light of contemporary philosophical debates (phenomenological, hermeneutic, and deconstructive). These new readings will challenge the classic metaphysical tendency to subordinate the possible to the actual as the insufficient to the sufficient. Instead of seeing possibility as some want or lack to be eradicated from the divine so that it be recognized as the perfectly fulfilled act that it supposedly is, I proffer the alternative view that it is divinity's very potentiality-to-be that is the most divine thing about it.

Refusing to impose a kingdom, or to declare it already accomplished from the beginning, the God-who-may-be offers us the possibility of realizing a promised kingdom by opening ourselves to the transfiguring power of transcendence. Each human person carries within him/herself the capacity to be transfigured in this way and to transfigure God in turn—by making divine possibility ever more incarnate and alive. This capacity in each of us to receive and respond to the divine invitation I call *persona*. In this sense, one might even say that it is, paradoxically, by first recognizing our own powerlessness—vulnerability, fragility, brokenness—that we find ourselves empowered to respond to God's own primordial powerlessness and to make the potential Word flesh.

According to this reading, God can be God only if we enable this to happen. Or to quote the poignant words of Etty Hillesum, shortly before she was executed in a Nazi concentration camp: "You (God) cannot help us, but we must help you and defend Your dwelling place inside us to the last."[1] This dwelling place—which transfigures and is transfigured by turn—is what I term *persona*.

The God of the possible—which I call *posse* in a liberal borrowing from Nicholas of Cusa—is one who is passionately involved in human affairs and history. And my basic wager is that this God is much closer than the old deity of metaphysics and scholasticism to the God of desire and promise who, in diverse scriptural narratives, calls out from burning bushes, makes pledges and covenants, burns with longing in the song of songs, cries in the wilderness, whispers in caves, comforts those oppressed in darkness, and prefers orphans, widows, and strangers to the mighty and the proud. This is a God who promises to bring life and to bring it more abundantly. A God who even promises to raise the dead on the last day, emptying deity of its purported power-presence—understood metaphysically as *ousia, hyperousia, esse, substantia, causa sui*—so that God may be the promised kingdom.

In this wager, I subscribe to that new turn in the contemporary philosophy of religion which strives to overcome the metaphysical God of pure act and ask the question: what kind of divinity comes after metaphysics? Here I acknowledge the formative influence of a number of thinkers, such as Emmanuel Levinas, Jacques Derrida, and Paul Ricoeur, with whom I had the good fortune to work during my doctoral studies in Paris in the late seventies and after. From Ricoeur and Levinas—the director and examiner, respectively, of my doctoral thesis *Poétique du possible*—I learned that the philosophical question of God is far from dead and may in fact be revived by innovative methods of thinking proposed by phenomenology and hermeneutics. Again from these thinkers—and from others such as Jean-Luc Marion, Stanislas Breton, Jean Greisch, and Jean Beaufret who also participated, along with Ricoeur and Levinas, in the 1980 conference "Heidegger et Dieu," which I co-organized in the Irish College in Paris—I learned that the dialogue between philosophy and religion is one of the most burning intellectual tasks of our time. And this conviction was further confirmed by my ongoing encounters with Jacques Derrida in Paris, beginning with our published dialogue "Deconstruction and the Other" (1982).[2] This contact was to prove for me a highly fruitful one, despite our philosophical differences, and took on an even deeper complexion during our exchanges at the Villanova conferences of 1997 and 1999 on Postmodernity and Religion.[3] It was during these same conferences, moreover, that I came into more immediate contact with the invigorating thought of John Caputo, co-director of these events. Indeed I would say that without the stimulation of these extraordinary colloquies, which brought together many of my French interlocutors (Derrida, Marion, Greisch) with a rich variety of Anglophone philosophers of religion (Westphal, Tracy, Taylor, Hart, Schwartz, Milbank, Dooley, and Richardson), this current volume would not have been written.

In this respect, I see the present work as a conjoining of my Parisian studies in the late seventies—culminating in the publication of *Poétique du possible* and *Heidegger et la question de Dieu*[4]—with my regular visits to Boston College and Villanova in the late eighties and nineties. And it is perhaps indicative of this debt that the first four chapters of this volume draw much of their material from both *Poétique du possible* (especially parts 3 and 4) and two of my Villanova Conference lectures.

But speaking of debts, it would be quite remiss of me not to also acknowledge here the dialogue I have been conducting over the years with several of my Irish colleagues who first reminded me of the importance of religious thought and kept my mind ticking over with their encouragements and enthusiasms: I am thinking particularly of Joseph O'Leary, Mark Hederman, William Desmond, Joe Dunne, Josephine Newman, Patrick Masterson, and Dermot Moran (the last three, former colleagues at University College Dublin).

What these respective dialogues—French, American, and Irish—taught me is that God is not a dead letter but a vibrant concern for our time. In spite of the vagaries of fashion, and interminable apocalyptic pronouncements on the death of God, the task of questioning the divine has arguably become more urgent than ever. Indeed, when UNESCO distributed a questionnaire to leading thinkers throughout the world several years ago asking what they considered to be the most important issue for our new millennium, the majority replied: religion. My question here is of course more specific and focused: it asks how we may overcome the old notion of God as disembodied cause, devoid of dynamism and desire, in favor of a more eschatological notion of God as possibility to come: the *posse* which calls us beyond the present toward a promised future?

This kind of questioning breaks open a space where what the prophets called "the Lord of History" may find a voice. It retrieves the inaugural name of the God of Exodus 3:14 not as the I-am-who-am of abstract subsistent being (as scholastic theologians assumed) but as the one who-will-be. Read from an eschatological, rather than purely ontological perspective, the God of Exodus and Transfiguration can be heard to say: "I am the one who will always be faithful, and by my faithfulness all future generations will know me and call me: I am the promise to remain with my people and they can all count on me in the future. I am the God not only of their memories and of their fathers and mothers, but also of their hopes and aspirations, of their sons and daughters."[5]

God will be God at the eschaton. That is what is promised. But precisely because this promise is just that, a *promise*, and not an already accomplished possession, there is a free space gaping at the very core of divinity: the space of the possible. It is this divine gap which renders all things possible which would be otherwise impossible to us—including the kingdom of justice and love. But because God is *posse* (the possibility of being) rather than *esse* (the actuality of being as fait accompli), the promise remains powerless until and unless we *respond* to it. Transfiguring the possible into the actual, and thereby enabling the coming kingdom to come into being, is not just something God does for us but also something we do for God. As the proverb goes, "God made the sea, we make the ship; He made the wind, we make a sail; he made the calm, we make oars."

This is why I suggest that the God of Exodus and Transfiguration, the God of Eros and Possibility, is a God who may be. And, by extension, this is why I argue throughout this volume that it is wiser to interpret divinity as a possibility-to-be than as either pure being in the manner of onto-theology, or as pure non-being in the manner of negative theology. To this end, I propose to rethink history as a chiasmus where God traverses being, the biblical *'esher* intersecting with the Greek *einai* and transfiguring it according to its image and desire. In this scenario, we may speak of God putting being into question just as being puts flesh on God. Or we may invoke, as I do in chapter 2 below, Eckhart's wonderful reading of the burning bush deity as *ebullutio*—an overflowing of light within light, traversing everything as it passes through air. (A sort of eschatological *nous poetikos*.) The divine possible takes its leave of being having passed through it, not into the pure ether of non-being, but into the future which awaits us as the surplus of *posse* over *esse*—as that which is more than being, beyond being, desiring always to come into being again, and again, until the kingdom comes. Here at last we may come face to face with the God who may be, the deity yet to come.

But does thinking of God as possibility make a difference? Does it really matter to us? I suggest it does.

First, it means that the presuppositions and prejudices that condition our everyday lives are put into question in the name of an unprogrammable future. For it is the divine "perhaps," hovering over every just decision or action that ensures that history is never over and our duty never done. The *posse* keeps us on our toes and reminds us that there is nowhere to lay our heads for long. God depends on us to be. Without us no Word can be made flesh. If Moses, for example, had not listened to the voice of the burning bush, there would have been no Exodic liberation. If the Shulamite woman had refused Solomon's advances, there would have been no theo-erotic song of songs. If a young maid from Nazareth had not said yes to the annunciating angel, there would have been no Christ. And if we say no to the kingdom, the kingdom will not come.

Second, the God-who-may-be reveals that since no die is cast, no course of action preordained, we are free to make the world a more just and loving place, or not to. We are thus reminded that if there is evil in our society—as there is—it is not the pre-established will or destiny of God (the error of metaphysical thinking about divinity as pure act and necessity) but *our responsibility*. For evil, as Augustine rightly noted, is the absence of God, the lack of divine goodness (*privatio boni*), the consequence of our refusal to remain open to the transfiguring call of the other *persona*—the summons of the orphan, widow, or stranger, the cry of the defenseless one: "where are you?" In short, interpreting God as *posse* rather than *esse* is a final "no" to theodicy. It reveals history to be a divine venture, and human adventure. This sentiment is strikingly echoed in Hans Jonas's statement in "The Concept of God after Auschwitz": "God divested himself of his deity—to receive it back from the odyssey of time weighted with the chance harvest of unforeseeable temporal experience: transfigured or possibly even disfigured by it. In such self-forfeiture of divine integrity for the sake of unprejudiced becoming, no other foreknowledge can be admitted than that of *possibilities*."[6]

Third, the God-who-may-be reminds us that what seems impossible to us is only seemingly so. For once transfigured by God all things are made possible again, disclosing the eschatological potentials latently inscribed in the historically im-possible. So that if we continue to look at the same event in the light of God's transfiguring power, we can now see (like Wittgenstein's experiment of seeing the cutout as a rabbit or a duck) the hitherto impossible as possible. The *posse* keeps us open to hope, even if it is hope against hope. In other words, the hope that in spite of injustice and despair the *posse* may become more and more incarnate in *esse*, transmuting being as it does so into a new heaven and a new earth—into what Cusanus (in a sense somewhat different from mine) calls *possest*.[7]

* * *

So how would I respond to the standard hermeneutic question: Where do you speak from? (*d'où parlez vous?*) How do I identify my own position? Philosophically, I would say that I am speaking from a phenomenological perspective, endeavoring as far as possible to offer a descriptive account of such phenomena as *persona*, transfiguration, and desire, before crossing over to hermeneutic readings. In this domain my primary intellectual mentors are Husserl, Heidegger, Levinas, Ricoeur, and Derrida. Religiously, I would say that if I hail from a Catholic tradition, it is with this proviso: where Catholicism offends love and justice, I prefer to call myself a Judeo-Christian theist; and where this tradition so offends, I prefer to call myself religious in the sense of seeking God in a way that neither excludes other religions nor purports to possess the final truth. And where the religious so offends, I would call myself a seeker of love and justice *tout court*.

But regardless of labels, I would like to think that the kind of reflections advanced in this book are vigorously ecumenical in terms of interfaith dialogue. And I would suggest, for instance, that the kind of detachment from excessive ego drives and obsessions which a liberating *posse* solicits is one shared, in different ways, by all genuine spiritual movements, East and West. Here I wholeheartedly subscribe to the view of Charles Taylor that Christianity and Buddhism display a common commitment to transcendence and the love of life. "In Christian terms, if renunciation decenters you in relation with God, God's will is that humans flourish, and so you are taken back to an affirmation of this flourishing, which is biblically called agape. In Buddhist terms, Enlightenment doesn't just turn you from the world, but also opens the floodgates of *metta* (loving kindness) and *karuna* (compassion) . . . the highest Buddha acts for the liberation of all beings."[8] If I do not make reference to non-Western religious thought in the chapters below, it is not, therefore, out of any Euro-centric presumption but because my limited competence confines me to the Judeo-Christian and Greco-Roman traditions.

Is there a name for the kind of philosophy of God I am adumbrating here? Not really. But I am tempted to float, nonetheless, a number of tentative quasi-names—or what I might call methodological pseudonyms. The first is *dynamatology*. This term derives from the Greek *dynamis*, meaning potentiality or potency, used by both Aristotle and the writers and commentators of the scriptures. The neologism, *dynamatology*, first came to me in conversation with an Irish playwright friend of mine, Tom Murphy, in the early eighties in Dublin when we were discussing some ideas for a new play he was working on, *The Gigli Concert*. In it there is a character who wants to teach people to "sing like Gigli," the great genius of Italian opera, thereby inviting them to come into contact with their innermost potential. The term Murphy and I hit upon to convey the meaning of this "logic of the dynamizing possible" was *dynamatology*. There was of course a certain ludic poetic license to this coinage which perhaps renders it more suited to theater than to philosophy in the strict sense. But then maybe philosophy needs a little poetics betimes.

A second name I would consider for this philosophy of *posse* is *metaxology*. This is a neologism borrowed from another Irish friend of mine; in this case a philosopher, William Desmond. Even though Desmond's understanding of the term differs somewhat from mine—he rethinks transcendence in largely Platonic-Augustinian terms—we share a common determination to choose a middle way (Greek, *metaxy*) between the extremes of absolutism and relativism.[9] In my own case, this middle space, or as I prefer to call it *mi-lieu*, is chosen as an alternative to what I consider to be two polar opposites in contemporary thinking about God (which sometimes end up colluding with each other), namely: (a) the hyper-ascendant deity of mystical or negative theology; and (b) the consigning of the sacred to the domain of abyssal abjection. In the first instance, God can take the form of a divinity so far beyond-being (Levinas, Marion, and at times even Derrida) that no hermeneutics of interpreting, imagining, symbolizing, or narrativizing is really acceptable. Indeed God's alterity appears so utterly unnameable and apophatic that any attempt to throw hermeneutic drawbridges between it and our finite means of language is deemed a form of idolatry.[10] In the second instance, the divine slips *beneath* the grid of symbolic and imaginary expression, back into some primordial zero-point of unnameability which is variously called "monstrous" (Campbell, Zizek), "sublime" (Lyotard), "abject" (Kristeva), or "an-khorite" (Caputo). While both positions push the notion of God to opposite extremes—to the highest of heights or lowest of depths—they share a common aversion to any mediating role for narrative imagination. For both, the divine remains utterly unthinkable, unnameable, unrepresentable—that is, unmediatable. The hermeneutic approach to religion I am espousing here, by contrast, seeks to engage just such a mediating function.

This brings me to a third pseudonym for my approach to the possible God: *metaphorology*. I use this term to convey my understanding of religious language as an endeavor to say something (however hesitant and provisional) about the unsayable. Here I borrow liberally from Ricoeur's notion that inventive hermeneutic readings of religious texts can spark off a rich play of metaphoricity resulting in a radical semantic augmentation (or "surplus of meaning"). In relation to hermeneutic interpretations of the Song of Songs, which I analyze in chapter 4, Ricoeur makes the point that no single writing or reading can capture the meaning of divine desire indicated in these verses. Hence it is by interanimating this text with other texts from the Scriptures and later traditions of interpretation (Talmudic, theological, Cabbalistic, mystical, psychoanalytic, etc.) that we can begin to approximate to some notion of divine desire with live metaphors that conjoin heterogeneous semantic fields.[11] Here the term metaphor regains some of its original etymological charge as *meta-phora*, meaning to transfer, transit, or carry across.

Rejecting the narrowly Platonizing use of allegory, which admits of only vertical transfer from the sensible to the intelligible and from the human to the divine, this new model of religious hermeneutics seeks a two-way production of metaphorical meaning—like Jacob's ladder with angels passing up and down. Taking the example of the two lovers in the Song of Songs, Ricoeur offers the following suggestive gloss: "The idea of an intersecting metaphor invites us to consider the different and original regions of love, each with its symbolic play. On the one side, the divine love is invested in the Covenant with Israel and later in the Christic bond, along with its absolutely original nuptial metaphorics; on the other, there is human love invested in the erotic bond and its equally original metaphorics, which transforms the body into something like a landscape. The double 'seeing as' of intersecting metaphors then finds itself as the source of the 'saying otherwise.' "[12] From which he concludes, astutely, that it is the mark of the "power of love to be able to move in both senses along the ascending and descending spiral of metaphor, allowing in this way for every level of the emotional investment of love to signify, to intersignify every other level."[13]

To acknowledge the deeply diverse ways in which we metaphorize the desire of God is already to admit that no one of them can be held hierarchically superior to any other. Indeed it is from the productive friction of their "intersignification" that some transfer (*metaphora*) of meaning is eventually, if always tentatively, achieved. It is, moreover, by recognizing the fecund metaphorical interplay at work in the reading of all great religious texts that we become more capable of hermeneutically retrieving certain lost meanings—in this case, eschatological ones—within and between (*metaxy*) the texts themselves.

To rephrase this metaphorizing role of hermeneutic mediation in more theological terms, we might say that it charts a winding path between the apophatic and cataphatic approaches to God. For if the apophatic tradition—from negative theologians like Clement of Alexandria and Dionysius to Levinas, Derrida, and Marion—stresses the impossibility of saying anything meaningful about God,[14] the opposing cataphatic tradition runs the risk of embracing overly "positive" and foundationalist propositions. If the former, in short, tends to place God too far beyond being (so that there is no way back to the flesh of the face), the latter is sometimes tempted to reduce God to being (either as the most general or highest being: *ontos on—theion*).

Between these poles of negative theology and onto-theology I propose to navigate a third channel approaching God neither as non-being nor as being but as the possibility-to-be. This third way, where the infinite eschaton intersects with the finite order of being, I call onto-eschatology. It is here that we encounter the nuptial nexus where divine and human desires overlap. The still point of the turning world where the timeless crosses time. The milieu where, in T. S. Eliot's words, the fire and the rose are one.

This is a frontier zone where narratives flourish and abound. It is a place where stories, songs, parables, and prophecies resound as human imaginations try to say the unsayable and think the unthinkable. The five chapters of this volume are tentative hermeneutic endeavors to sound out some of these narratives, from the burning bush and Song of Songs to the testimony of transfiguration on Mount Thabor. Drawing from a wide variety of sources—biblical, scriptural, rabbinical, patristic, theological, and philosophical—I will try in what follows to sketch the outlines of a narrative eschatology.

The current work is the third and final volume of a trilogy entitled "Philosophy at the Limit." The first two volumes, *On Stories* and *Strangers, Gods, and Monsters*, are published by Routledge.

Toward a Phenomenology
of the *Persona*

I begin by exploring the theme of transfiguration, first in terms of a phenomenology of the *persona*, and then in subsequent chapters with more specific reference to defining epiphanic moments such as the burning bush (Exodus 3:15), the transfiguration narratives of Christ on Mount Thabor (Mark 9, Matthew 17, Luke 9, John 12) and the story of divine-human love in the Song of Songs. In each instance, I will be seeking to address what I consider to be crucial contemporary debates on the notion of an eschatological God who transfigures and desires. What follows is not, let me make clear at the outset, a strictly theological or exegetical account—a task beyond my competence—but an attempt to chart a hermeneutic path of thinking along the tracks and traces of the Possible God who comes and goes. My approach here, as elsewhere in this volume, draws liberally from post-Heideggerian accounts of the self-other relation (Levinas, Merleau-Ponty, Kristeva, Ricoeur, and Derrida), taking, in this instance, an additional cue from the Johannine promise: "A little while and you will no longer see me; and again a little while and you will see me" (John 16:16–20).

Figure of the Other—*Persona*

Each person embodies a *persona. Persona* is that eschatological aura of "possibility" which eludes but informs a person's actual presence here and now. I use it here as another word for the otherness of the other; just as I use "person" to refer to my fellow in so far as he/she is the same or similar to me (empirically, biologically, psychologically, etc.). At a purely phenomenological level, *persona* is all that in others exceeds my searching gaze, safeguarding their inimitable and unique singularity. It is what escapes me toward another past that I cannot recover and another future I cannot predict. It resides, if it resides anywhere, beyond my intentional horizons of re-tention and pro-tention. The *persona* of the other outstrips both the presenting consciousness of my *perception* here and now and the presentifying consciousness of my *imagination* (with its attempts to see, in the mode of *as-if,* that which resists perceptual intuition). The *persona* of the other even defies the names and categories of *signifying* consciousness. It is beyond consciousness *tout court.* Though this "beyondness" is, curiously, what spurs language to speak figuratively about it, deploying imagination and interpretation to overreach their normal limits in efforts to grasp it—especially in the guise of metaphor and narrative.

This *persona* is what Levinas names *la trace d'autrui*; and it is not unrelated to what Derrida calls the enigma of "alterity"; nor ultimately to what, in many religions, goes simply but often quite misleadingly by the term "spirit" (*pneuma/anima/âme/Geist*). I will endeavor here to develop the notion of *persona* in terms of a radical phenomenology of transfiguration.[1]

* * *

I never encounter others without at the same time configuring them in some way. To configure the other as a *persona* is to grasp him/her as present in absence, as both incarnate in flesh and transcendent in time. To accept this paradox of configuration is to allow the other to appear as his/her unique *persona.* To refuse this paradox, opting instead to regard someone as pure presence (thing), or pure absence (nothing), is to disfigure the other.

To be sure, this is not an easy matter. The other always appears to us *as if* s/he were actually present. And it is all too tempting to ignore this *as if* proviso and presume to have others literally before us, to appropriate them to our scheme of things, reading them off against our familiar grids of understanding and identification. (Especially since the otherness of the other is not located some*where* else—for example, in some Platonic form or noumenal substance.) Accepting the other as a "stranger" in our midst is an uncanny and often threatening experience.[2] Far easier to take the other as given, to take him/her for granted, as no more than what we can grasp—following the logic: what you see is what you get. For if it is true to say that we do somehow "see" the *persona* in the face of the person, we never *get* it. It always exceeds the limits of our capturing gaze. It transcends us.

Or, going to the other extreme, it is easier to mistake the other's *persona* for an idol than accept it as an icon of transcendence.[3] In this case, the *as if* presence of the *persona* is suspended in the interests of deification or apotheosis: a phenomenon not confined to religious idolatry (where an ordinary human person is revered as a divinity) but also evidenced daily in the cult of stardom (where Madonna replaces the Madonna . . .). Just think of Andy Warhol's multi-series of famous faces, which send up the whole media obsession with mass celebrity. In short, we disregard others not just by ignoring their *transcendence* but equally by ignoring their *flesh-and-blood thereness*. There is a thin line, of course, between seeking to capture the other as divine (qua idol) and receiving the divine through the other (qua icon). But thin lines are no excuse for fusion or confusion. They call rather for acute hermeneutic vigilance. Because the *persona* is at once so near and so far, we easily fall for the lure of possession.

The enigma of *persona* as presence-absence is usually betrayed in the name of some fictitious totality. Such betrayal derives from the fact that the fictitious character of this totality is unacknowledged. We simply forget the *as-if* strategy that affects the illusion of full presence. We succumb to *literalism:* masking the figural in the literal. Or what, paradoxically, amounts to the same thing in this instance: *fetishism.* For both literalism and fetishism conflate the orders of the possible and the actual, the fictional and the empirical. A strange convergence this, witnessed in the surprising collusion in our time between the ostensibly opposite pulls toward a positivist science of facts and a postmodern culture of fantasies. Or in the religious world, between the seeming extremes of fundamentalism and New Ageism. But more on this below.

We live more and more under the eclipse of the *as if.* Which doesn't mean that the *as if* no longer functions. It might even be argued that it functions more effectively today than ever before to the extent that it operates behind our backs, unbeknownst to us—a process of concealment actually abetted by the postmodern cult of simulation. Indeed, as critics of ideology, from Marx to Ricoeur, have observed: ideology is a "false consciousness" which, like the camera obscura, works by inversion, in the dark, to give us what seems like a perfectly believable illusion.[4]

Fetishism hides itself and gleans power from its stealth. One doesn't have to look far for examples of this. One finds it recurring, on the scale of persons, in the wild obsessions of fans and fanatics, ranging from stalker- and voyeur-fantasies to the mass-media apotheosis of certain figures of fame and charisma (a postmodern version of the modernist personality cult). But fetishism doesn't always involve a human person. Nations, states, and empires are also subject to idolatrous personifications. Think of the sacralizing cults of national sovereignty and territory. Here too we find disfiguring practices.

Persona as **Eschaton**

What characterizes the eschatological notion of *persona*, by contrast, is that it vouchsafes the irreducible finality of the other as eschaton. I stress, as eschaton not as telos (i.e., a fulfillable, predictable, foreseeable goal). And I understand eschaton here precisely in the sense of an end without end—an end that escapes and surprises us, like a thief in the night—rather than some immanent teleological closure. Eschatologically considered, the *persona* of the person brings home to us that we have no power over her/him. Or as Levinas puts it, *"nous ne pouvons plus pouvoir."* Before the other we are no longer able to be able. If anything, it is the other who, once we first confront our primary disablement, re-enables us. But this reality of the ego's fundamental insecurity and frailty is something most prefer to ignore, compensating instead, from childhood on, with fantasies of power and omnipotence. (A point noted by Freud when he claimed that every child is a megalomaniac.) In our contemporary society, as in previous ones, such infantile imperiousness—concealing the breach of its own inner brokenness—is rampant. Hitler, Mussolini, Stalin: these are extreme examples of this widespread human cover-up. By contrast, if anyone can make me truly capable, it is the other who entrusts power to me. The other empowers me by saying: "Even though you are powerless, I believe you can do this."

The eschaton, as *persona*, is precisely the other's future possibilities which are impossible for me (to realize, possess, grasp). The vertical "may-be" of the other is irreducible to *my* set of possibilities or powers: my "can-be." That is why "the future is that which is not grasped . . . the relation with the future is the relation with the other."[5] In other words, if we could figure out—in the sense of knowing and appropriating—the other's *persona*, it would no longer be other. We would have denied the other's temporality, futurity, alterity. We would literally *have* them by the tail. But the otherness of the other is precisely that which cannot be had, however much we fool ourselves into thinking it can. Just when it seems we hold it in our hands, it absents itself, resists the lure of presence. "The relation with the other is the absence of the other; not absence pure and simple, not absence as pure nothing *(néant)*, but absence in a futural horizon, an absence which is time."[6] It is in this temporal sense that we might say that my *persona* is both younger and older than my person—pre-existing and post-existing the seizure of myself as presence (qua sum of totalizable properties). The *persona* is always already there and always still to come.

Put in another way, the *persona* is there where there is no one *(il y a persona là où il n'y a personne)*;[7] This u-topian no-place of *persona* might be said to correspond in some way to what Winnicott called the "potential space" which exceeds the dualism of internal subject and external object, being and non-being. Indeed we should understand its status of no-place in the context of the Pauline view that God chooses "things that are not *(ta me onta*) in order that he might cancel things that are" (1 Corinthians 1:28). It is in a similar Pauline sense that we will understand the analysis of *persona* as *personne* below.

Persona takes the place of the no-place; but it does not itself take place. Yet it does *give place* to the person and without it the person could not take its place. It is the non-presence that allows presence to happen in the here and now *as* a human person appearing to me in flesh and blood. It is, in short, the quasi-condition of the other remaining other to me even as s/he stands before me in this moment. But however non-present it is, *persona* is not to be understood as some impersonal anonymous presence (i.e., a Monarchian *deus absconditus*). Nor is it to be taken as a merely formal condition of possibility (Kant); nor indeed as some archaic and formless receptacle (Plato's and Derrida's *khora*). *Persona* is always inseparable from *this* person of flesh and blood, here and now. In fact, it may even be said to constitute this very thisness (*haeccitas*). "Lovely in limbs, and lovely in eyes not his / To the Father through the features of men's faces" (Gerard Manley Hopkins).

The *persona* is there to remind us that there is always something more to flesh and blood than flesh and blood.[8] Hence the inevitable frustration of the torturer—so acutely observed by Sartre in *Being and Nothingness*—when he discovers that the tortured is dead but unvanquished: the torturer now has a corpse (*Körper*) in his hands, but he has lost precisely that which he was seeking to possess—the free transcendence incarnate in that person's living body (*Leib*). The tortured *persona* always escapes the torturer.

The *persona* also resists, at an everyday level, my countless attempts often benevolent—to turn it into an alter ego. I might cite here the futility of Husserl's attempts in the fifth of his *Cartesian Meditations* to ground intersubjective relations in an imaginative projection of one ego onto another. What he describes, in his efforts to eschew the solipsism of the transcendental ego, is a reciprocating process of apperception, pairing, and empathy (*Aneignung/ Paarung/Einfühlung*);[9] And we realize, on observing this heroic but doomed Husserlian enterprise, that it is not only I-It relations of coercion that compromise the irreducible alterity of the other's *persona*. Such compromise can also take the more subtle form of symmetrical I-Thou relations, especially where the Thou plays the role of another I: my mirror-image, myself by proxy, ego in drag.

This *egoisme-à-deux* frequently goes by the name of "love." Time and again, lovers seek to appropriate each other's *persona* as if it could be magically conjured in its present-at-hand thereness (*Vorhandensein*); They fall for the lure of fusion, that is, for the illusion that some ecstasy or addiction might make us *one with the other*. But it cannot. The other will never *be* me, nor even *like* me. Whence the shock, for example, of a spouse reading his partner's private diary and discovering he never really knew the person (i.e., *persona*) he lived with for so many years. Whence also the post-coital *tristesse* that derives from the awareness that no amount of intimacy can ever grasp the other. We do grasp something of course—the other person, in their delectable givenness—but not the other's *persona*.

And so, in a curious reversal of received opinion, it is the transcendent *persona* who marks the uniquely differentiating character of the finite person. For us, while the "person" is a token of sameness *(idem)*—all that is statistically, logistically, metrically, anatomically computable and therefore comparable in the order of like-with-like—it is the *persona* who is guarantor of singularity. The *persona* tells us more about the uniqueness of the person than can be captured on any identity card.

You can fake a person's ID but never their *persona*. Despite the most ingenious efforts, you can never quite take on another's *persona*, anymore than you can imitate their fingerprint. The body—lest we forget Merleau-Ponty's reminder—is the primary locus of incarnate *persona*. It inscribes a singular style and manner of existing that is unique to each person. Whence Merleau-Ponty's quip about the transcending-transfiguring nature of our experience as body-subjects: "perception already stylises."[10] Even our most involuntary alimentary and libidinal functions—ingestion, excretion, copulation—have their symbolic charge, as psychoanalysis reminds us; and as religious apologetics sometimes forgets. Contrary to spiritualist illusions, the *persona* is not some disembodied soul. It gives itself in and through the incarnate body. Just as it absolves or withholds itself. There and not there; but never somewhere else. *Lovely in limbs and eyes. Through the features of faces.*

Beyond Fusion

But the drive to fuse with the other is not always carnal, or even personal. The unconscious has countless ruses up its sleeve to transfer libidinal fixations onto sublimated, impersonal Figures. The Eternal Feminine, the Absolute Sovereign, the Replacement Lost Object, and so on.[11] Such projections subordinate singular others to some totalizing One: the Same-One who is, at bottom, no more than the sum of our ego-fantasies. The transcendent *persona* is thereby reduced to the surrogate "object-other," the unconscious illusion standing in for absence. But unlike its fraudulent usurpers, the *persona* gives, calls, loves, solicits, and even (Levinas would have it) forbids murder. The other as fetish-object does not. It does not care. Indeed, as Lacan reminds us in his unmasking of such fantasy figures as *La Femme* and *Le Phallus*, the fetishized Other is precisely that which does not exist.[12]

A more benign but no less compromising version of the fetishized *persona* is to be found in Plato's theory of eros where what is desired is, at best, no more than an exemplification of an Idea. In the *Symposium*, Plato invokes the Form of Beauty which is always one and the same (like the permanent Oneness it reflects). The so-called Platonic love which reveres a woman as exemplary of the Eternal Feminine is not love of the other's unique singularity *(persona)* but love of the Same-One. We thus assume we are participating in what Augustine would later describe as the Self-Loving-Love of the divine (*amor quo Deus se ipsum amatur*). And we find similar approximations of this Self-Loving-Love in the metaphysical paradigms of Self-Thinking-Thought (*nous tes noeseos*), Self-Causing-Cause (*ens causa sui*) and, perhaps, most suggestively, in the Plotinian paradigm of Self-Desiring-Desire (*autou eros*). " 'God is love' can indeed be found in Plotinus," remarks Kristeva, "meaning a self-sufficient love that radiates in itself and for itself—a felicitous, dazzling return of Narcissus. The One 'is simultaneously the *loved one* and *love*; He is *love of himself*; for He is beautiful only by and in Himself' (*Enneads* VI, 8, 15). That *autou eros* that I see as sublime hypostasis of narcissistic love was to constitute the decisive step in the assumption of the . . . introspective space of the western psyche. God is Narcissus, and if the *narcissistic* illusion is for Myself a sin, my ideal is nonetheless *Narcissan*."[13] Kristeva adds, tellingly from my point of view: "In this autarkic love, which leads to union with a divinity that is itself autarkic, there is no other but nothingness."[14] In short, what we forfeit in the game of self-regarding love is the alterity of the other person.[15]

The stakes are high. I am contrasting here the eschatological relation of one-for-the-other with the onto-theological relation of one-for-one, or if you prefer, of the one-for-itself-in-itself. The latter comprises a long logocentric tradition running from certain aspects of Plato, Aristotle, and neo-Platonism (cited above) to Hegel and Heidegger. And the political implications of this legacy are not always propitious. As Levinas points out: "Plato constructed a Republic which must imitate the world of Ideas . . . and on this basis the ideal of the social will be sought in an ideal of fusion. One will assume that the subject relates to the other by identifying with him, collapsing into a collective representation, into a common ideality."[16]

To this fusionary sameness of the One I would oppose the eschatological universality of the Other. This latter notion of the universal is more ethical to the extent that it is conceived in terms of a possible co-existence of unique *personas*, whose transcendence is in each case vouchsafed. That such an ethical universal remains a "possibility" still to be attained—heralding from an open future—resists the temptation of acquiescing in the security of the accomplished. The fact that universal justice is an eschatological possible still-to-come creates a sense of urgency and exigency, inviting each person to strive for its instantiation, however partial and particular, in each given situation.

To put this in terms of a more patristic metaphor, we might say that the eschatological universal holds out the promise of a perichoretic interplay of differing *personas*, meeting without fusing, communing without totalizing, discoursing without dissolving. A sort of divine *circumin(c/s)essio* of the Trinitarian kingdom: a no-place which may one day be and where each *persona* cedes its place to its other (*cedere*) even as they sit down together (*sedere*). The Latins knew what they were about when they played on the semantic ambidexterity of the *c/s* as alternative spellings of the phonetically identical root term *cessio/sessio*.[17] They knew about the bi-valent promise of *persona* as both there and not there, transcendent and immanent, visible and invisible.

The eschaton is just that: a promise, not an acquisition. A possibility of the future to come, impossible in the present where the allure of total presence risks reigning supreme. As such, the eschatological *persona* defies my power—even if I have all the weapons in the world and it has none. The *persona* transfigures me before I configure it. And to the extent that I avow and accord this asymmetrical priority to the other, I am transfigured by that particular *persona* and empowered to transfigure in turn—that is, to figure the other in their otherness.

The asymmetrical priority of the other's *persona* over my person (qua ego-cogito) finds expression in the fact that the other comes to me not as some fulfillment of my intentional consciousness; but as a figure-face which eludes and shatters my intentional horizons. The face of the *persona* discountenances me before I countenance it. Which is another way of saying that the *persona* never actually appears at all, as such, in that it has *already come and gone*, leaving only its trace; or is *still to come*, outstripping every figuration on my part. The *persona* hails and haunts me *before* I even begin to represent it *as if* it were present before me.[18]

These idioms of "already," "prior," "before," "after" and "still to come" signal a new kind of temporality—a specifically *ethical* time. This ethical relation expresses itself in the temporal ek-stasis of the self, surpassing itself toward the other who surpasses it, responding to the call of the *persona* issued from a time which exceeds my beginning and my end. That is why the *persona* assumes the form of an *achronic* figure that disrupts me before and after every *as-if* synchronism I impose upon it. In the very proximity of the other—which itself attests to the distance of the *persona* vis-à-vis the present person—an ethical summons is heard: a call coming to me from some immemorial past. It is this aspect of the proximate neighbor as transcendence that Levinas terms "*visage*."[19]

Persona as Chiasm

Strictly speaking then, we might say that the phenomenon of the *persona* surpasses phenomenology altogether. At least phenomenology understood in the Husserlian sense of an eidetics of intentional consciousness (striving toward a rigorous science of transcendental immanence). The phenomenon of the *persona* calls for a new or quasi-phenomenology, mobilized by ethics rather than eidetics. The enigmatic *persona* supersedes every presentation or re-presentation which seeks to apprehend it as intuitive adequation. It flouts the *adequatio intellectus ad rem*. Which is another way of saying that the figure-face is, at bottom, not literally a figure at all, but only figuratively so—that is, a quasi-figure which appears *as if* it was an appearance, as a pre-figuration or re-figuration of that which effaces itself as it faces us. So doing, and always avowing its own *as-if* conditionality, the *persona* of the other announces a difference which differentiates itself ad infinitum. *Persona* is infinitely premature and invariably overdue, always missed and already deferred. *Persona* comes to us as a chiasmus or crossover with person—as in Merleau-Ponty's crisscrossing lines or two-sided sleeve.[20] Which is why we cannot think of the time of the *persona* except as an immemorial beginning (before the beginning) or an unimaginable end (after the end). That is precisely its eschatological stature—the messianic achronicity which breaks open the continuous moment-by-moment time of everyday chronology.

Persona has always already crossed the person and yet is still always about to do so. That is why it can never be caught in the lure of some pure moment cut off from the differentiating traces of past and future. It marks a time that is always *more*, remaindered, excessive, sabbatical, surplus. And yet this extra-time reveals itself in time, in what Walter Benjamin called the *Jetzzeit*—the incursion of the eternal in the moment.

The time of the eschaton is, as it were, anti-clockwise. Or if one prefers, post-clockwise. It cannot be accounted for in terms of prevision. The inexhaustible alterity of the *persona* remains forever anterior—and posterior—to its manifestations and so baffles every cognitive interpretation I project onto it. That is why it deranges me so, why it retards and pre-empts me, knocks me off kilter, out of synch.[21] (I shall return to this enigma in the discussion of "messianic time" below.)

In sum, the *persona* is never there on time. Indeed, because it is never adequately there at all, we might say that *persona* is literally *personne*. It is *no*-one, if *some*-one means a person who is phenomenally symmetrical to me. But it is *this* one and no one but *this* one, if my neighbor appears to me eschatologically, defying the *as-if* figurations by means of which I try to tell its story. For the *persona* is always other than the other-for-me here and now. It is the figure which transfigures by absenting itself as *personne* in the very moment that it hails and holds me. Like Celan's *Niemandsrose*. Or what Franz Rosenzweig, in his essay on "The Eternal" (1929), refers to as the paradox of the "distant uniting with the near," the "whole" traversing "one's own."[22] The eternal sounds through (*per-sonans*) the momentary person before me, sounding and seeking me out.

In this sense we might best describe ourselves as actors (*figurants*) in a play authored by *personne* (the French carries the dual sense of "person" and "no-one"). To interpret our role is, in this respect, to respond to the script of the *persona* who speaks through the other, to figure and play out this role as a one-for-the-other, as a one through (*trans*) the other. It is to behold the other as an icon for the passage of the infinite—while refusing to construe the infinite as some other being *hiding behind* the other. This is not Platonism. Nor Kantianism. *Persona* is neither Idea nor Noumenon. Neither pure form nor *Ding-an-sich*. Nor any other kind of transcendental signified for that matter. No. *Persona* is the in-finite other in the finite person before me. In and through that person. And because there is no other to this infinite other, bound to but irreducible to the embodied person, we refer to this *persona* as the sign of God. Not the other person as divine, mind you—that would be idolatry—but the divine in and through that person. The divine as trace, icon, visage, passage.

Persona as **Prosopon**

This is what the Greeks—poets and church fathers alike—called *prosopon*. Whence the English rhetorical term *prosopopoeia*, a figure by means of which an absent one is represented as speaking or acting, a sort of poetic personification, impersonation, or embodiment of some other self.[23] I use this term of prosopopoeic substitution, however, in a more strictly phenomenological and ethical sense—and without its theatrical connotations of feigning or make-believe. For me it signals the otherness of the other in and through the flesh-and-blood person here before me. Trans-cendence in and through, but not reducible to, immanence. *Prosopon* is the face of the other who urgently solicits me, bidding me answer in each concrete situation, "here I am."

This hermeneutic retrieval of the term *prosopon* finds support in the original Greek usage. As John Manoussakis reminds us, the etymology of the term *prosopon*—later translated into Latin by Tertullian and others as *persona*—carries the dynamic sense of being-for-the-other. The term is made up of the two parts: *pros* meaning "in front of" or "toward"; and *opos*, as in optics, meaning a face or more particularly an eye, countenance, or vision. More precisely, *prosopon* refers to the face of the person as it faces us, revealing itself from within itself. One "is" a *prosopon* but never "has" a *prosopon* as such; it lets us see the very soul of the person in a new light. So to be a *prosopon* is to be-a-face-toward-a-face, to be proximate to the face of the other. And, tellingly, the term rarely appears in the singular but almost always as a plural noun (*prosopa*), signaling that the *prosopon-persona* can never really exist on its own (*atomon*), but emerges in ethical relation to others. In this sense, the *prosopon-persona* may be said to be radically intersubjective, invariably bound up in some ethical vis-à-vis or face-to-face. "Being-towards-a-face always presupposes the other, in front of whom we stand. This other, in turn, by standing in front of me, has to be a *prosopon* as well."[24] Reinterpreted hermeneutically from a post-Levinasian perspective, one can see just how appropriately this Greek-Latin pair of *prosopon-persona* may serve to translate the Judeo-Christian primacy of ethics. It perfectly captures the double sense of someone as both proximate to me in the immediacy of connection and yet somehow ineluctably distant, at once incarnate and otherwise, inscribing the trace of an irreducible alterity in and through the face before me.

I call this paradoxical phenomenon of the *prosopon transfiguration*, bearing in mind that *figura* also carries the sense of face and inscription. Transfiguration is something that, in the last analysis, we allow the *persona-prosopon* to do to us. Something we suffer to be done unto us. Like the summons of the distressed other. Or the eyes of the icon that look through us from beyond us.

Or the thin small voice of Elijah's cave. Or the cry in the wilderness. A far cry from the Sartrian world where hell is other people. The only hell in this scenario is that of self condemned to self. *Atomon.* The empty choosing will cut off from all others. The ideology of each-for-itself.

What I am proposing, therefore, is a version of the old preference for icons over idols, recalling that *persona* and *eikon* were originally used synonymously by certain early Christian sources such as Procopius of Gaza (c. 538).[25] If the tradition of onto-theology granted priority to being over the good, this counter-tradition of eschatology challenges that priority. Herewith the good of the *persona* takes precedence over my drive to be (*conatus essendi*) and holds it to account. And, where possible, cares for it. Against Heidegger I say: it is not our being that cares for itself, as being-toward-death, but the good of the *persona* that cares for being, as promise of endless rebirth. Natality transfigures mortality.

Openness to the *persona* of the neighbor in each instant is, as Matthew 25 reminds us, the ultimate in eschatological awareness. And so we find ourselves, on foot of the above analysis, at the threshold of a phenomenology of religion.

I Am Who May Be

The epiphany of the burning bush provides my first example of religious transfiguration. I start with a brief account of this dramatic encounter between Moses and his Lord, before proceeding to a hermeneutic retrieval of several decisive readings of this passage—rabbinical, exegetical, and philosophical. My aim is to identify and address the hidden crux of this enigma: the extraordinary phenomenon of a deity which appears and disappears in a fire that burns without burning out, that ignites without consuming, that names itself, paradoxically, as that which cannot be named, and that presents itself in the moment as that which is still to come.

* * *

In Exodus 3:14 Moses meets his maker. Leading his flock to the desert mountain of Horeb, he happens upon a voice speaking from the midst of a flaming thornbush. From this transfiguring fire which flares up without being extinguished, the voice of an angel calls and Moses answers "Here I am." The voice bids him to stand back and remove his sandals. And revealing himself as the Lord of his ancestors—of Abraham, Isaac, and Jacob—God says he has heard the cry of his people and has come to deliver them from bondage.

But it's not enough for Moses. Standing there under the midday sun, he wonders if this is not some mirage, some hoax. Perhaps the voice is an inner demon prompting him to a fit of madness. After all, wasn't it just such a strange angel who appeared to Jacob late one night and shattered his hip, before disclosing the name of Israel? And wasn't it another elusive voice which summoned Abraham to Mount Moriah to murder his own son? That was a cruel command. A trick of course. Only a test of faith. He must tread carefully. Moses wasn't quite sure he wanted to do business with such a mercurial God: one who sent visitors to maim you in the middle of the night and commanded blood sacrifice (even if he wasn't really serious). Every angel was terrible in a way, wasn't it?

Moses longed for a God of justice and liberty. Someone who'd remain faithful to his people. But who was *he* to question God—if this really *was* God and not some counterfeit conjured by his dizzy mind? He would have to proceed cautiously. So instead of asking straight out: Who are *you?* Moses puts it another way, the other way around: "Who am *I?*" "Who am I," he inquires, that I should go unto Pharaoh and lead the children of Israel out of Egypt? To which God replies, with a second, though still indirect revelation of himself: "I will be with Thee." The ancestral God is now declaring himself a *constant* God—one who will stand by Moses as he embarks on his mission to a promised land. Not only is the bush transfiguring itself but so too is the God who speaks through it (*per-sona*). And it threatens to transfigure Moses too.

Still Moses is unsure; but he is beginning to like the sound of things. There is maybe more to this deity than meets the eye? Something more than the tribal divinity of his forebears? A hint of something new? Not just a God of ancestry, it seems, but a God of advent: a promise for the future.

Emboldened by this surmise, Moses asks God, one last time, to reveal himself, to say who he truly is, to disclose his name. Feet still bare on the hot sand, Moses takes a small step forward. He wipes perspiration from his forehead, and addresses the burning bush: "When I come unto the children of Israel and shall say unto them, The God of your fathers hath sent me unto you; and they shall say to me, What is his name? What shall I say to them?" (Exodus 3:13). To which God responds, bolder and brasher this time—his third and final reply: "*'ehyeh 'asher 'ehyeh.*" The New Jerusalem version reads: "God said to Moses, 'I am he who is.' And he said, 'This is what you are to say to the Israelites, 'I am has sent me to you.'" [1]

So there we have it. Holy Moses, a tired shepherd with a price on his head, dusty and parched after days of wandering about with his father-in-law's sheep in the desert, is confronted with an angel who eludes him, a fire that won't burn out, and a voice that answers his questions with a riddle! If Moses is to lead his people out of bondage in Egypt, he needs to know a little more about the credentials of the one who speaks to him through the voice (*per-sona*) of this angel of the thornbush. He must be able to convince his own people, after all, that this God is a better bet than the magic deity of Pharaoh and the Egyptians. So how does God respond to Moses? How does he reassure His bewildered shepherd, racked with doubt and insecurity? He reassures by repeating Himself, by not really replying at all, turning his answer into a tautology, an enigmatic turn of phrase which not only puzzles Moses but all those after him who profess the Name: *'ehyeh 'asher 'ehyeh!*

This formula, translated into Greek as *ego eimi ho on*, into Latin as *ego sum qui sum*, and into English as "I am who am" or "I am he who is," has fascinated commentators for centuries.[2] Talmudists and exegetes, mullahs and prophets, church fathers and angelic doctors, theologians and philosophers, have pored over this riddling Name and offered countless conjectures. But the riddle remains. In Exodus 3:14, God declares his own *incognito* and manifests himself in terms of a divine self-definition which cannot be defined. Unlike other passages in the Torah where God reveals himself in the position of the divine "I" ("I Yahweh"), this passage is rare in that it adds the verbal promise to be. Indeed it adds it twice, first in terms of *'ehyeh* and then by adding *'asher 'ehyeh*. The Tetragrammaton thus appears to partake in the semantic field of the verb traditionally rendered as "to be"—in the constative or conditional mood. How best to translate this verb is a complex matter dividing scholars throughout the ages and resisting final consensus. In more contemporary idiom, this verbal play compels us to wonder if God is here reducing himself to a metaphysics of presence or rendering himself immune to it for good and all.

In what follows, I discuss two main traditions of interpretation under the headings *ontological* and *eschatological*, before offering a third or median option which I call *onto-eschatological*. My ultimate suggestion is that we might do better to reinterpret the Transfiguring God of Exodus 3 neither as "I who am" nor as "I who am not" but rather as "I am who may be"—that is, as the possibility to be, which obviates the extremes of being and non-being. *'Ehyeh 'asher 'ehyeh* might thus be read as signature of the God of the possible, a God who refuses to impose on us or abandon us, traversing the present moment while opening onto an ever-coming future. That, in a word, is my wager.

The Ontological Reading

From the outset the Greeks rendered Exodus 3:14 in terms of the verb "to be," or *einai*. Inheriting the Hellenic formula *ego eimi ho on*—I am the one who is—Augustine and the Latins claimed there was no fundamental difference between this *ego sum qui sum* and the *esse* of metaphysics. The Exodic formula was considered by early and medieval Christian theologians to be the highest way of saying *vere esse, ipsum esse*, that is, Being-itself, timeless, immutable, incorporeal, understood as the subsisting act of all existing. While the human soul is split apart into memory (it was), attention (it is), and expectation (it will be), God suffers no such *distentio animi*. The God revealed in Exodus is what He is in Himself, one and the same: his own *essentia—Idipsum esse* existing beyond all time, all history, all movement.[3]

Already in the *Confessions* (13.31, 46), Augustine turns the verbal "is" of God into a substantive formula. And this move becomes more explicit when Augustine comments directly on Exodus 3:14 (which he renders as *Qui est, misit me ad vos*)—"Because he is *Is*, that is to say God is Being itself, *ipsum esse*, in its most absolute and full sense. '*Esset tibi nomen ipsum esse*,' he says to God (*Enarrationes in Psalmos* 101.10)."[4] Consolidating this quasi-Parmenidean reading, Augustine makes an important distinction between what God is for us (his *nomen misericordiae*) and what He is in Himself (his *nomen substantiae*). While the former more historico-anthropomorphic perspective is conveyed by the formula "I am the God of Abraham, Isaac, and Jacob," the latter—safeguarding the absolute, inaccessible, and transcendent character of God—is expressed by the *ego sum qui sum*. It is this latter sense that Augustine has in mind in the *De Trinitate* when he identifies the God of Exodus with the Greek-Platonic notion of substance (*ousia*) understood as an a-temporal, immutable essence: "He is no doubt *substania*, or if one prefers, he is the *essentia* which the Greeks called *ousia* . . . *essentia* comes from *esse*. And who 'is' more than He who said to his servant Moses: '*ego sum qui sum*' . . . That is why there is only one substance or immutable essence which is God and to which being itself (*ipsum esse*) properly belongs" (*De Trinitate* 5.2, 3). Augustine concludes from this that anything that changes or is capable of "becoming something which he was not already" cannot be said to possess being itself. We can say of God therefore that "He is" precisely because he is that which does not change and cannot change.[5]

Aquinas developed the Augustinian view that the *qui est* of Exodus is the principal name of God and the highest formulation of being. The revelation of Exodus, he affirmed, designates "true being, that is being that is eternal, immutable, simple self-sufficient, and the cause and principle of every creature."[6] For Aquinas, as for Augustine, the *esse* of God is nothing other than his *essentia*, and as such exists eternally in the present without past or future: that is, without movement, change, desire, or possibility—*Deus est actus purus non habens aliquid de potentialitate* (*Summa Theologiae* 1.3.4c). With Aquinas and the scholastics, the God of Exodus is thus enthroned as the most fully-fledged "act of Being." In both his *Commentary on the Sentences* and *De Substantiis Separatis*, the Exodus verse is invoked by Thomas to corroborate speculative thought about the most ultimate mode of Being. For Being says more of God than either the Good or the One. The proper name of God revealed in Exodus 3:14 is none other than the absolute identity of divine being and essence. *Esse is the essentia of God.* This obtains for Aquinas no matter how much the divine essence surpasses the limits of rational speculation, approaching God only in an analogical way in the proofs for his existence. Aquinas concedes, after all, that while we can prove *that* God exists we cannot know *what* he is. But these reservations notwithstanding, Aquinas has no hesitation in citing Exodus 3:14 as confirmation of his proofs in the *Summa* (ad 3). This is how he justifies his conviction that the Exodic formula provides us with the ultimate name for God: "The reason for this name is that, in its reference, it exceeds every form, because it signifies being itself (*ipsum esse*). Moreover, the less determined the names the better they pertain to God, by virtue of their common and absolute character. Every other name in fact connotes a restrictive modality. Now 'He who is' does not define any particular modality of being; but it envelops all indeterminate modes. Nevertheless, the sacred Tetragrammaton preserves better still the incommunicability and singularity of God" (*Summa Theologiae* 13.11).

Without the encounter of Greek metaphysics with biblical religious thought, philosophers "would have never reached the idea that Being is the proper name of God and that this name designates God's very essence."[7] Or as Etienne Gilson remarked in *The Spirit of Mediæval Philosophy*, "Exodus lays down the principle from which Christian philosophy will be suspended. . . . There is but one God and this God is Being, that is the corner-stone of all Christian philosophy."[8] With this scholastic verdict, the traditional notion of faith seeking understanding reaches its logical culmination. The conflation of Yahweh with the supreme Being of the philosophers is sealed. And this conjunction of God and Being was to survive for very many centuries—from Bonaventure and Aquinas to Gilson and the neo-Scholastics. Thus did the God of Exodus secure ontological tenure in the God of metaphysics. And this tenure has come to be known, after Heidegger, as "onto-theology": a tendency to reify God by reducing Him to a being (*Seiende*)—albeit the highest, first, and most indeterminate of all beings.[9]

Onto-theology, we might say, sought to have its cake and eat it: to equate God with a modality of being while safeguarding His ultimately ineffable and transcendent nature. Unlike the negative theology of Dionysius and the Christian Neoplatonists, however, most Scholastics identified God with Being by means of proofs and analogies, seeking some sort of balance between Being's universality and indeterminacy on the one hand, and God's density as a quasi-subject or person (which holds God from infinite dispersion) on the other.[10] It is, some argue, a short step from such onto-theological equilibrium to Hegel's notion of a "concrete universal"; or Schelling's famous equation of the divine "I AM" with the self-identification of the transcendental Ego. Indeed, Schelling will go so far as to claim that the I AM is "one and the same thing with our immediate self-consciousness."[11] This unification of divine and human consciousness finds modern echoes not only in German idealism and romanticism (Schelling, Fichte, Hegel, Coleridge), but also in a contemporary strand of New Age mysticism.[12]

In short, if one pole of the ontological reading of the I AM leads to *onto-theology* (the conceptual capture of God as a category of substance), another pole comprises what we might call *mystical ontologism* (the conflation of divine and human consciousness).[13] I shall briefly revisit these positions in the third part of this chapter, entitled "Critical Considerations."

The Eschatological Reading

There is a powerful counter-tradition which resists ontological approaches to God. This second tradition of interpretation—which I call eschatological—is arguably more attuned to the original biblical context of meaning. Here the emphasis is on the ethical and dynamic character of God. The very framing of the Exodic self-revelation in terms of a response to Moses' question—who shall I say sent me?—opens the phrase toward the "mark of becoming."[14] This reading points to the fact that Exodus 3:14 falls within the framework of a solicitation—that is, assumes the task of summoning us toward an eschatological horizon. Such an understanding of the Exodic Name contrasts sharply with the more essentialist conceptions of divine Being in medieval and post-medieval metaphysics.

The God Who Promises—The Ethical Mandate

The great medieval Jewish commentator Rashi (Rabbi Solomon ben Isaac, 1040–1105) renders the burning-bush encounter as follows: "And God said unto Moses, 'I shall be what I shall be.' And he said, 'so shall you say to the children of Israel, I shall be has sent me to you.'" And lest there be any lingering doubt, God adds the binding promise: "This is my name for ever and this is my remembrance from generation to generation."[15]

Rashi interprets the "name" in terms of mandate and mission. He offers this daring commentary on God's address to Moses on Mount Horeb: "the vision that you have seen at the thornbush is the sign for you that I have sent you—and that you will succeed in My mission, and that I have the wherewithal to save you. Just as you saw the thornbush performing My mission without being consumed, so too, you will go on My mission and you will not be harmed." And Rashi adds, tellingly, that this mandate itself prefigures the fact that three months later Moses and his followers would receive the Torah upon the very same mountain.[16] Going on to render the key passage of Exodus 3:14, he writes, in very much the same spirit of futural promise: "I shall be what I shall be—I shall be with them during this trouble what I shall be with them at the time of their subjugation at the hands of other kingdoms." In other words, Rashi tells us, the transfiguring God of the burning bush is pledging to remain with those who continue to suffer in future historical moments, and not just in the present moment. Rashi attributes a similar sense to the phase "This is My Name forever, and My Remembrance from generation to generation" (Exodus 3:15). The transfiguring God is not a once-off deity but one who remembers the promises of the past and remains faithful to them into the eschatological future.

One of the best ways to ensure this fidelity is by refusing to yield up the secret of the Name here and now. As Rashi notes, the terms of Remembrance and Name are linked through the common experience of discretion and passing beyond. The word for "forever" in this verse is spelled in such a way that it takes the form of a word which normally says to "hide the Name." The reference to Remembrance means, accordingly, that God "taught Moses how the Ineffable Name which is to be concealed is to be pronounced (. . . other than it is written)."[17] Finally, and reinforcing his general reading of Exodus 3:15 in terms of mission, drama, and venture, Rashi points out that when God tells Moses that he will go to the king of Egypt and say that the God of the Hebrews "happened upon us" (Exodus 3:18), the phrase itself communicates a crucial sense of "chance occurrence,"[18] that is, of unpredictable surprise, serendipity, and grace. The future of the covenant is wide open—nothing is predetermined. It is up to us to remain as faithful to God as God promises to remain faithful to us.

It is important to recall here that Moses responds to the call of the burning bush—"Moses! Moses!"—with the reply "Here I am." The self-revelation of God that precedes and follows Moses' reply is less predicative than appellative. Above all else, it is a promise: "This is the name I shall bear forever, by which future generations will call me" (Exodus 3:15). We should be wary, then, of hypostatizing the "name" and seek to resituate it within the context of a dynamic mandate.[19] Amplifying the meaning of 'ehyeh 'asher 'ehyeh in this manner allows for a plurality of interpretations of the verb "to be" used by God in his address to Moses. And this means reading the formula in terms of function rather than substance, in terms of narrative rather than syllogism, in terms of relation rather than abstraction. God's "I shall be" appears to need Moses' response "Here I am" in order to enter history and blaze the path toward the Kingdom.

One consequence of the infiltration of this transfiguring God into the history of Greek and Latin metaphysics was to inject the latter with a specifically *ethical* charge. Smoke from the burning bush blurred the clear blue sky of Greco-Roman assurance. Nobody slept quite so well at night anymore, or breathed quite so easily during the day. There was a whiff of anxiety and expectation in the air. Dogmatic definitions of God began to fritter and come undone. And even those Neoplatonists who recognized the unknowable nature of God found it difficult to handle the urgency of this eschatological summons. God, it seemed, was undergoing an identity crisis. (Though not a gender one yet; He was still called He for a long while.) And though it was all very well to agree with the likes of Dionysius that the accompaniment of every affirmation with a negation points, apophatically, to a God beyond the proper names of Being, one was still left facing the quandary: if God is devoid of *all* historical being, is He not then also deprived of the power to act and call and love—a God so distant as to be defunct? So whether it was a question of the metaphysical God of essence or hyper-essence, it was hard to square either with a burning-bush God resolved to retrieve the past and inaugurate a new beginning.[20]

But let us return to Moses in front of his bush. A little context may be helpful here. Moses raised the question of God's identity in the light of the cultic-magical power systems prevalent at the time in most religions of the ancient Near East. Near Eastern gods bore a variety of names for general consumption but were considered to have a secret inaccessible name, unavailable to humans, and bearing enormous power. One exegetical commentator, André LaCocque, suggests that Moses' question to God may in part be an attempt to acquire this unknown name of divine power, particularly when we remember his competition with the Egyptian magicians. Moses' request, on this reading, is for such a name of power; and God's response to his request may be read accordingly as a *refusal* of this request. The very circularity and indeterminacy of the nameless name—*'ehyeh 'asher 'ehyeh*—confounds the attempt to glean magical profit from it. What God resists is not being addressed by Moses as such—He is invoked on countless occasions in the personal form of "Thou" throughout the Psalms (e.g., Psalm 99:6). No, what he resists is being reduced to the status of an idol. In short, God is repudiating any name that would seek to appropriate Him here and now as some thaumaturgical property. Instead, God keeps Himself open for a future, allowing for a more radical translation of his nameless name as "I am as I shall show myself."[21] In this respect, the linguistic root *hyh* in *'ehyeh 'asher 'ehyeh* is to be understood, LaCocque argues, less as a mere copula than as a token of agency: more like "to be with, to become, to show oneself . . . to befall, to happen" (*cadere, evenire*).[22]

Other paraphrasitic translations of Exodus 3:14 include Buber's "As the one who will always be there, so shall I be present in every time"; or Rosenzweig's "I will be there as I will be there."[23] These commentators share the view that what the suffering Hebrews needed from Moses was not some metaphysical proof about the existence of God as *ipsum esse* but an assurance that He would remain close to them. The promise of the speaking God which begins with the word *'ehyeh*, "I shall be," means a pledge to his people that he will not abandon them. It is not, Buber observes, the self-exposure of some occult magical power but a clarification of the *kind* of God he is, an indication of the eschatological "meaning and character of a name (YHVH)."[24]

The God revealed in Exodus is more, however, than a demystification of pagan tendencies to invoke divine names as mythical powers. It also marks a step beyond the capricious deity inherited by the Hebrews themselves from certain ancestral narratives recorded in Genesis—in particular the "sacrificial" account of Abraham and Isaac on Mount Moriah in Genesis 22 or the burnt sacrifices performed by Abraham in Genesis 15. Exodus 3:14 may be read accordingly not only as a biblical critique of other mystery-rite religions but as a self-critique of such traces in biblical religion itself![25]

According to my eschatological view, the Greek rendition of Exodus 3.14

as *ego eimi ho on* / *I am the one who is* misses too much of the original dynamism of the Hebrew expression, and concedes too much to Hellenistic ontology.[26] So doing it misses its mark. The burning bush epiphany is to be understood less as an ontological substance in opposition to non-being than as a self-generating event. In this annunciation, an agent is designated whose "work is actualized in Israel's exodus from Egypt"—namely, the self-revealing agency of the "Thou in dialogue with the divine I."[27]

In such light, Moses' question in Exodus 3:14 may be reinterpreted as a radical challenge to the One who has revealed himself as the God of his ancestors to proclaim a new plan of action by *becoming different* from what he has been until now.[28] The fact that Moses returns to Egypt and delivers a message of emancipation to his people signals the inauguration of an utterly novel mode of relation.[29] The One who was experienced by them as the God of their Fathers now discloses himself as the God of their sons and daughters.

So the Exodic name, we may now surmise, is *both* an I that is identical with itself in its past *and* a Thou that goes forth into the future. It reveals God as he is, at the same time as it commits God, and his emissary Moses, to an action of salvation. This is why the Name is both theophanic and performative.[30] It serves as the pre-name and sur-name of that which cannot be objectively nominated. And it is this excess or surplus that saves God from being reduced to a mere signified—transcendental or otherwise. The transfiguring God of the burning bush remains a trace which explodes the present toward the future, a *trait* which cannot be bordered or possessed. As Derrida notes in his comment on the eschatological tension within the Tetragrammaton: "the self-eclipsing *trait* cannot even say itself in the present, since it is not gathered, since it does not father itself, into any present, 'I am who I am' (a formula whose original grammatical form, as we know, implies the future). The outline or tracing separates and separates itself; it retraces only border lines, intervals, a spacing grid with no possible appropriation."[31] Which is why Derrida claims that "God deconstructs," and later again, that "deconstruction is justice."[32]

In short, the nameless Name is not an *acquis* but a promissory note. Its self-disclosure is inextricably tied to Moses' commission to go and announce to his fellow Hebrews their liberation and redemption. "You shall know that I am Yahweh your God, who frees you from the burden of the Egyptians. . . ." Henceforth, Yahweh is to be experienced as a saving-enabling-promising God, a God whose performance will bear out his pledges. As Psalm 138 makes clear, "you have made your promised word well above your name."[33]

It is worth repeating here that this eschatological promise is granted within an I-Thou relationship (of God with Moses), thereby indicating *two* sides to the promise, human *as well as* divine. The double relation in turn carries a dual responsibility not to become too distant or too familiar with God. Moses, remember, is summoned to approach, but also to remove his sandals and keep his distance. A safe distance, a sacred reserve. This twofold summons—come! but not too near!—is itself parallel to the shift from past to future. The revelation of Exodus 3:14 thus marks a displacement from an ancestral deity (of magic, territory, and inheritance) to a salvific God who vows to free the faithful from bondage in Egypt and prize open the more universal horizon of a Promised Land. Here God commits Himself to a kingdom of justice if his faithful commit themselves to it too; the promise of Sinai calls forth a corresponding decision on behalf of the people. To phrase this otherwise: the I puts it to the Thou that the promise can be *realized* only if those who receive it do not betray its potential for the future. Not that this is a matter of conditional exchange—turning the Exodus revelation into an economy of give-and-take. No, the promise is granted unconditionally, as pure gift. But God is reminding his people that they are free to accept or refuse this gift. A gift cannot be imposed; it can only be offered. A gift neither is nor is not; it gives.

This liberty to receive or reject the promise of the Name is epitomized by the character of *discretion* contained in the paronomasis—that is, the circular, tautological, indeterminate quality of the expression (similar to the proverbial shaggy-dog story that undoes itself: a literary device not unknown to several postmodern narrators from Beckett and Borges to Calvino and Eco). Indeed, even when Moses reports the revelation of the Name to his people, he does not do so in the objectifying form of the third person but once more in repetition of the I-Thou commission "*'ehyeh has sent me.*" In this manner also, the unnameable Name refuses not just the temptation of ritual incantation but the danger of ideological appropriation. Yahweh does not possess and cannot be possessed. Paronomasis serves, accordingly, as a guarantee of *radical dispossession.*[34]

God does not reveal himself, therefore, as an essence *in se* but as an I-Self for us. And the most appropriate mode of human response to this Exodic revelation is precisely that: *commitment to a response.*[35] Such commitment shows Yahweh as God-the-agent, whose co-respondents, from Moses to the exilic prophets and Jesus, see themselves implicated in the revelation as receivers of a gift—a Word given by someone who calls them to cooperate with Him in his actions. That is why Moses is called to be as "God for Aaron" and "for the Pharaoh" (Exodus 4:16 and 7:1). Moses and the prophets are *implicated* in the revelation showing us how Yahweh acts concretely through his human emissaries. With the revelation of his Name, God says of himself something like "with you Moses—and with Israel throughout history—I stand or fall!" Exodus 3 is the proclamation that God has invested the whole of Himself in his emissary's history.[36]

The God Who Comes—Historical Mandate

We may say, consequently, that the Exodic act of disclosure signals an inextricable communion between God and humans, a radically new sense—as Levinas points out—of fraternity, responsibility, and commitment to a shared history of "becoming," beginning with emancipation from bondage in Egypt.[37] God may henceforth be recognized as someone who *becomes with us*, someone as dependent on us as we are on Him. God's relation with mortals is, in other words, less one of conceptuality than of covenant. From which it follows that most philosophical reflections on God are in need of revision. And certainly, the orthodox onto-theological categories of omnipotence, omniscience, and self-causality, originally forged *sub specie aeternitatis*, could do with a radical rethink *sub specie historiae*. Faced with the burning bush, one doesn't merely speculate; one runs, or if one holds one's ground, one praises, dances, acts.[38]

The eschatological wager reaches here its most dramatic stakes. Once the "unaccomplished form of the verb"—*'ehyeh*—is taken in its full implications, one realizes that God is what he *will* be when he becomes his Kingdom and his Kingdom comes on earth. At the eschaton, God promises to be God (cf. Isaiah 11:9; Psalms 110:1; Zechariah 14:9; 1 Corinthians 15:24–28). Meanwhile, God is in the process of establishing his lordship on earth and the *'ehyeh 'asher 'ehyeh* may be rendered accordingly as "I will be what I will be; I will become what I will become." In addition, therefore, to the unaccomplished form of the verb, we find an "uncannily taut drama" signaled by the relative pronoun *'asher* (what/who) "for its content essentially depends on the quality of history that Moses and his people will pour into it."[39]

Thus does the Exodic Name come to supplement Elohim as the name for the living God. For if Elohim—a name derived from a common noun—is the transcendent God who sat in heaven (Psalm 47), created earth and demanded sacrifice (e.g., of Isaac), Yhwh is more a name-of-invocation which makes the living God more accessible to human relation and history (i.e., more personal and more eschatological). With the revelation of Exodus, "God ceases to be the Unnameable, the inaccessible, the one *a se et per se*. He ceases to be impassible—if he ever was."[40] Yhwh is now revealed as affected and vulnerable, showing himself henceforth as one who wrestles with himself (Hosea), laments (Jeremiah), regrets (Samuel), seduces and forgives (Psalms). Here we witness a God who persuades rather than coerces, invites rather than imposes, asks rather than impels. This God of Mosaic manifestation cannot be God without relating to his other—humanity.[41] And seldom has this wager been so dramatically expressed as in the following midrash on Isaiah 43:12: "If you are not My witnesses, I am, as it were, not God."[42]

In the final analysis, what makes Exodus 3:14 a call to human attestation through a history of effectivity (*Wirkungsgeschichte*) is not just the unaccomplished nature of the verb and pronoun but the first-person voice: I-may-be. The formulation is performative rather than constative. It takes the form of an address that solicits action from the addressee, rather than some kind of super-determination from on high which leaves us too cold, or too hot, to act. It always leaves us, in short, the option of response. This is surely why commentators like Fromm, Ricoeur, and LaCocque see the first person call to a Thou as the condition of an eschatological colloquy where I and Thou engage in a relationship of *mutual answerability and co-creation*.[43]

The existential implications of this inauguration of a personal God are revolutionary. For what we are witnessing here is a radical alteration of the metaphysical use of the copula. What was crucial for Greek thought was *to be* since divine being was ultimately deemed timeless and permanent, ontological rather than moral. (Just think of Aristotle's God.) For the Hebrews, by contrast, what is most important is to *become, to be able.* Thus while the Hellenists translate Exodus 3:14 as "I am the Being who is eternal," a non-Hellenic Jew like Maimonides encourages us to conceive of Yhwh as an agent with an active purpose, a God who *does* rather than a *being who is* (*Guide of the Perplexed* 1.54–58).[44]

The consequences for a Christian reading are no less radical. The early Church saw the incarnate Christ as the Exodic Name made flesh. As Revelation 1:8 proclaims: "I am the one who is, who was, and who is to come." In this manner the recognition of the Name as eschatological vocation is charged with a goal which for Christianity finds its realization in the coming, or second coming, of Christ. In several passages in John we find the formula *ego eimi*/I am (John 4:26, 6:35; 1 John 1:1). And it is also in John that we find Christ identifying himself explicitly with the Name: "I have made your Name known to those whom you gave me from the world . . . now they know . . . in truth that I came from you" (John 17:6).

The unnameable Name is, in short, God's way of transfiguring—that is, of appearing-disappearing—in a bush that never burns away. The Exodic epiphany is an ingenious wordplay which heralds an eschatological transcendence: a transcendence with the wherewithal to resist the lures of logocentric immanence.

Critical Considerations

Transcendence can, however, become too transcendent. If removed entirely from historical being, God can become so unknowable and invisible as to escape all identification whatsoever. Such a numinous deity often takes the form of a "negative" or "apophatic" theology.

This tendency to construe the transfiguring God of Exodus as a God without being is especially evident in a contemporary thinker like Jean-Luc Marion.[45] Marion cites Dionysius and the apophatic tradition in his argument that the whole metaphysics of *naming* God must give way to a new understanding of God as pure *giving*. To subordinate the God of love to speculative distinctions of being and non-being is to resort to principles of reason which God radically transcends. Indeed for Marion the conceptual atheism of modern thinkers like Nietzsche and Heidegger is, curiously, one of the best weapons against the "conceptual idolatry" of onto-theology. Why? Because by deconstructing the old idols it can permit a new logic to emerge: that of superabundance and gratuity. The statement "God is One" may thus give way—for Marion, if not for Nietzsche and Heidegger—to the utterance "God loves."

But there are problems with Marion's mystical theology when it comes to the name of God. In *God without Being*, Marion directly relates Exodus 3:14 to what he considers to be privileged mystical revelations in the Christian scriptures (John 8:24 and 58; or Luke 24:39 where Christ says "I am myself," *ego eimi autos*). So doing, Marion invokes the authority of a Eucharistic hermeneutic. The "hermeneutic of the text by the community," he writes, is conditioned by that community itself being "interpreted by the Word." But this can only be ultimately guaranteed "thanks to the liturgical service of the theologian par excellence, the bishop."[46] In the heel of the Marionesque hunt, "only the bishop merits, in the full sense, the title of theologian."[47] To remain true to such an ecclesiastical hermeneutic we must accept that the "saturation" of signs (words, names, texts, speech) by the "unspeakable Word" means that "we find all already given, gained, available."[48]

The transfiguring Word, in short, does not depend on us in any way. It does not really need our response in order to be more fully fulfilled. Once it is revealed through such a saturated phenomenon as the burning bush (or, Marion adds, the Eucharist), there is nothing further for us to think, say, or do to make the Word more fully alive in this world. We have little or no part to play in the transfiguring mission of the Word—e.g., the quest for historical justice. The referent of the religious sign is not, Marion makes plain, something to be "taught," and by extension debated or developed. No, it is encountered *as is* "by mystical union."[49] Consequently, only he who knows the "Word nonverbally," in mystical communion with the Eucharist, has the wisdom to subsequently interpret it.[50] (A confessional move which, on the face of it, does not seem very inclusive of non-communicant non-Catholics.)

But how does Marion come to such a conclusion? In his essay "In the Name," Marion clarifies the underlying implications of his thinking. Here he points to a God beyond both the affirmation and negation of names, where words assume a purely pragmatic function: "beyond every name and every denegation of the name . . . the word says just as little as it negates—it acts by referring to the One who de-nominates (*dé-nomme*)."[51] As such, Marion argues that the "hyper" invoked by Dionysius and others to indicate the "ineffability" of God (*Divine Names* IV, I, 865c), is not of the order of essence or knowledge but transgresses both in favor of a praise of that which precedes every essence. The "hyper" of negative theology would thus point to a God radically devoid of being and safely beyond the reaches of onto-theology understood as metaphysics of presence. Marion distills negative theology (as enunciated by Dionysius and Gregory of Nyssa) into an uncompromising "theology of absence." The "saturated phenomenon" of mystical eucharistic encounter with the divine is informed by such a *hyper*-excess that it cannot be seen, known, or understood. Its very superabundance surpasses all predication and narration. Or to put it in Marion's own words: this mystical experience takes the form of a certain "stupor" or "terror" which its very "incomprehensibility imposes on us."[52]

We hit here upon a serious hermeneutic muddle. If the saturating phenomenon is really as bedazzling as Marion suggests, how can we tell the difference between the divine and its opposites? How are we to distinguish between enabling and disabling revelations? Who is it that speaks when God speaks from the burning bush? And if it is true indeed, as Saint Paul concedes, that the Messiah comes like a thief in the night, in the very same passage (1 Thessalonians 5), Paul, *pace* Marion, calls for sober and enlightened vigilance: "But you, beloved, are not in darkness, for that day to surprise you like a thief; for you are children of light and children of the day; we are not of the night or of darkness. . . . So let us keep awake and be sober." Such Pauline sobriety seems a far cry from Marion's celebration of blind mystical rapture. Or as John Caputo adroitly inquires—when we are confronted with the saturated phenomenon of God how can we discriminate between excess and defect—"how do we know that we have been visited by a supereminent excess and not just invaded by *khora*?"[53] How indeed!

＊＊＊

But in addition to conceptual atheists (like Nietzsche) and negative theologians (like Marion), there exists a further strand of mystical postmodernism which challenges attempts to reduce divine alterity to the level of human hermeneutics. This third approach I term—borrowing from medieval parlance—a *teratology of the sublime* in that it focuses on the "monstrous" character of God. One finds examples of this in certain New Age invocations of a neo-Jungian or neo-Gnostic "dark god"—an ambivalent deity which transcends our conventional moral notions of good and evil and summons us to rediscover our innermost unconscious selves, to "follow our bliss." A typical instance of this is Joseph Campbell's reference to the "monster God" whose very horrendousness explodes all categories of judgment and shatters our accredited "standards for harmony, order and ethical conduct."[54] In this order of spellbinding sublimity, "God is horrific."

Some postmodern advocates of the monstrous God find intellectual precedents in a particular strain of German idealist mysticism running from Schelling's writings on the "dark side of God" (the groundless ground of divine nature whose obverse is the burning bush epiphany) to the later Heidegger's "Last God."[55] Such Gods are considered monstrous in so far as their very sublimity reveals itself as ultimately indistinguishable from abjection and evil. In the realm of the sublime, vertical excess and abyssal excess easily collapse into one another. Alterity becomes the flip side of the void. And this reversibility of opposites prompts a provocative Slavoj Zizek to suggest that Judaism, as a cult of utterly unnameable, unimaginable, inaccessible transcendence, is itself a religion of the sublime: "Judaism is the religion of the Sublime (in that) it tries to render the suprasensible dimension . . . in a purely negative way, by renouncing the images altogether."[56] God becomes so unfamiliar and ineffable as to be traumatic—that is, *horrible*. So horrifying indeed as to assume the form of the "Real of the primordial violent thing."[57] In other words, Zizek is suggesting that the monotheistic God can sometimes appear *so alien* as to be not just strange but radically estranging. Which prompts certain critics to suggest that even Levinas's pursuit of a radically other God can go to such extremes that he becomes a master of the "literature of horror"![58]

But whatever the accuracy of such critiques, I remain persuaded that it is still possible to respect the otherness of the Exodic God without succumbing to the extremes of mystical postmodernism, and in particular its dispensing with ethical and historical judgment.

While acknowledging therefore how salutary it is to shock theological orthodoxies and unsettle the self-righteous, I do believe that certain postmodern teratologists revel in excess for its own sake. By contrast, a rebel iconoclast like Moses already showed us how we can break open a new order of existence without dissolving into a void. He confronted the burning bush without succumbing to the monstrous. His encounter with the absolutely Other revealed a deity who, as noted, calls us to an ethico-political task—the eschatological quest for liberty and justice. To the cult of apocalyptic traumatism (and masochistic *jouissance*) advanced by some of my postmodern colleagues, I might oppose Rashi's radical reading of the burning-bush God as mission and promise; a reading reinforced by Moses Hess's own bracing version of Exodus 3:14: "As God has redeemed the people from Egypt, so he will be the Redeemer from every other social slavery (whether material or spiritual, bodily or moral) in the future."[59]

In sum, the danger of God without being is that of an alterity so "other" that it becomes impossible to distinguish it from monstrosity—mystical or sublime. To avoid this, it may, I suggest, be wiser to reinterpret the God of Exodus 3:14 as neither being nor non-being, but as something before, between, and beyond the two: an eschatological *may be?* Such a third way might help us eschew the excesses of both *ecclesiastical mysticism* on the one hand (Marion and certain negative theologians) and *apocalyptic postmodernism* on the other (Zizek and the prophets of the sublime).

The God Who May Be—A Via Tertia

In conclusion I will sketch a hermeneutic retrieval (*Wiederholung*) of the Exodic name with a view to charting an itinerary beyond the polar opposition between onto-theology and negative theology. My wager here is that at the chiasmus where *'ehyeh* meets *einai* a seismic shift occurs—with God putting being into question just as being gives flesh to God. At this border-crossing, the transfiguring Word struggles for carnal embodiment even as it dissolves into the flaming bush of its own desire.

From this onto-eschatological perspective, I will try, by way of a few final tentative remarks, to reread some highpoints in the historical interpretations of Exodus 3:14.

When Philo invoked the Greek translation of the Exodus passage—*ego eimi ho on*—he insisted that God here reveals not his content (whatness-essence) but only *that* he exists (the verb *einai*). Christian commentators would later render this passage in the light of self-revelations of Jesus—e.g., "The one who is, and who was, and who is coming," or again, "Before Abraham was, I am" (8:58). This translation of the Hebrew into Greek (*einai*) and later into Latin (*esse*) was to radicalize the existing plurality of terms for being. It provoked an extraordinary variety of interpretations throughout the history of Western thought. Indeed, it is Paul Ricoeur's view that this very pluralism of interpretation actually safeguards against the danger of "conceptual idolatry" (so rightly feared by Marion and other postmoderns) and reinforces the enigmatic resonance of the original phrase heard by Moses and his Hebrew followers.[60] In short, why not assume that Exodus 3:14 was "ready from the very beginning to add a new region of significance to the rich polysemy of the verb being, explored in other terms by the Greeks and their Muslim, Jewish and Christian heirs?"[61]

The prefatory command of God to Moses to remove the sandals from his feet may now be seen in its original innovative implications. As also the fact that it is far from his own people, captured in Egypt, that Moses receives his revelation from God. For it is only in the solitary estrangement from Moses' native home that the Other shows itself to Moses as self-consuming fire. In this manner, the "dangerous liaisons" between being and God are, as Stanislas Breton suggests, a way of signaling God in his transcendence without neglecting his carnal desire. For if there was no burning bush to see or no voice, however riddling, to hear, there would be nothing to witness, and so nothing to remember or promise! There would only be regress to the chaos of pre-creation: the dark before the Word. *Tohu bohu.*

Revisiting Meister Eckhart's much neglected intervention in the Exodus 3:14 debate, one remarks how this subtle Dominican managed to skew ontological categories in the direction of eschatological intent. Under his gaze, the "I" of the Exodic tautology is seen to accentuate the sense of God's *difference*: for example, the epithet *discretivum*, with which Eckhart qualifies the "I," connotes a measure of distance.[62] By extension, Eckhart's use of the term *substantia* may be understood in the curious sense of a "being that stands on its own, by its own energy"—the quasi-being encountered at the heart of nothingness, which "carries all things according to the Word." This pure separateness of the divine "I" declines all additions of "this or that" and outstrips the familiar Aristotelian categories of substance deployed by conventional scholasticism.

Eckhart's commentary on the verb *sum* also invites us to reinterpret the traditional being of God. "Being-as-copula" becomes being in "solitude and separation."[63] Qua *sum*, God here absolves himself from all predication, announcing both the ontological difference between Being and beings and the theological difference between divine and human. Here is a *sum* whose very burning-bush indeterminacy, in Breton's words, "expresses the purificatory fire of a certain iconoclasm."[64]

And what, finally, of the *who*? Here, Eckhart may be seen as stressing the *dynamism* of the self-giving God: "The repetition which says twice "I am who I am" is the purity of affirmation which excludes all negation . . . it indicates a certain reflexive conversion in itself and on itself, a sanctuary or repose which holds in itself; what is more, it indicates a specific effervescence (or bubbling over) or birth of self: this being, in fact, conceals a fervor which expands within itself and onto itself in a sort of bubbling; light within light, it penetrates everything. . . ."[65] By means of such hyperbole, Eckhart's rendering of the Exodic verse actually destabilizes and reworks traditional metaphysics. Behind their ostensible orthodoxy, the ontological proposition *esse est Deus* and the theological proposition *Deus est esse* mutually deconstruct each other. This bilateral deconstruction does not ignore the fundamental implication of God in flesh. On the contrary, it shows that God's self-nomination cannot dispense with the detour through amorous being, lest it become so unknowable as to pass us by unseen and unheard. There's more to God than being. Granted. But to pass *beyond* being you have to pass *through* it. Without the flesh of the world, there is no birth.

And I might add here that it is in this passing through flesh that God made flesh liberates and transfigures the *persona* in each one of us. Indeed Eckhart even goes so far (perhaps too far) as to suggest that "between the Son and the soul there is no distinction" and so "the eye by which I see God and the eye by which God sees me are one and the same."[66] But already in the transfiguring fire of the burning bush, Eckhart, like Rosenzweig, identifies a similar overlapping "of the distant God with the near."[67]

Thus the ontological commentaries on the *ego sum qui sum* found in Eckhart may be seen—from an eschatological viewpoint—to carry a presentiment of God as pure *gift* and *passage*. Pure gift in the sense of self-giving beyond the economic condition of return. "Being," as Eckhart put it, "is so superior in rank and purity and so much God's own that no one can give it but he—as he gives himself."[68] But God is also pure passage in the sense that while he always stays faithful to his promise, He never stays put. Eckhart's own best defense against the charges of onto-theology or mystical ontologism is the reminder that he deemed the dialogue between God and being to be *provisional* rather than final. God passes through being just as beings pass through God. But the primary verb is just that: *passage*, understood as transition and migration. Reinterpreted from an eschatological angle, God is the *imperative of transit*. "This is a God who disturbs, uproots, reiterates the call of Yahweh to Abraham to 'leave his house'; a God who shakes every edifice, even the venerable *esse subsistens*."[69] Which is surely why Eckhart takes his leave of being only after he has rendered homage to its imprescribable necessity as passage.

His famous formula—"I pray God to rid me of God"—may be read consequently as an echo of the imperative to transit. The move beyond ontology has
as corollary the move beyond essentialist theology, surpassing the essence of
God toward God's ultimate promise. In this wise, the metaphysics of exodus
(being-word-abyss) becomes an exodus of metaphysics. A self-emptying movement of metaphysics beyond itself. The revelation of God as traversal—or as
what I have called in the opening chapter *transfiguration*.[70]

Transiting through and beyond metaphysics, God reveals himself, in
keeping with his promissory note in Exodus, as a God that neither is nor is not
but *may be*. And here I might add the intellectual dexterity of Cusanus to the
deconstructive daring of Eckhart. God, as Nicholas of Cusa puts it, is best
considered neither as *esse*, nor as *nihil*, but as *possest*. Transgressing the traditional scholastic capture of God as *esse*, Cusanus redefines God as *possest*
(absolute possibility which includes all that is actual). "Existence (*esse*) presupposes possibility (*posse*)," writes Cusanus, "since it is not the case that
anything exists unless there is possibility from which it exists." God alone, he
concludes, "is what he is able to be."[71] It is arguably this same hidden intellectual heritage which resurfaces, however obscurely, in Schelling's definition of
the God of Exodus 3:14 as the "possibility to-be" (*seyn wird*) or the "immediate
can-be" (*unmittelbar Seyn-konnende*); or again in Heidegger's later understanding of the gift of being as a "loving-possibilizing" (*das Vermögen des
Mögens*). Indeed we may even detect distant traces of it in Derrida's enigmatic
description of the transfiguring power of the messianic Perhaps: "There will
occur, perhaps, the event of that which arrives, and this will be the hour of joy,
an hour of birth but also of resurrection . . . the promise promises in that
fundamental mode of perhaps. . . . The possibilisation of the impossible possible must remain at one and the same time as undecidable—and therefore as
decisive—as the future itself. . . ."[72] This counter-tradition of readings, which I
will revisit in subsequent chapters, calls I believe for a new hermeneutic of
God as May-Be. What I term an onto-eschatological hermeneutics. Or more
simply, a *poetics of the possible*.[73]

Does all this amount to a *conditional* God? No. For if God's future being is
indeed conditional on our actions in history, God's infinite love is not. As a gift,
God is *unconditional* giving. Divinity is constantly waiting.

* * *

Let me conclude with the following surmises: In the circular words, I-am-
who-may-be, God transfigures and exceeds being. His *esse* reveals itself, surprisingly and dramatically, as *posse*. The Exodus 3:14 exchange between God
and Moses might, I have been suggesting, be usefully reread not as the manifestation of some secret name but as a pledge to remain constant to a promise.
God, transfiguring himself in the guise of an angel, speaks through (*per-sona*)
a burning bush and seems to say something like this: *I am who may be if you*

continue to keep my word and struggle for the coming of justice. The God who reveals Himself on Mount Horeb is and is not, neither is nor is not. This is a God who puns and tautologizes, flares up and withdraws, promising always to return, to become again, to come to be what he is *not yet* for us. This God is the coming God who may-be. The one who resists quietism as much as zealotry, who renounces both the onto-theology of essence and the voluntarist impatience to appropriate promised lands. This Exodic God obviates the extremes of atheistic and theistic dogmatism in the name of a still small voice that whispers and cries in the wilderness: *perhaps.* Yes, perhaps if we remain faithful to the promise, one day, some day, we know not when, I-am-who-may-be will at last be. Be what? we ask. Be what is promised as it is promised. And what is that? we ask. A kingdom of justice and love. There and then, to the human "Here I am," God may in turn respond, "Here I am." But not yet.

Transfiguring God

I say more: the just man justices;
Keeps grace: that keeps all his goings graces;
Acts in God's eye what in God's eye he is—
Christ—for Christ plays in ten thousand places,
Lovely in limbs, and lovely in eyes not his
To the Father through the features of men's faces.

—*Gerald Manley Hopkins, ["As kingfishers catch fire"]*

In this third chapter, I turn to the more explicitly incarnational accounts of the *persona-prosopon* as it features in the Christian narratives of transfiguration on Mount Thabor and the paschal apparitions in Emmaus, Jerusalem, and Galilee. My approach remains, however, in spite of invoking several scriptural and patristic texts, that of a phenomenological-hermeneutic retrieval rather than that of theological exegesis per se.

Messianic Transfiguration

The act of transfiguration finds canonical expression in the testimony of Mount Thabor. Here the person of Jesus is metamorphosed before the eyes of his disciples into the *persona* of Christ. The alteration—from one to the other—is Christ's coming into his own, fully assuming his messianic calling announced by the prophetic tradition from Moses to Elijah. It is marked not by Jesus abandoning his original person to become *someone* else, but by a change of "figure" which allows his divine *persona* to shine forth—in singular fashion —through his flesh-and-blood embodiedness. Jesus comes into his own by being "othered" as Christ. His person transforms into the *persona* latent in his self, the very divine otherness of his finite being, his in-finity. He becomes the *prosopon par excellence,* or as Stanislas Breton might add, *par excès.*

It is no accident that the episode occurs just eight days after Jesus announced the first prophecy of the Passion and the coming of the kingdom: the double act of death and promised resurrection which sets the condition for following Christ, "anyone who loses his life for my sake will save it" (Luke 9:23–28). Nor is it adventitious that prior to this announcement, Jesus had challenged Peter with the question of his identity—"who do you say that I am?"—receiving Peter's response: "The Christ of God" (Luke 9:21). What occurs shortly afterward on Mount Thabor, in the presence of Peter and two other apostles, is surely Jesus' own way of confirming this mystery of messianic incarnation: the word made flesh, the Christ made man in and through the *prosopon* of Jesus. *To the father through the features of man's face.*

The *Dictionaire de la Bible* says: "The transfiguration of Our Lord, which ancient tradition locates on Mount Thabor, is indicated by the verb *metamorphothe, transfiguratus est,* which supposes a change, not in the person itself, but in the *figure* in which it normally appears."[1] Saint Luke's Gospel tells us that as Jesus was praying, "the aspect of his face (*prosopon*) was changed and his clothing became sparkling white" (Luke 9:29–30). Note that it is the *face* that registers the transfiguring event, marking an ethical openness to transcendence which refuses idolatry. The Greek is very instructive here, *prosopon heteron,* means literally "his face was othered." And yet he somehow remained *some* one, for he was *still recognized* as himself.

A similar distancing precaution is also evidenced in the mention of "whiteness," a common metaphor for the infinite character of divinity (see also Matthew 17:2). Indeed the manner in which the narrative shows Jesus carefully preparing his three disciples, James, John, and Peter, by leading them to a sequestered high mountain to pray, and by covering himself in a cloud, suggests further measures of protection against idolatrous appropriation. It would seem to be in this same spirit that Christ insists, after the event, that the disciples build no monuments and keep their counsel—that is, avoid making him into an idol. As we are told, "the disciples kept silence and, at that time, told no one what they had seen" (Luke 9:36).[2] This is an echo of Christ's admonition after Peter's profession of faith in the "Christ of God"—"he charged them not to say this to anyone" (Luke 9:21).

The Eschatological Legacy

I

It may be instructive to recall the famous *Homily on the Transfiguration* by Saint John Damascene. Here we read: "The holy body finds itself circumscribed because, at the very moment it stands on Mt. Thabor, it does not surpass the physical limits of the mountain; but the divinity (of Christ) is infinite; it is . . . beyond all."[3] Damascene goes on to make this connection between Christ's infinity and the whiteness of his transfigured aspect: "Just as the sun's light is other, so the visage (*prosopon*) of Christ shines forth like the sun and his garments white as light; they glisten with the splendour of the divine light."[4] But the author is adamant that the transfigured character of Christ's face does not mean his divinity is reducible to this appearance. The transfigured Christ "receives glory," he tells us, "by *investment* not by *fusion*."[5] In this sense we might say that the transfiguration signals a surplus or incommensurability between *persona* and person even as it inscribes the one in and through the other.

Hence the phenomenological logic behind the Chalcedonian formula of two-in-one. A startling chiasm of infinity in the finite. Certainly too much for his disciples, who are so baffled and bedazzled by Christ's whiteness that they immediately recoil in fear and must be reassured by the voice of the Father speaking from the cloud: "This is my Son, the Chosen One. Listen to him" (Luke 9:35). An echo perhaps of Moses' initial fright before the blinding brightness of the burning bush, removing his sandals in fear before he is summoned to his mission by God?

We might even recall here what Melville has to say about the strange and estranging quality of whiteness in *Moby Dick*: "But not yet have we solved the incantation of this whiteness, and learned why it appeals with such power to the soul; and more strange and far more portentous—why . . . it is at once the most meaning symbol of spiritual things, nay, the very veil of the Christian's Deity; and yet should be as it is, the intensifying agent in things the most appalling to mankind." Melville asks finally, "Is it, that as in essence whiteness is not so much a color as the visible absence of color, and at the same time the concrete of all colors; is it for these reasons that there is such a dumb blankness, full of meaning, in a wide landscape of snows—a colorless, all-color of atheism from which we shrink?"[6] The thin white line between atheism and theism marks the seemingly undecidable frontier of faith. God-man as double bind. The Christic crossing of *persona* and person.[7] A holy braille to be deciphered in blinding light. Which is why the transfiguring God calls at all times for hermeneutic vigilance and discernment, setting us at a critical distance—yet never so distant as to forfeit grace. Far in its very nearness, but not so far as not to be (or be read) at all. It bids us cast a cold eye but not the eye of death.

It is surely telling then that while the disciples who witness the transfigured Christ are filled with fright (Luke 9:34), his two Jewish forebears—the first and last prophets, Moses and Elijah—appear not in fear but "in glory" (Luke 9:31). The calm wisdom of the prophets as they converse with Christ stems doubtless from the fact that they have already encountered the infinite— and lived. (Moses in Exodus 3:14 and Elijah in Kings 19). And again in contrast with Peter, James, and John, the two Jewish prophets do not propose setting up tents of cultic adoration there on the mountain but choose to speak to the transfigured Christ about his coming mission—"his passing which he was about to accomplish in Jerusalem" (Luke 9:31).

The disciples' effort to fix Christ as a fetish of presence, imposing their own designs on him, make it necessary for God to intercede from the cloud and bid them attend to Christ's otherness: "Listen to *him!*" In this manner, the voice of transcendence speaks through Christ as divine *persona*, thereby arresting the idolatrous impulse of Peter, James, and John to fuse with his person or possess him as a cult object. The next line is especially telling. "After the voice had spoken, Jesus was found *alone*" (Luke 9:36). In other words, Christ is *set apart* from his followers by the divine voice-over (*per-sona*). And it is this very solitude of Christ, together with the consequent silence of the disciples as they follow him down the mountain that marks off this incident as an epiphany of radical alterity. Mount Thabor unfolds accordingly as a Gospel replay of Mount Sinai, with the transfigured Christ both re-figuring the burning bush and pre-figuring the coming of the messianic kingdom (when the resurrected Christ and the last prophet Elijah will return). Christ as a trans-figure *between* Moses and Elijah.

II

To reparse this in the phenomenological idioms of the opening chapter, we might say that the transfigured Christ breaches the limits of intentional consciousness. The very otherness and uniqueness of his *persona* exceed the horizontal reach of our three main modalities of noetic intentionality: It goes beyond *perception* (the dazzling whiteness and the cloud, recalling the veil protecting the holy of holies), beyond *imagination* (the refusal of Peter's cultic imaginings), and beyond *signification* (the observing of silence). This excess of transcendent *persona* over immanent person is what prompts John Damascene to portray Jesus cautioning Peter: "If Adam had not sought deification, before the time, he would have achieved what he desired. Do not seek goods before their time, O Peter!"[8]

Moreover, the fact that the day after their descent from Mount Thabor Christ makes his second prophecy of the Passion to come—announcing that he will be "delivered into the power of men" (Luke 9:44)—and then proceeds to declare that a helpless child on the street is greater than all the ambitious disciples, is a further indication of how the Transfiguration narrative is framed with scenes which resist attempts to apotheosize Christ as some magical power. The Transfiguration reminds us that when it comes to the *persona* of God—marking the unique thisness (*haecitas*) of each person—it is a question of the old enigma: now you have him, now you don't. One moment there, one moment gone.

From which it follows that the cult of the *historical* Jesus can be a form of idolatry just as compromising of Christ's *persona* as his reduction to some *a-historical* fetish (Gnostic or ecclesiastic). The infinite *persona* of Christ is not exhausted in the finite figure of Jesus of Nazareth. The Messiah is distinct, if by no means separable, from the Nazarene. For as John Damascene once again reminds us, God only becomes man "in an indivisible difference, in a union *without confusion*."[9] And this is reinforced by Saint John, the favorite apostle, when he identifies the transfiguring spirit of Christ with the eschatological Paraclete of the kingdom. Jesus the historical person must depart from this finite world so that the *persona* of the infinite Christ may return as the Paraclete who refigures all in a new heaven and a new earth (John 14:26). This is what the Homily of Saint Anastasius refers to as the "marvellous theophany on Mount Thabor in the guise of an image prefiguring the Kingdom."[10] For, according to this eschatologico-messianic reading, what we witness in the Mount Thabor narrative is nothing less than a preview of the "new creation," a call to "draw a recreated creation towards God."[11]

III

This audacious perspective is confirmed by many another post-Gospel commentary. Dionysius the Areopagite, for example, claims that to be perfect as the heavenly father is perfect means that the "Lord will appear to his perfect servants (in the kingdom) in the same guise as he was seen by the apostles on Mt Thabor."[12] And several other commentators find support for this radical interpretation in Mark's account of God reminding the three apostles that the transfigured Christ is his "beloved son" (Mark 9:7). So doing, God confounds the apostle's "natural" expectations and announces Christ as the possibility of all humans becoming "sons of God"—that is, by being transfigured into their own unique *personas*. Accordingly, Christ is held out to us as a promise inscribed in the long prophetic path pointing toward the coming kingdom, and already signposted by Moses and Elijah (the iconoclastic and messianic prophets, respectively). Indeed it is no accident that both these predecessors are harbingers of exodus (*ex-hodos*, the way outwards) rather than of closure. Their accompaniment of Jesus in his moment of metamorphosis on the mountain serves as reminder that the transfigured Christ is a *way* not a terminus, an *eikon* not a fundamentalist fact, a *figure* of the end but not the end itself. A point powerfully brought home to us by Christ's insistence on his own exodic "passing" in the days to come. The Mount Thabor narratives may thus be said to speak to us of a God of passage rather than of literal presence. God as way, truth and light—but never as fait accompli. The very discretion of Christ's *prosopon-persona* is a prohibition against premature possession. His face is too self-effacing to incite religious war.

It is perhaps fitting to mention at this point the vigorous attempts by the third-century Tertullian to emphasize the differential uniqueness of Christ's *persona* as an answer to those early sects—Sabellian, Patropassian, and Monarchian—who wished to reduce the Son and the Spirit to the single monarchy of the Father. Against this drive for paternalist hegemony, Tertullian translated the Greek *prosopon* into the Latin *persona* (apparently the first Christian commentator to do so), thereby reinforcing the irreducible singularity of Christ regarding human beings but also regarding the two other persons of the Trinity. By translating the already used Greek *prosopon* to reinforce the distinctness of the *tres personae* of the Trinity, Tertullian was ensuring that (1) the *persona* of Christ would be acknowledged as more than just a human person, albeit incarnate in and through the latter; (2) that He would be given his proper and equal role in the Trinity; and (3) that certain connotations of *persona* as a mere theatrical mask or pretense would be avoided in favor of Christ's uniqueness and authenticity.[13]

This last point is crucial for it suggests how the attribution of the *prosopon*/*persona* figure to Christ succeeds in *personalizing*—without either *literalizing* or *volatilizing*—the notion of the Son. Now Christ can be seen as *both* finite and infinite, eternal and carnal, *hypostasis* and *ekstasis*. For the early Church Fathers, the point of identifying Christ with the *prosopon*/*persona* was to suggest that he was neither an hypostasis without ekstasis (idolatry of God as merely human), nor an ekstasis without hypostasis (mysticism of God as inhuman). This is no doubt why Basil the Great felt compelled in a letter (no. 214) to make an important distinction between *prosopon* (face) and *prosopeion* (mask). For while there is clearly an etymological connection between the terms, the prioritizing of the latter would have made the *persona* of Christ into little more than a mouthpiece for the Father, a mere spectral apparition or divine ventriloquist's dummy. It would have totally ignored the crucial crossing between hypostasis and person which epitomized the singularity of Jesus (he was *this* embodied person and none other). And this very singularity was part of his transfiguring power. It is the personhood (*prosopon*) of Christ which marks the mode of divine self-generation into being.[14]

It is curious to note how many of these patristic references, dating back to the third century, have been revived today in a radically phenomenological context by thinkers as diverse as Levinas, Heidegger, Marion, and Caputo.

The Pauline Legacy

It is arguably Saint Paul, however, who most influenced the eschatological reading of the Transfiguration narratives. In 2 Corinthians 3:18, he invokes this perspective of the kingdom when he suggests that the scene on Mount Thabor is a call to each one of us to become transfigured in the light of Christ. Such transfiguring is something done onto us by the grace-giving *persona* of Christ; but it is also something we can do to others in turn. ("Anything you do for the least of my brothers and sisters you do for me"; Matthew 25:40). That is why we are left with an ethical choice: *either* to transform our world according to the Christic icon of the end-to-come; *or* to fix Christ as a fetish whose only end is itself. The choice is between transformation or fixation.

For Paul, therefore, Mount Thabor is to be reread within the broader biblical history as a re-figuration of Jewish messianic prophecy (e.g., the Psalms and prophets who already foretold the holiness of Mount Thabor) and a pre-figuration of the kingdom—when each human person will be metamorphosed in Christ's image (*eikon*). As Paul says, when the kingdom comes, the clouds and veils that protect God will be lifted so that we may see face to face: "And all of us, with our unveiled faces (*prosopa*) like mirrors reflecting the glory of the Lord, are being transfigured from glory to glory into his very figure (*eikon*); this is the working of the Lord who is the Spirit" (2 Corinthians 3:18). It is highly significant that the famous promised vision of the divine-human "face to face" is rendered in Greek as *prosopon.*

Elsewhere—1 Corinthians 15:49–58 and Colossians 3:10—Paul elaborates on these key metaphors of figuring, imaging, and reflecting. Referring to Christ as the final Adam (*eschatos Adam*), Paul suggests that the transfigured—or what he calls "heavenly"—body of Christ is in fact the secret goal of divine creation aimed at from the very beginning, though it is only fully revealed in the *eschaton.* And this eschatological revelation or *pleroma* will be one in which each person may find itself altered according to Christ's image and likeness. "And as we have borne the likeness (*eikon*) of the earthly man, so we shall bear the likeness (*eikon*) of the heavenly one . . . we are all going to be changed, instantly, in the twinkling of an eye, when the last trumpet sounds" (1 Corinthians 15:49–52). That at least is the promise of the messianic *persona.* It is *all* humanity that is invited to be transformed according to the image-*eikon* of Christ. In this universalist scenario, the "old self" is "renewed in the image of its Creator" (Colossians 3:10–11). As such, renewal is open to everyone: "in that image (*eikon*) there is no room for distinction between Greek and Jew . . . slave and free. There is only Christ: he is everything and he is in everything."

This eschatological promise requires not only grace but ethical action on our part. The advent of the *eschaton* of Creation is inseparable from human innovation.[15] In short, for Paul the transfiguring Christ is not some *eidolon* to be embalmed and enshrined but the *eikon tou epouraniou*: the icon of the ultimate *persona* prefigured from the origins of time. This divine *persona*, finally, safeguards what is unique in each one us—what stitches each in its mother's womb, what knows every hair of our head—while convoking us to a shared humanity. When Christ appears in the kingdom, as John (a narrative witness of Mount Thabor) writes, "we shall be like him, because we shall see him as he really is" (1 John 3:2).

Messianic Time

This brings me to the crucial question of what Levinas and Derrida call "Messianic time." Our story of transfiguration as epilogue of Adam and prologue of Christ-to-come-again surpasses the limits of what is ordinarily known as history.[16] The *persona* is "eternal" in its very unicity to the extent that it remains irreducible to the laws of a purely causal temporality. Its eschaton does not operate according to the objective laws of cause-effect or potency-act (though it does recognize that this is the chronological time in which human persons exist). Nor is it exhausted in the world-historical mutations of some teleological plan à la Hegel or Hartshorne. The reason that Paul says that the kingdom will come in a "blink of an eye" is to signal the utterly unpredictable and unprogrammable character of its coming. That is how we should understand the paradoxical language of anterior-posteriority which Christ, and later Paul, use to describe the eschatological kingdom. The kingdom is already "amongst us" even as it is still to come—like a lightning flash across the sky (Luke 17:20–25). Or as I might add, the eschatological *persona* is transfiguring always, in each moment, but always remains to be ultimately transfigured, at the end of time. Which is another way of saying, its temporality exceeds the limits of ordinary time.[17]

Walter Benjamin offers this intriguing gloss on the subject in his *Theologico-Poetical Fragment* (1921): "This future does not correspond to homogenous empty time; because at the heart of every moment of the future is contained the little door through which the Messiah may enter."[18] That is why we must always remain vigilant and expectant. There is no guarantee or calculus as to how the transfiguring Messiah will come. When he comes, if he comes, it will be a surprise. An instant event that takes us unawares (as it does the three apostles on Mount Thabor) even as it is signaled from the beginning of time (and prophesied by the three holy figures on the same mountain: Moses, Elijah, and Jesus). Maybe it is this very unpredictability which has Jesus swear his apostles to silence both after Mount Thabor, and after the critical exchange with Peter which precedes it. For remember, Jesus does not here declare himself the one and only Christ. No, he asks a question: "who do you say that I am?" And when the crowds and disciples seek to capitalize on his divinity, he invariably rebukes them, deferring them to the "Father in heaven"—the same father of Moses and Elijah and every son of man.

True, the Father calls him his "chosen one." But does not Christ's *persona* do the same for each of us? Are we not all called to be chosen ones? If you do it to the least of these you do it to me. *For Christ plays in ten thousand places . . . To the Father through the features of men's faces.*

Some early Christian commentators seem to suggest as much. The *persona* of the transfigured Christ is, as John Damascene suggests, "both this and that, of the same essence as the Father (the universal kingdom) and of the same race and nature as us (the particular descendants of Adam)."[19] The transfiguration thus is as much about us as it is about God, for the transfigured Christ "renews our nature in himself restoring it to the pristine beauty of the image charged with the common visage of humanity."[20] Such a transfiguring mission includes all who seek justice-to-come. Or as John Damascene's version promises: "It is thus that the just will shine at the resurrection, transfigured into [Christ's] condition . . . according to this image, this figure (*prosopon*), this light, as they sit with the son of God."[21] Perhaps it is also this universal invitation of the christic *persona* that Saint Anastasius has in mind when he urges us to waste no further time but hurry toward the kingdom: "We should make speed towards it—I say this boldly—like Christ our precursor with whom we will all shine with spiritual eyes, renewed in the features of our souls, configured to his image and like him forever transfigured."[22] This understanding of the eschatological transfiguration of the face does not seek to *exclude* other messianic (or non-messianic) religions in the name of some Christo-centric triumph. On the contrary, what a Christian means by the *persona-visage* of Christ is very similar, one could argue, to what a Jew like Levinas believes when he says that one of his own preferred images of the "face" is that of Jesus.[23]

The New Age Controversy

The fact that the transfigured Christ is not all there, so to speak—that is, is not reducible to his actual personal presence there and then—means that his *persona* remains to be perpetually interpreted. The surplus meaning of Mount Thabor, marked by this incommensurability of *persona* vis-à-vis person, invites a history of plural readings. (Though this chiasm of incommensurable aspects does not for a moment belie the indivisibility of Christ Jesus—any more than two sides of a sleeve, to reiterate Merleau-Ponty's image, belie the indivisibility of that sleeve.) Indeed it is, paradoxically, the very silence which surrounds the event that in turn provokes a plurality of competing and often conflicting interpretations. Its ineffability becomes the motor of its *fability*—its translation into a variety of accounts, testimonies, fables, narratives, and doctrines ranging from the initial versions of John and his fellow evangelists, to the multiplicity of later readings offered by Paul and patristic authors and extending down through the entire "effective-history" (*Wirkungsgeschichte*) of Christian theology.

Paul was not insensitive to the various ways, good and bad, that Christ's promise of metamorphosis could be read. He was as enthusiastic about the eschatological reading, where Mount Thabor pre-figures the kingdom to come, as he was suspicious of the various disfigurations of this same promise— including those attributed to the power of pseudo-prophets to "transform themselves" (*transfigurantes se*) into manipulators of souls (2 Corinthians 11:13–15). Even Satan, Paul warns, deploys such fake mutations—turning himself into an angel of light just as his followers pretend to "transfigure" themselves into ministers of justice. The very fact, he notes, that the life and death of the transfigured Christ comes down to us in words and "figures"—in spite of the injunction to keep silent—means that it is always open to both transfiguring and disfiguring interpretations: the former construing Christ as an icon of alterity, the later misconstruing him an as idol of presence (1 Corinthians 4:6).[24]

The controversies continue in our own postmodern times. One of the most recent involves Slavoj Zizek's neo-Pauline reading of Christ versus the neo-Gnostic nostalgia for the historical Jesus. Zizek's basic point, for which I have much sympathy, is that we are currently witnessing a suspension of the "authentic kernel of Christianity"—to wit, the promise of a New Beginning, epitomized by such "symbolizing" events as the Transfiguration and Resurrection. These events represent the true "scandal" of Christ as herald of a messianic time of miracle and grace: a time which can undo the sins of the past (brushing history backward) while simultaneously invoking a universal kingdom that is both now and still to come (that is, "eternal" or *sur-chronic*).

What the advocates of New Age Gnosticism promote, by contrast, is a return to the historical or material Jesus. This Jesus is all too literal—however shrouded in fake mystique—and supposedly escaped from the tomb to live on in the south of France, marry Mary Magdalene, and leave several descendants behind him! This hypothesis ignores the rupturing of chronological history by the transfigured Christ in favor of a banalized Jesus, now little more than a guru-cum-escape-artist who teaches DIY self-improvement techniques: a sort of glorified maharishi-Houdini.[25] But the banality of this particular New Age thesis has not prevented the emergence of a whole spate of pseudo-scientific bestsellers recounting various attempts to reveal the secret of Jesus, suppressed for millennia by the churches—viz. that he was a crypto-Gnostic preaching inner journeying and "purification of the soul": a man with brothers and brides and babies and all such things besides.

How different these New Age narratives are from the marvelously faithful *Last Temptation of Christ* by Kazantzakis, which portrays such a naturalist scenario as pure *fantasy*. Unlike Kazantzakis, the neo-Gnostic craze to literalize the historical line of Jesus takes the eschatological harm (i.e., grace) out of the transfiguration. It makes it utterly immanent. Or to use Zizek's Lacanian language, it contrives to reverse the transfiguration, qua radical "symbolic" event (*creatio ex nihilo*), back into the order of the "real."[26] In the process the very transcendence of Christ's *persona* is disavowed. The revolutionary challenge of transfiguration is defused. It is emptied of alterity.[27] Explained away.

What is important here, I submit, is not just to expose such pseudo-scientific fabulations but also to recognize them as precisely that: *fabulations*. In other words, rather than demonizing such Gnostic fictions, it is perhaps wiser to consider them—however fanciful they may be—as part of the inevitable excess of fantasy generated by the very *figurative* character of the transfiguration itself. An excess, moreover, which is symptomatic of our times. The point is not to repudiate such a multiplicity of interpretations but to enter the conflict and *take sides*. And the choice of sides is determined ultimately by which interpretations we deem more faithful to the ethico-eschatological import of the Christ-event. Which readings, in other words, best testify to the transfiguring (i.e., singularizing-universalizing) power of the *persona*?[28]

Testimony is the bottom line. Faithful and discerning testimony—known by its fruits. Fruits of love and justice, care and gift. We have to try to tell the difference, in sum, between narrative testimonies that transform or deform lives. The rest is indeed silence.

Paschal Testimonies

In this closing section, I offer a number of more personal reflections on the enigma of transfiguration, as it relates to the specifically paschal testimonies of the resurrected Christ.

I begin with Jesus appearing to his disciples on the road to Emmaus (Luke 24:13–35). One of the most striking things about this Luke narrative is how the two disciples walking on the road *failed* to recognize their Messiah when he appeared. In a wonderful twist of irony, Jesus asks them what they were talking about: to which they reply that he must be about the only person in Jerusalem who *hasn't* yet heard about Jesus being crucified! Continuing the game, Jesus asks the disciples to tell him all.

They do, even mentioning—with doubled irony—how the apostles who went to the empty tomb on hearing that Jesus had risen, *"did not see him."* Jesus scolds them gently for not believing what the prophets had taught, thus making it necessary for the Messiah to suffer crucifixion before entering into his glory. But still they do not see him. Only, finally, when Jesus agrees to stop off at the village of Emmaus and share their evening meal are the scales lifted from their eyes. In the breaking of the bread they at last recognize him. As soon as their "eyes are opened," however, Jesus "vanishes from their sight." No sooner does he appear than he disappears. Now they see him, now they don't.

Several things about this story recall the enigma of the Transfiguration. We do not recognize the sons of God when they appear to us as we wander along the road of life. So full of great expectations are we that we fail to see the divine in the simplest of beings: we overlook the *persona* in the person. Second, the embodied God *cares* for our physical and material being: it is in the sharing of food that the divine becomes visible. And third, rather than glorying in some kind of I-told-you-so posthumous triumph, Jesus takes his leave. As soon as he is seen, he absolves himself, goes invisible, refuses to be appropriated, enthroned, idolized. He becomes little or nothing again. Or as Paul says in 1 Corinthians, God chose things that are not (*ta me onta*) to cancel things that are.

In John (20:11–18) we read of how the posthumous Christ also appeared to Mary Magdalene and said more or less the same thing he said to the disciples at Emmaus: "Do not hold onto me!" (John 20:17). Here Jesus chose to make himself visible to the most despised of beings—a fallen, scorned prostitute, then considered the lowest of the low—and to make her the premier evangelist of his risen message.

It was in a closed room in Jerusalem that Jesus made his third apparition after his death: this time to the disciples (including the two just returned from Emmaus). Once again, we encounter one of the simplest messages of the post-paschal transfiguration—the overcoming of fear. The apostles are so "terrified" by what they see that they cannot recognize Jesus at first (Luke 24:35–48). They actually mistake him for a ghost. Doubts invade their hearts. But Jesus tells them not to be afraid—to approach and touch his wounds. And seeing that they are still "disbelieving," still not accepting that his wounded body is transfigured, he resorts once more to the nourishment motif. "Have you anything to eat?" It is only then, when he takes some broiled fish and sits and eats with them, that they finally recognize him. They see and hear his message of dying and rising again: a message of transfiguring that comes—paradoxically but tellingly—through the body, a broken body, bruised and hungry for something to eat. Not at all through hyper-power and glory, but through woundedness and want does the risen *persona* make itself known.

The fourth and final story of Jesus appearing after his death—on the shore between Tabha and Capernaum—recounts the miracle of bread and fish: the story of Christ himself as *gift* of food and life. (The only trace remaining in Tabha in our own day is, fittingly, a faded fresco of two small loaves and fishes.) The miracle of multiplication from next to nothing, the mystery of excess from paucity, of surplus from scarcity. The mystery of less as more. Of person as *persona*. Divine crisscrossing. Chiasm. Monstrance of the not-there in the there.[29]

The gospel narrative in question (John 21:1–14) tells how the disciples "did not know that it was Jesus" standing on the shore. The transfigured *persona* was again incognito, unrecognizable to them in his person as he called across to them in their boat just offshore, asking if they had any fish, and they replied no. It was only when he instructed them to cast their nets out the other side of the boat, resulting in the famous catch, that the most impetuous of them all, Simon Peter, the one who'd denied him three times a few days earlier, finally identified him. And jumped into the water! Coming ashore, Peter—and the other disciples who *still* did not recognize Jesus—found a charcoal fire already prepared for them with fish and bread. "Come and have breakfast," said Jesus. For he knew their hunger. He knew their want, their lack, their need, their desire. He invited them to sit and eat; and it was *then* and only then, the narrative tells us, that their eyes were opened.

Once more, the seeing comes in the sharing of bread and fish. It is, as the narrative attests, in the carnal giving of his *persona*—in the transubstantiation of his *persona* as an embodied giver of nourishment—that the transfigured-resurrected Christ reveals his identity. As John writes: "Now none of the disciples dared to ask him, 'Who are you?' because they knew it was the Lord. Jesus came and took the bread and gave it to them, and did the same with the fish." Here we witness the power of transfiguration as ultimate answer to blood-sacrifice—epitome of an ethics of *kenosis* and gift.

Seen thus as *kerygma* of Transfiguration-Passion-Resurrection, the message of Christ's paschal visitations might go something like this: If you are hungry and need bread and fish, ask for it and you shall have your fill. If you see a lost loved one standing on the shore and are filled with joy, throw decorum to the wind, jump into the waves, and swim to them. If someone gives you food, do not ask for identity papers or credentials ("Who are you?"); just sit and receive. If you are wanting in body or mind—crippled, despised, rejected, downcast, disabled, despondent—and your nets are still empty after many tries, do not despair; someone will come and tell you where to cast your net so that you may have life and have it more abundantly. Indeed the most transfiguring thing about this God of little things is that he gives with a gratuity that defies the limits of space and time. Now he's gone, now he's here, now he's gone again. Now he's dead, now he's alive. Now he's buried, now risen. Now the net is empty, now it's full. And more surprising still, the fish is cooked for us even before we get ashore and unload our nets. "Come and have breakfast," Christ says as the boat touches land.

Conclusion

The post-paschal stories of the transfiguring *persona* remind us that the Kingdom is given to hapless fishermen and spurned women, to those lost and wandering on the road from Jerusalem to nowhere, to the wounded and weak and hungry, to those who lack and do not despair of their lack, to little people "poor in spirit." The narratives of the transfigured-resurrected Christ testify that after the long night of fasting and waiting and darkness and need—afloat on a wilderness of sea—breakfast is always ready. The transfiguring *persona* signals the ultimate solidarity, indeed indissociability, of spirit and flesh.

Today a triumphal monument crowns the hill of Thabor, compromising Christ's request for discretion, for nothing, no tents, no temples, no memorials, at most a trace or scripted testimony. Today Christians, Jews, and Muslims are still fighting over who should own or exercise "sovereignty" over the places of their sacred stories—the tomb of Abraham in Hebron, the Wailing Wall, the Dome of the Rock on Mount Moriah, the "millennial" space in front of the Church of the Annunciation in Nazareth (a giant edifice towering over the ground where a humble young woman once knelt). And various Christian sects—Armenian, Greek Orthodox, Coptic, Protestant, and Catholic—still skirmish with thuribles, bibles, and crucifixes over rights of priority procession through the Church of the Nativity in Bethlehem or the Holy Sepulchre in Jerusalem. The message of transfiguration so easily disfigured.

How ironic it is to observe so many monotheistic followers still failing to recognize the message: that God speaks not through monuments of power and pomp but in stories and acts of love and justice, the giving to the least of creatures, the caring for orphans, widows, and strangers; stories and acts which bear testimony—as transfiguring gestures do—to that God of little things that comes and goes, like the thin small voice, like the burning bush, like the voice crying out in the wilderness, like the word made flesh, like the wind that blows where it wills.

And since the enigma of transfiguration never ceases to remind us that we are *embodied* creatures who inhabit lands in space and time, and still need pilgrimages to holy places at sacred times, I would tentatively add these scattered testimonial traces of the transfigured Christ which I witnessed during a recent visit to Israel—for as a Christian it is all I have any competence to invoke: the ruins of Capernaum and Tabha where Jesus and the apostles took refuge after their expulsion from Nazareth; the vacant hill-caves of Sitve and Avdat where the Christian Naboteans (a people of the Spice Trail now extinct) rested on their passage through the Negev desert; or the sequestered, humble hermitages of Saint George and Maar Saba carved into rockcliffs in the hills of Judea. These fragments of stone and story, these traces of fragile testimony, still resist—as they have resisted for centuries—the triumphalism of ecclesiastical empire. Hideouts, off the beaten track, without foundation. Cut against the grain. Self-effacing, modest, vulnerable, welcoming. Sanctuaries for migrants. Shelters for the exiled. Footholds for the forgotten. Arks. Perfect places for rejected *personas* to come and lay their heads. Ciphers, perhaps, of a transfiguring God.

Desiring God

Another way of speaking of the transfiguration of God is to speak of the desire of God. It is through such desire that the God-who-may-be finds voice, and does so in many different *personas*. We have been looking above at such epiphanic examples as the burning bush on Mount Horeb and the trans-figured face of Jesus on Mount Thabor. In this chapter I focus on more secular and sensual ways in which the transfiguring God elects to show himself—through the faces of eros. Here *persona* becomes passion—the passion of burning love and of endless waiting. Though my analysis opens here with the chant of the Shulamite woman in the Song of Songs, the readings of Levinas and Derrida which follow extend the range of reference to a phenomenology of largely non-scriptural experience.

Biblical Readings: The Song of Songs

I

How are we to understand the *desire of God?* Is it God's desire for us? Or is it our desire for God? Or both? One of the most revealing verses on this question is the Song of Songs 3:1–4, where the anxious, expectant seeking of the love-struck bride is reversed into a *being-found*, that is, a *being desired*. Here the desire of God takes the form of a sentinel who finds you out by asking "where are you?"—"Who goes there?"—and you reply, "Here I am! It is me." The lover of God, this verse tells us, exists in the accusative as well as the nominative. "The bride speaks of her beloved: upon my bed at night I sought him whom my soul loves; I sought him but found him not; I called him, but he gave no answer. So I said to myself, 'I will rise now and go about the city, in the streets and in the squares; I will seek him who my soul loves.' . . . I sought him, but found him not. The sentinels *found me*, as they went about the city. I asked, 'Have you seen him whom my soul loves?' Scarcely had I passed them, when I found him whom my soul loves." I repeat, it is only *after* the bride has passed the sentinels who found *her*, that she finds *Him* whom her soul loves!

God, it seems, is the other who seeks me out *before* I seek him, a desire beyond my desire, bordering at times, in the excess of its fervor, on political incorrectness! "You have searched me and you know me Lord. . . . You search out my path and are acquainted with all my ways. . . . You hem me in, behind and before, and lay your hand upon me. . . . Where can I flee from you? If I ascend to heaven, you are there; if I make my bed in Sheol, you are there. . . . If I take the wings of the morning and settle at the farthest limits of the sea . . . your right hand shall hold me fast" (Psalms 139). A hot God if ever there was one! This desire of God is no mere deficiency but its own reward—excess, gift, grace. "Those who seek the Lord *lack* no good thing" (Psalms 34). Why? Because such desire is not some gaping emptiness or negation (as Sartre and certain existentialists held) but an affirmative "yes" to the summons of a superabundant, impassioned God—"Here I am. Come. Yes, I will Yes, I will Yes."

II

The lovers' discourse in the Song of Songs testifies to the traversing of sensuality by transcendence. On the one hand, Solomon compares his beloved's breasts to "two fawns, / twins of a gazelle" (7:4) while she compares his eyes to "doves at a pool of water" (5:1). On the other hand, the amorous passion serves as a *persona-trace* testifying to the unnameable alterity of God: there is even a telling allusion to the burning bush episode of Exodus 3:14 in the beloved's claim that "love is as strong as Death. / . . . The flash of it is a flash of fire, / A flame of Yahweh himself" (Song 8:6). The transfiguring fire of the burning bush here becomes the fire of a devouring desire—the Shulamite woman tells us she is "sick with love" (5:8)—where the ecstasy of the beloved crosses over with, without consuming or being consumed by, the incarnational love of God. And in this crisscrossing *persona* of lover and beloved, both are transfigured. Divine desire is embodied. Human desire is hallowed.

If Exodus 3 allowed of a God speaking through an angel and a burning thornbush, the Song of Songs amplifies the range of divine speech to include lovers' bodies and, by analogy, entire landscapes. The lands in turn are brimming with fruits (nuts, figs, pomegranates), harvests (wine, honey, wheat), plants (lilies, cedars, roses, apple-trees), and animals (gazelles, stags, and turtledoves). The desire of Yahweh's flame here appears to embrace all that is alive. As though the seed of the thornbush has spread from the dusty heights of Mount Horeb and disseminated its fecundity throughout the valleys and planes below. But above all, the seed has found its way into the embrace of lover and beloved. The free nuptial love celebrated in this song challenges the cheerless moralism of tribal legalities (the Shulamite's proprietal brothers oppose the relationship). And, so doing, it miraculously echoes the innocence of eros prior to the Fall, when God made the first lovers of "one flesh" and declared it "good" (Genesis 2). Perhaps even more radically, it looks *ahead* to an eschatological kingdom where such innocence may flourish again once and for all. The reference (backward and forward) to paradise is reinforced by the startling and suggestive verse: "Under the apple-tree I awakened you?" (8:5), an allusion reiterated in the fact that the lover-king-shepherd is himself referred to as an apple tree. These ostensibly retrospective echoes of a lost Eden are transformed here into a celebration—without the slightest hint of melancholy—of a passionate desire *in the here and now* for a fuller consummation *still to come*. This latter eschatological horizon is indicated by verse 5:1, among others, which sings of the lover entering a garden full of milk and honey (Song 5:1).

The influential nineteenth-century rabbi Hayyim de Volozhyn corroborates the reading of the songs in the double light of Exodus and eschatology. He takes the beloved's famous apostrophe—"Let him kiss me with the kisses of his mouth" (Song 1, 2)—as a plea that the Exodic revelations on Mount Sinai may eventually be given *directly* through the mouth of the lover.[1] No longer obscurely—through a voice disguised as an angel or bush or the "back of God's head"—but *mouth to mouth*.[2] And this intrepid reading is born out by Volozhyn's conviction, deeply influenced by the Cabbalistic Books of Creation, that the cosmological orders of nature and the human body are themselves incarnational metaphors for the eschatological expression of a divine flame. Volozhyn cites Jewish sources which attribute different powers and names of God to different parts of the body, reserving the nameless name of Exodus 3:15 (*Ehyeh* or "I shall be") as the only one which perdures throughout the entire history of creation. The Rabbi interprets the invocation of song 5:2—"My dove, my perfect one"—as an indication of God's deep association with the universe of creatures and, more precisely, of his eschatological "orientation towards the creation of worlds and His union with them."[3] Indeed Volozhyn will read verses 5:1 and 4:15 as allusions to the three "sacrificial" organs of the created body—the heart, the liver and the brain—in which the three main aspects of the divine spirit (*nefesh, ruah, neshama*) are said to reside. And he goes on to interpret verse 1:11—"we will make you golden earrings and beads of silver"—in the light of the Cabbalistic teaching that the former signify those parts of speech (accents and vowels) which come directly from the head of the divine soul and animate the voice of the body (represented by "silver" consonants).[4]

We see thus how certain rabbinical traditions—which exerted considerable influence on contemporary thinkers like Levinas, Rosenzweig, and Scholem—came to read the texts of Genesis, Exodus, and the Song of Songs in the light of Cabbalist texts (e.g., the Book of Creation/*Sefer Yetsirah*), premised on the idea that Creation is, in part at least, God's body and points toward the transfiguration of a new world.[5] In this respect, the Song of Songs may be said to reveal how eschatology repeats cosmology, taking the form of a dramatic filling out of the incarnational voices of Genesis, Exodus, and Isaiah. The nuptial promise reads accordingly as a reprise of the promise of Sinai, while the lover longing for his "promised bride" anticipates the promised kingdom.

III

It is this underlying eschatological intent which has prompted several contemporary commentators to identify a "subversive" intent behind the songs' lyrical tones.[6] But we would be mistaken to see this subversiveness as somehow turning the lovers into cardboard characters of abstract allegory. The lovers are not mouthpieces for some spiritual message. They are much more than "personifications" of spiritual wisdom or "representations" of Yahweh's continuing love for Israel in spite of its infidelity.[7] These things too perhaps, but much more. The lovers come across as carnal embodiments of a desire which traverses and exceeds them, while remaining utterly themselves. Hence the candid corporality of references to limbs, mouths, breasts, hands, navels, and so on. Not to mention the sense of deep inner yearning and the sheer naturality of description which brings this to life: the woman is a lily, garden, mare, vineyard, dove, sun, moon; while the lover is a gazelle, king, fawn, bag of myrrh, and cluster of blossoming henna. The powerfully erotic charge of many of the amorous verses defies any purely allegorical interpretation: "his left arm is under my head and his right makes love to me" (2:6 and 8:2); he "pastures his flock" among the lilies (6:3); his "fountain makes the garden fertile" (4:15); or "my beloved thrust his hand/through the hole in the door; / I trembled to the core of my being" (5:4). Doesn't get much hotter than that.

This kind of language was, according to André LaCocque, almost unprecedented in the bible. And it was to prove so controversial in the later rabbinical and Christian monastic traditions as to be frequently laundered, chastened, or censored. As a certain puritanical mind-set took hold, the songs were often explained away in terms of a Platonizing dualism which contrived to take the harm out of its sensual-sensible-sexual content by attributing its *real* meaning to some supra-sensible metaphysical message—a reading typified, for example, in the refrain "wisdom, *not love*, is divine."[8] Equally unique in this biblical chant is the fact that divine love finds privileged expression in the voice of a young woman. It is the Shulamite who takes most of the initiative and does most of the talking in the Song of Songs. And if the lover-king-Solomon speaks at some length in his own voice, his discourse often quotes the Shulamite and harks back to her as its source of reference. It is a "woman's song" from first to last and it keeps the heroine center stage.[9]

Moreover, since this freedom and centrality of the woman's point of view suggests an Egyptian influence, one might even see the songs as an extension of God's exodic "flame" (8:6); that is, an amplification of the voice of the burning bush, which pitted Israel *against* Egypt, to a more inclusive voice which brings them together again in some kind of actual, or promised, nuptial bond.[10] The fact that the Shulamite's passion represents free love—she is faithful to her lover "outside matrimonial bonds and social demands" (e.g., demands to remain a servant, wife, child-bearer, mother, or commercial exchange object)—corroborates the view that the songs put the entire societal orthodoxy into question.[11] The Israelite poetess is not just seeking to entertain her public but also, deep down, to shock them. "The family and familiar guardians of women's chastity, namely the 'brothers' and the night watchmen in the songs, are largely outdone by events over which they have lost control. Those who consider the future marriage of their son or daughter as a commercial transaction are derided. The institution in general is swept aside and the event of love is glorified."[12]

This breaking open of divine desire beyond tribal or familial confines is in turn reinforced by three crucial references in the songs. We have, first, the reference to the Shulamite as a "chariot" (6:12), that is, as one who may be said to carry the Ark of the Covenant—marking God's love for his people—to those hitherto considered beyond the acknowledged bounds. Second, we have the reference to a "dance" (6:13), which seems to allude to the naked David "swirling with all his might" before the Ark (2 Samuel 6:14), another gesture of human desire for God; but which may equally allude to the eschatological figure of a divine-human love-dance in the last days (explored in the conclusion below). And, third, we have the verbal play between the terms "Shulamite" and "Shunamite"—the latter being the "extremely beautiful girl" brought to warm King David's bed but ultimately shunned and left a virgin. The fact that the formerly rejected Shunamite is here reprised as the liberated Shulamite who captivates her shepherd king indicates how these revolutionary biblical songs succeed in turning the once "passive and reified" woman into an "active subject whose first-person pronoun" dominates the love-talk and celebrates the love.[13]

These references, to be sure, are metaphorical, intra-textual, and indirect. But they show how a powerful religious poetics can sing the unsayable and intimate the unnameable by means of an innovative and insubordinate language, a language resistant to both allegorist abstraction and metaphysical dualism. By intimating a "perfect similarity of relations between two quite dissimilar things" (Kant's analogy of faith), this song of eros creates a surplus of meaning. It twists and turns accredited words and thoughts so as to bring about a sort of catachresis or mutation within language itself. And it is this very semantic innovation which transforms our understanding of both God and desire. So that engaging in the Song of Songs we can, in Paul Ricoeur's words, think *more* about desire and *more* about God.[14] We can think each of them otherwise.

All of this indicates that burning, integrated, faithful, untiring desire—freed from social or inherited perversions—is the most adequate way for saying how humans love God and God loves humans. It suggests how human and divine desire may transfigure one another. A radical suggestion, to be sure, and one which confirms the highly controversial claim of Rabbi Aquiba that if "all the Scriptures are holy, the Song of Songs is the Holy of Holies."[15]

IV

In a striking section of *Tales of Love*, Julia Kristeva pushes the incarnational reading of the Song of Songs even further. This biblical poem, she argues, captures a dynamic tension between a "present, incarnate loved one," identified with the shepherd, and "another nonrepresentable one, holder of authority and taboo, forever out of reach although he conditions the lover's existence and who is God" (here identified with Solomon).[16] According to this reading, the amorous verse might be said to epitomize the *persona* paradox of the transfiguring God in that it keeps God invisible while enabling him, simultaneously and paradoxically, to be experienced as carnal lust. "Supreme authority, be it royal or divine, can be loved as flesh while remaining essentially inaccessible; the intensity of love comes precisely from that combination of received jouissance and taboo, from a basic separation that nevertheless unites."[17] This paradoxical movement epitomizes a radical form of biblical desire, specifically in its fourth or fifth century A.D. expression in the post-exilic Song of Songs.[18] Kristeva makes much of the fact that as soon as God is evoked in terms of amorous passion, we enter a poetic realm of uncontained figurative meaning—e.g., "your love is more delightful than wine; / delicate is the fragrance of your perfume etc." The transfiguring divine is named here at the same time as it remains nameless—a double movement of epiphany and withdrawal, which we have also witnessed in the burning bush narrative and in the Christian testimony of the transfigured Christ on Mount Thabor (see chapters 2 and 3 above). This double move manifests itself in the Song as a desiring *persona* who is both overwhelmingly there and yet ultimately transcendent of our appropriating grasp. The unique Name evoked almost from the outset induces a certain intoxication, notes Kristeva, "an overflowing of meaning, a flow of significations and sensations comparable to that produced by caresses, perfumes and oils. The sensitive and the significant, the body and the name, are thus not only placed on the same level but fused in the same logic of undecidable infinitization, semantic polyvalence brewed by the state of love."[19]

This erotics of incarnation is described by Kristeva from both a psychoanalytic and linguistic perspective. Citing the suggestive verse 5:4, already mentioned above—"My Beloved thrust his hand / through the hole in the door; / I trembled to the core of my being"—she proffers a new take on religious sublimation. Due to its sexual idioms, inextricably linked to the prevailing theme of absence and yearning to merge, carnality in the Song leads directly to the dialectic of incarnation. "The loved one is not there, but I experience his body; in a state of amorous incantation I unite with him, sensually *and* ideally."[20] And Kristeva goes so far in her ecumenical interpretation as to suggest that the Talmudic reading that recognizes Yahweh himself in the loved one supports the incarnational implications of the Song's rich metaphoricity. How could it be otherwise, she asks, "if I love God, if the loved one is, beyond Solomon's body, God himself? As intersection of corporeal passion and idealization, love is undisputably the privileged experience for the blossoming of metaphor (abstract for concrete, concrete for abstract) as well as incarnation (the spirit becoming flesh, the word-flesh)."[21]

The psychodrama of incarnation here is, of course, provisional and premonitory: the love metaphor is conjugal but also and inescapably marks a movement of deferral. And this surplus of eschatological sense in and through the five erotic senses of carnal contact is evidenced, at the linguistic and rhetorical level of the Song itself, as an almost inexhaustible proliferation of innovative figures of speech. In short, unlike Platonic love, this incarnational love of the Bible *does* involve all the senses—sound, odor, touch, sight, taste—but unlike the old pagan rites of sexual fusion and sacrifice, it resists the phallic illusion of totality, finality, or fullness (the Shulamite reminds us that even though she seeks her lover on her bed at night she does "not find him" (3:1).

V

This surplus of metaphoricity, whereby an eschatological symbolism of nuptial love is enmeshed in an erotics of the body without ever being reducible to it, gives rise in turn to what Paul Ricoeur calls "a phenomenon of indetermination."[22] This is evinced in the fact that many readers have difficulty identifying the lover and the beloved of the poem, for the lovers never clearly identify themselves or go by proper names (the term Shulamite is not a proper name). So we find ourselves forced to admit that we are never really sure who exactly is speaking, or to whom. We can even imagine that there are up to *three* different characters involved—a shepherdess, a shepherd, and a king (Solomon).[23] This puts us on a constant state of alert, like the amorous fiancée herself, as we keep vigil for the arrival of the divine lover. "Who is coming up from the desert?" (3:6), we too find ourselves asking. Or to frame the question in more eschatological terms: "Is it not from the end of the world and the depth of time that love arises?"[24] Moreover, it may be precisely the primacy of the fluid "movements of love" (Origen's phrase in his famous Homily on the Song), over the specific identities of the lover and the beloved, which guards the door open. We are kept guessing. This guarding of the Song as an open text of multiple readings and double entendres—divine and erotic, eschatological and carnal—provokes a hermeneutic play of constant "demetaphorizing and remetaphorizing" which never allows the song to end.[25]

In sum, what we have here is a story of transfiguring eros as the making possible of the impossible—"an impossibility set up as amatory law," as Kristeva puts it. This sets the biblical eros celebrated in the Song off from other kinds of erotic expression: for example, romantic infatuation, mystical ecstasy, or courtly *fine amour*, not to mention the more extremist genres of matrimonial moralism or libertine pornography.[26] But if the Song, informed as it is by Egyptian influences, extends the standard range of Western love literatures, it also amplifies the range of religious expression. The Song marks an opening of religion—understood by Kristeva as "the celebration of the secret of reproduction, the secret of pleasure, of life and death"—to aesthetics and ethics.[27] Or to what we might call an ethical poetics of religion. The *persona* of the Shulamite's song may thus be seen as a figure who promises the coupling without final consummation of God and desire—"sensuous and deferred love . . . passion and ideal."[28] Claiming that the Shulamite woman transfigured by love is—in her inner longing, division, and desire—arguably the first "Subject" in the modern sense of the word, Kristeva concludes her analysis with this account of the great paradox: "Love in the Song of Songs appears to be simultaneously in the framework both of conjugality and of a fulfilment always set in the future (recognition of amorous alteration as unavoidably missing the other who was barely touched and immediately lost . . .). . . . The Unique is imagined, seen, sensed—witness all the visual, tactile and olfactory descriptions of the lovers' corporeal qualities—in opposition to the postulate of God's irrepresentableness. God is seen and heard by chosen ones, by lovers, rather feminine lovers; but never merging, never definitively offered for an incarnation that would be accomplished once and for all."[29] In short, the Song of Songs confronts us with a desire that desires beyond desire while remaining desire.

Metaphysical Readings

But how account for this puzzling phenomenon of desire beyond desire—this hysteron/proteron of eschatological eros? I propose to hazard something of a hermeneutic guess in what follows by citing, first, certain key pronouncements on "divine desire" in the Western metaphysical tradition, before then exploring some intriguing contemporary accounts of this paradox from a phenomenological perspective—in particular those by Levinas in *Totality and Infinity* and by Derrida in *On the Name*.[30]

I

The history of religious thought in the West suggests that there are two main ways of desiring God—namely, *onto-theological* and *eschatological*. First, what (following Heidegger) I refer to as the onto-theological paradigm construes desire as *lack*—that is, as a striving for fulfillment in a plenitude of presence. Here desire expresses itself as a drive to be and to know absolutely. *Conatus essendi et cognoscendi.* This relates back to the biblical tales of Adam's Fall and the Tower of Babel. What Genesis, and later the Talmud, referred to as the "evil drive" (*yezer hara*) to be God by refashioning Yahweh in our own image.[31] It is also, no doubt, what 1 John had in mind when it warned against the "lust of the eyes" for what shines and seduces—a theme taken up by the Pauline preference for what is unseen over what is seen (Romans 8:18); and again by the Augustinian critique of the *concupiscentia oculorum*: the ocular-erotic drive to appropriate the ephemera of the visible universe. At its most sophisticated, this lust of the eyes took the form of an obsessive epistemological *curiositas* with regard to absolute knowledge. "This empty curiosity is dignified and masked by the names of learning and science," wrote Augustine; "it is called in the divine language the lust of the eyes. . . . Hence also men proceed to investigate the concealed working of nature beyond our ken, which it does no good to know and which men want to know only for the sake of knowing."[32]

This influential passage of Augustine prefigured a whole legacy of suspicion toward the desire for absolute knowing, culminating (as Heidegger noted in his 1920–21 Winter Semester lectures) in Luther's fulminations against the *fornicatio spiritus* which seeks to reduce God to a possession of metaphysical vision (*visio dei*).[33] The attempt by certain philosophers to objectify the *deus adventurus* into an onto-theological object is nothing but a "desire to dominate and master," argued Luther. For such philosophers "elevate their own opinion so high into the heavens that it is no longer difficult for them . . . to make judgments about God in the same way that a poor shoemaker makes a judgment about leather." So doing, they prefer "power to weakness," the *superbia* and *securitas* of speculative constructions to everyday acts of faith.

Thus the futural coming of the kingdom finds itself compromised—as does the eschatological yearning invoked by Paul when he described the desire for the kingdom as "hope for what we do not see" (Romans 8:25).[34] Viewed from such a Pauline-eschatological perspective, the ontology of presence (*ousia*) is a travesty of the *parousia* still to come (*apousia*). Only in the light of *parousia* can we speak of realizing our desire to see God's *persona*, "face to face." Until then we live our eschatological desire as a yearning for an Other who beckons but has not yet fully arrived, who is present in absentia (Philippians 2:12), a *deus adventurus* who seeks me yet still promises to come, unpredictably and unexpectedly, in the twinkling of an eye (1 Corinthians 15:52), like a thief in the night (1 Thessalonians 5:2).[35]

II

This critique of onto-theological desire should not, however, be read as a rejection of desire per se. The Nietzschean verdict that "Christianity gave eros poison to drink" is not quite as evident as it seems. On the contrary, the destruction of onto-theological desire might be more properly conceived as a spur to transcend our captivation by all that is (*ta onta*) for another kind of desire—a desire for something that eye has never seen nor ear heard. That is to say, *eschatological* desire. Here I might cite not only the Song of Songs itself but also those wonderful psalms which speak of humans craving for their Creator, for example, as "flesh fainting for God" (Psalms 63); or, later again, the erotico-ecstatic writings of many Jewish and Christian mystics, not least of all Augustine when he speaks of the erotic restlessness of the soul in search of God—*inquietum cor nostrum*. Read for instance how Augustine addresses God as impassioned lover: "You shed your fragrance about me; I drew breath and now I gasp for your sweet odour. I tasted you and now I hunger and thirst for you. You touched me and I am inflamed with love . . ." (*Confessions*, bk. 6).

What is perhaps most telling here is the *active-passive* character of this divine eros. Augustine reveals the double genitive at work in the "desire of God." It is because the Creator has first shed fragrance and touched Augustine that Augustine is inflamed with such passion. Augustine's desire of God is a fervid *response* to God's desire of Augustine. An echo surely of the Song of Songs 3:1–4.

Phenomenological Readings—From Hegel to Levinas

Emmanuel Levinas's major work, *Totality and Infinity*, opens with a definition of eschatology and proceeds, in one of its initial sections, to a detailed description of desire. Though Levinas is a believing Jew and a disciple of Rabbi Volozhyn in his Talmudic readings, he sets out in this book to write a strict phenomenology. So that if he is influenced by Cabbalistic or rabbinical discussions about eschatology or eros, he is doing his best here to bracket such religious presuppositions in the name of pure description. But Levinas's phenomenology of eros, as we shall see, stands in direct opposition to Hegel's phenomenology of consciousness.

I

The question immediately arises as to how these two central terms—eschatology and desire—are related for Levinas. It does not take long to realize that both have the same *ethical* structure—namely, a relationship with the other "beyond the totality." By "totality" Levinas means being as encompassed by history, reason, representation, horizon, and power, in brief—*ontology*. Totality, Levinas explains, is all that can be thought and said in terms of objectivity. This includes the object-presences of representation—as evinced in the *libido dominandi* of speculative epistemology. But it also extends to (a) the *archeological* obsession with First Causes (a retrospective account of desire running from Neoplatonic metaphysics right through to Freudian psychoanalysis) and (b) the *teleological* drive toward a Final End (a prospective account of desire proffered by the Hegelian model of history). By contrast, Levinas defines *eschatology* as a relationship of desire which breaches totality, opening up what he terms "infinity." It is a relationship, he explains, "with a *surplus always exterior to the totality*, as though the objective totality did not fill out the true measure of being, as though another concept, the concept of *infinity*, were needed to express this transcendence with regard to totality, non-encompassable within a totality."[36]

Levinas suggests, rather boldly, that a phenomenology of desire holds the key to this eschatological infinity. He thus confronts us with the paradox that the infinite is inscribed *within* our historical experience of totality precisely as a "trace" which betrays that which is "beyond" it. And this trace, he argues, is evinced, first and foremost, by *desire* and *responsibility*—desire of the other and responsibility for the other. Eschatological desire is, in short, desire of the infinite.

Contrary to the judgment of history in which Hegel wrongly saw its rationalization, eschatology calls for a different kind of judgment—one which breaks with the totality of wars and empires, and which (*pace* Hegel's phenomenology) does not envisage the end of history within the totality of being. Throwing down the gauntlet to Hegel in the opening arguments of his preface, Levinas writes: "The eschatological, as the 'beyond' of history, draws beings out of the jurisdiction of history and the future; it arouses them in and calls them forth to their full responsibility. Submitting history as a whole to judgment, exterior to the very wars that mark its end, it restores to *each instant* its full signification in that very instance . . . it is not the *last judgment* that is decisive, but the *judgment of all the instants of time*, when the living are judged" (my italics).[37] Here already, Levinas touches on one of the most puzzling features of the desire of God—its yearning for an eschatological kingdom *beyond history* while welcoming the coming of what comes *in each instant*!

The way we get from totality to infinity is, Levinas suggests in the first chapter of *Totality and Infinity*, by following the way of desire. Here, in a section entitled "Desire for the Invisible," Levinas describes a desire for the absolutely other whom we cannot see, consume, or represent. This desire is not only different from biological *need*, but from all dialectical concepts of eros considered as *lack* driving toward fulfillment (e.g., desire as unconscious libido in Freud-Lacan or as struggle for power and recognition in Hegel-Kojève. One thinks especially of Kojève's phenomenological take on desire as an "emptiness that wants to be filled by what is full").[38]

Let me briefly rehearse some decisive steps in Levinas's critique of Hegel. We begin our existence in sensible immediacy and familiarity—a *chez soi*—only to be turned toward an "elsewhere," an "otherwise," an other. Desire thus arises as an inaugural movement toward an other-than-self; and this other cannot be reduced to a thing that one needs or consumes—the bread I eat, the water I drink, the land I appropriate. Things one possesses in this manner are not "absolutely other."

So far, Levinas merely confirms the standard Hegelian distinction between desire and need; but he then marks his departure from the dialectical account of desire as a longing for some coveted object. The desire that Levinas calls *metaphysical* (and sometimes eschatological) tends toward something entirely different. "The metaphysical desire does not long to return, for it is desire for a land not of our birth, for a land foreign to every nature, which has not been our fatherland and to which we shall never betake ourselves."[39] This is not the desire of absolute consciousness to return to its own essence. Nor, in spite of Levinas's respect for certain forms of Zionism, is it a promised land that could ever be occupied. No, this most fundamental desire of all desires, *prior* to all needs and inclinations, is the desire of the good.

Here Levinas turns from Hegel to Plato. Heeding the Socratic preference for Diotima over Aristophanes in the *Symposium*, Levinas claims that metaphysical desire "desires beyond everything that can simply complete it. It is like goodness—the Desired does not fulfil it, but deepens it."[40] The desired is like the good precisely because it cannot be possessed, because it is invisible, separate, distant, different, transcendent. This is not to say that desire is without relation; only that it is related to a desired that is never *given*, to an otherness that is absolute precisely because it absolves itself from the intentionality of adequation and appropriation. In other words, desire is a relation that is unequal to itself, asymmetrical.

The desired of eschatological desire exists before memory and beyond anticipation. It is immemorial and unimaginable, exceeding the horizons of historical time. But if the desired good gives itself thus from "beyond" history, it is nonetheless inscribed, as vigilance and summons, in each instant of our existence. It is in-coming at all times. It is, moreover, on embracing this eschatological paradox that Levinas goes beyond Plato.

In contrast to both Hegelianism and Platonism, it is not the accomplishment of knowledge but its very *inadequacy* which exposes the inordinateness of our desire for the absolutely other. This exteriority of the desired vis-à-vis the desirer cannot, however, be understood in terms of horizontal questing—as an endless restlessness that satiates itself in some dialectical infinity. Exhausting every "passion of the possible," it marks an ethical relation to the infinite as verticality—transcending all dialectical models of *Wesen* and *Gewesen*, of *anamnesis* and *mneme*, of *Möglichkeit* and *mögen*. Alluding, discreetly, to the language of the Torah, Levinas writes: "For desire this alterity, non-adequate to the idea, has a meaning. It is understood as the alterity of the Other and of the Most-High. The very dimension of height is opened up by metaphysical desire."[41] But this elevation of desire towards the Most-High does not imply (as one might think) a Platonic elevation to a transcendental hinterworld. On the contrary, the experience of height arises, once again, *in the midst of* my relation to the concrete living other. The good *beyond* finds itself inscribed *between* one and another. Desire here again reveals itself not as deficiency but as positivity. Not as *manque-à-être* but as grace and gratuity, gift and surplus. Less as insufficiency than as the bursting forth of the "more" in the "less."[42]

II

We have seen from the above how an eschatological understanding of eros charts a course beyond both the Hegelian and Platonic dialectics of desire. In the fourth and final part of *Totality and Infinity*, Levinas embraces this challenge under such headings as "The Ambiguity of Love," "Phenomenology of Eros," and "Subjectivity in Eros."

Levinas here acknowledges the rapport between intersubjective desire and language. Desire is at once language and that which exceeds language. The "erotic" is the "equivocal" par excellence—a simultaneity of need and desire, of concupiscence and transcendence, which reaches the interlocutor and goes beyond him. Eros—as word inscribed in flesh—discloses the "ambiguity of an event situated at the limit of immanence and transcendence."[43] It highlights the oscillation between the Hegelian tale of eros as return-to-origin and Plato's vision of metaphysical elevation. Levinas states the equivocation thus: "Love remains a relation with the Other that turns into need, and this need still presupposes the total, transcendent exteriority of the other, of the beloved. But love also goes beyond the beloved. This is why through the face filters the obscure light coming from beyond the face, from what *is not yet*, from a future never future enough."[44]

This future never future enough signals the messianic advent of eschatological infinity. But if "love" of the other bears ambiguous witness to this on the plane of affective or sexual immanence, it is desire as such which points us toward transcendence in its absolute exteriority. *Desire beyond love* would thus appear to be a higher ethical relation to the other than *desire with love*. Although Levinas never spells this out, it seems a logical consequence of his reasoning in this section and one quite in keeping with his trenchant critique of "love" in his 1954 essay "Le Moi et la totalité": "L'amour c'est le moi satisfait par le toi, une société à deux, société de solitudes. . . . L'amour ne contient pas la réalité sociale. . . . Le 'tu' véritable n'est pas L'Aimé, détaché des autres. Il se présente dans une autre situation. La crise de la religion dans la vie spirituelle contemporaine tient à la conscience que la société déborde l'amour, qu'un tiers assiste blessé au dialogue amoureux, et qu'à l'égard de lui, la société de l'amour elle-même a tort. . . .Tout amour—à moins de devenir jugement et justice—est l'amour d'un couple. La société close, c'est le couple."[45] If love stops short at couples and coupling, desire cuts through toward the other. Desire is always more than a purely romantic or bourgeois *égoisme à deux*.

But we are compelled to ask here if it is possible ever to fully separate out the strands of desire and love that mesh so intimately in the term *eros* (as we saw in the opening section on the Song of Songs). Can one desire the infinite—including infinite justice—without first loving the finite beings in front of us? Can one desire the alterity of goodness without loving *human* others? Can an eschatology of eros ever be wholly disengaged from an intersubjective relation of one-with-another?

III

In the section "Phenomenology of Eros," Levinas attempts to tease out some of these puzzles. The analysis is as dense as it is daring. First, he offers a phenomenological description of the feminine erotic as epitome of *equivocation*—the simultaneity of the clandestine and the exposed, of not-yet being and being, fragility and weight, violability and inviolability, modest inwardness and profane nudity. But the feminine already signals a secession from Hegel's master-slave dialectic. The feminine remains untouchable in the contact of voluptuosity, "not as a freedom struggling with its conqueror, refusing its reification and its objectification, but a fragility at the limit of non-being wherein is lodged not only what is extinguished and is *no longer*, but what is not yet."[46]

From this account of the feminine as witness to an eschatological not-yet, Levinas moves on to a phenomenology of the *caress* (echoing Sartre's analysis in part 3 of *Being and Nothingness*). He here construes the caress as an erotic surge into the invisible, a transcendence in and through the immediately sensible—what he calls future in the present, "seizing upon nothing, soliciting what ceaselessly escapes its form toward a future never future enough, in soliciting what slips away as though it *were not yet*."[47] This is why Levinas insists that desire is not adequately understood, with Hegel and Sartre, in the terminology of subject and object, consciousness for- and in-itself, possibility and actuality. The erotic, Levinas avers, is not reducible to the *Bildungsprozess* of a subject seeking meaning. Already in the erotic we glimpse the epiphany of the face as eschaton of exteriority; we begin to understand that being-for-the-other escapes the dialectic of antecedence and finality, in that in existing for another I exist otherwise than in existing for me. This erotic epiphany is the portal to ethics itself, the carnal trace of *goodness*.

Levinas is in fact taking issue here with a long tradition—running from the Stoics to Hegel and Sartre—which argued that desire and ethics are opposed. And in doing so he also appears to take his distance at this point from the phenomenological-hermeneutical approach to desire advanced by Ricoeur in *Freud and Philosophy*. For Levinas's phenomenology, the signification of the *face* is presupposed by and makes possible the symbolism of the *sign*. Ethics *precedes* hermeneutics. In this sense even the equivocation and double meaning of eros presupposes the face: the feminine is erotic by virtue of the blurring of the face in the ambiguous play of lust. Lust is the mixing of the metaphysical and the animal. In the "lasciviousness of erotic nudity one plays with the Other as with a young animal."[48] In its feminine epiphany, says Levinas, the face that I desire dissimulates, allures, alludes with innuendo, speaks by not speaking. But it is by virtue of this very indirection and obliquity that *eros* represents a sort of *via negativa* from below, its ludic voluptuosity breaching the master-slave dialectic of possession and totalization. "Nothing is further from *Eros* than possession. In the possession of the Other I possess the Other inasmuch as he possesses me: I am both slave and master. Voluptuosity would be extinguished in possession."[49]

It is here, finally, that Levinas chooses to replay Hegel's desire of desire *against itself*. For while admitting that voluptuosity aims not at the Other but at the other's voluptuosity—voluptuosity of voluptuosity—he reads this not as a struggle for self-recognition but as *trans-substantiation* through the engendering of a child. Here erotic love seeks what is to be engendered—the "infinitely future"—where same and other are not fused or balanced but, "beyond every possible project, beyond every meaningful and intelligent power—engender the child."[50]

IV

Let us pause at this rather startling turn in Levinas's argument. Levinas is speaking here, we recall, in eschatological rather than merely biological terms. Engendering the child goes beyond questions of genes and genealogy, of primogeniture and property rights. It goes beyond even the ontological *Eigentum* of *Ereignis* and *Eigentlichkeit*, so central to both Hegel and Heidegger.

Striking out on a new phenomenological path, Levinas insists that if desire begins in voluptuosity, it excels in *paternity*. And this excellence is the very opposite of a *privatio* or *steresis*. Paternity, argues Levinas, allows the lover who "loves the love of the Beloved" to return to himself while at the same time moving beyond himself in the coveting of the child, both other and myself. We are here before a new category: the paternal relation with the child as a "desire that is not extinguished in its end nor appeased in its satisfaction."[51]

The transcendence of trans-substantiation—marked by paternity—is one where the I is, in the child, an other, itself as another, one-for-another. The child is the stranger, as Levinas reminds us (invoking Isaiah 49), who is me as a *stranger to myself*. But the future of the child could not come to pass from beyond the dialectical horizons of power and project were it not, to repeat, for the erotic encounter with the other as feminine—an encounter which breaks the relation with the future as a solipsistic project of the subject, as a power of mastery over possibilities, replacing it with a very different relation to the future which Levinas calls "fecundity." (At the mention of fecundity, all card-carrying Platonists, Hegelians, and Sartrians clear the room!)

V

In fecundity the subject finds itself again as the self of an other: there is a leave-taking of one's former self as "virile and heroic I," a reversal of one's initial subjectivity into infinite recommencement. *Eros* goes toward a future which *is not yet*. Lured by the alterity of the feminine, it leaves behind the imperial subject which from every adventure returns to its Ithaca, like Ulysses. Finding itself the self of an other, erotic subjectivity remains a future by transcending absolutely in fecundity. This freedom of absolute commencement opened up by fecundity has, Levinas claims, nothing to do with a subordination of desire to some impersonal or neutral force—such as Hegel's universal or Freud's unconscious.[52] "It is precisely as itself that the I is, in the relation with the other in femininity, liberated of its identity. . . . In the I being can be produced as infinitely recommencing, that is, properly speaking, as infinite."[53] Thus, in contrast to Heidegger's being-towards-death, Levinas (like Arendt) here promotes the idea of beginning-again-through-the-birth-of-another. Ethics as natality rather than as mortality. As the yes of woman rather than the *nom-du-père*. As *autrement qu'être* rather than *manque à être*.

And so out of the ambiguity of voluptuosity, which remains a quest of desire even in profanation, we discover the fecundity of "infinite being" as a being that is forever *recommencing*, establishing a relation with the child as the other that is not power over the future but a relation with the absolute future of infinite time. In fecundity the obsessional neurosis of the self seeking to repeat itself or return to itself is breached. Indeed, the relationship with the alterity of the child inaugurates the time of the other as alteration of one's very substance, the time of a "third" exploding the lovers' *société à deux*.

Accordingly, through a phenomenology of voluptuosity-paternity-fecundity, the desiring self moves from *reiteration* of the self as ego to *initiation* into the enigma of oneself-as-another. It rediscovers within the very depths of voluptuosity a movement of transcendence toward to an Other beyond my ken.[54] Levinas concludes his phenomenology of desire at this point by reasserting the eschatological infinity of desire: "The Other is not a term: he does not stop the movement of Desire. The other that Desire desires is again Desire; transcendence transcends toward him who transcends—that is the true adventure of paternity, of the transsubstantiation which permits going beyond the simple renewal of the possible in the inevitable senescence of the subject. Transcendence, the for the Other, the goodness correlative of the face, founds a more profound relation: the goodness of goodness. Fecundity engendering fecundity accomplishes goodness . . . the gift of the power of giving, the conception of the child. Here the Desire which in the first pages of this work I contrasted with need, the Desire that is not a lack, the Desire that is the independence of the separated being and its transcendence, is accomplished—not in being satisfied and in thus acknowledging that it was a need, but in transcending itself, in engendering Desire."[55] In paternity, as Levinas concludes in a related passage, desire is maintained as "insatiate desire, that is as goodness."[56]

VI

So what do we make of this? The most arresting claim in Levinas's analysis of voluptuosity-fecundity-paternity is that it is desire that keeps love vigilant and asymmetrical. With regard to paternity, we might conclude that the parent loves the child in a way that the child can never be expected to love the parent, but only its own child in turn in the *next* generation—in a future never future enough. The parent who seeks to appropriate the child's desire, compelling the child to return to the parent who engendered it (like Chronos devouring his offspring), twists fecundity back onto itself and forfeits the eschatological infinity of desire. Desire of the other as separate and transcendent is desire as gift rather than appropriation. It is the refusal of incest—the renunciation of tribal closure. Desire thus engenders an ethics of asymmetrical fecundity finding its epitome in the desire of God.

But aporias abound. Is Levinas's account of eros a purely phenomenological description as he likes to claim? Or is it not already to some extent an *interpretation* of desire according to certain biblical and Talmudic precepts? Secondly, we might ask if Levinas's notion of eschatological desire is ever actually *possible?* On the face of it, it appears to be endlessly deferred to some messianic moment of peace—a future never future enough? Is the desire we invariably encounter as erotic love, voluptuousness, and fecundity not fundamentally at variance with a metaphysical desire for the invisible? Is not paternity—as desire through surplus, selfhood through otherness, recommencing through rupture—not itself an *impossible way of being*, replacing human time with the "messianic time" of prophetic eschatology? Or as Levinas himself puts it: is the eschatological time of eternity—which fecundity and paternity desire—"a new structure of time, or an extreme vigilance of the messianic consciousness"?[57] This problem, Levinas concedes, "exceeds the bounds of this book."[58] Perhaps indeed of any book. For the very hyperbolic excess of Levinas's ethics is, arguably, the very token of its impossibility. An impossibility which, understandably, prompts John Caputo to claim that "the work of Levinas comes over us today like the voice of a Jewish prophet . . . inspiring a prophetic postmodernism. We are awed, shocked, even scandalized by the sublimity, by the excess, of what Levinas demands, which is clearly too much. . . . What Levinas asks is not possible."[59]

But for Levinas the demands of eschatological desire are impossible in a second and more final sense. In his last major philosophical work, *Otherwise than Being*, Levinas actually cites, in reference to the Song of Songs, the Shulamite's declaration that she is "sick with love" (5:8). In this later reading, however, the desire of the beloved for her transcendent lover has turned from infinite yearning to an almost pathological passivity and paralysis. This malady of desire is now defined as a modality of abduction by the other to the point of becoming, through subjection, a hostage or victim. The sickness unto love sung in the Song of Songs re-emerges here as a form of corporal uneasiness and heaviness which, Levinas insists, has nothing to do with the "gift of fine words or of songs."[60] An impossible, terrifying love, not embraced but suffered, not offered but inflicted. A "psychosis" bordering, at times, on theo-erotic masochism.

Deconstructive Readings—From Derrida to Caputo

I now look, finally, at how certain deconstructionists have responded to this dilemma of eschatological desire. I begin with Derrida's own curious comments on Levinas's allusion to the "sick with desire" verse of the Song of Songs.[61]

I

The first point that Derrida makes is that the identity of the "self" who is sick with love is undetermined in Levinas's text. Is it the beloved, as the footnote assignation to the Song suggests? Is it Levinas himself? Or the self, as accused and accosted by the other's love? Or God? Derrida proceeds to rehearse the full verse of the Song (5:6–8) which precedes the sick-with-love declaration: "I opened to my love, / but he had turned and gone. / My soul failed at this flight, / I sought but could not find him, / I called, but he did not answer . . . (They beat me, they wounded me) / they took my cloak away from me: those guardians of the ramparts! / I charge you, / daughters of Jerusalem, / if you should find my love, what are you to tell him? / —That I am sick with love." It is odd that Derrida omits the one sentence about beating and wounding which most powerfully captures the Levinasian sense of persecution, violation, and alienation "in the name of love." He also omits the immediately preceding reference to the beloved's invasion by her lover, an act of metaphorical "breaking and entry" whose erotic and orgasmic connotations are veiled but vivid: "My love thrust his hand / through the hole in the door; / I trembled to the core of my being / Then I got up / to open to my love, / myrrh ran off my hands, pure myrrh off my fingers, / on to the handle of the bolt" (5:4–5).

Derrida's editing of this passage indicates perhaps not only a scruple of discretion concerning Levinas's idioms of masochistic eros, but a determination to focus on the grammatical performance of the beloved "I" whose sickness of love is a *response* to the other. Derrida implies that such a response pre-exists voluntary choice to the extent that the love-sick "I" comes to be in the accusative mode—that is, as someone who says "here I am" in visceral response to an erotic other whose language "interrupts," "deranges," "haunts," and "extradites" (all words used in Derrida's commentary).

Derrida's analysis here is linguistic and micro-logical rather than psychoanalytical or theological. And what interests him is how Levinas endeavors, in spite of all, to say the unsayable—regarding the sickness of love—by indirectly invoking *another* language behind the surface language of the text. This other text, masked by the thematizable text, manages to "disassimilate" and "interdict" our normal way of speaking and thinking. Referring specifically to Levinas's citation of the sick-with-love verse, Derrida writes: "The verse quoted and translated from the Song of Songs, which we should recall is already a response, and a response more or less fictive in its rhetoric, and made moreover to be *cited* in its turn, transmitted and communicated in indirect discourse, the accusative thus finding its grammatical credibility . . . this verse is torn from the mouth of a woman to be given to the other."[62] This very function of indirect, estranging, and elusive citation is for Derrida a typical linguistic ploy to capture what Levinas means by the "extradition of subjectivity to the other."[63] Through this curious disruption of our grammar and lexicon, Levinas attempts to do the impossible—to somehow utter what is unutterable about the enigma of desire, to compel language itself to make a contract with the alien outsider: that other which language—like the lovesick bride—"can only embody but not assimilate."[64]

So is it God we are still ultimately talking about here? Or is the divine paramour of the Song of Songs being replaced by another kind of other— atheistic, anarchic, perhaps even monstrous? This brings me to Derrida's intriguing statement in *On the Name* (1995): "The desire of God, God as the other name of desire, deals in the desert with radical atheism."[65] The most immediate difference with Levinas here is Derrida's linking of the desire of God with atheism. So doing, Derrida appears, on the face of it, to be reversing the Levinasian position. But what exactly does Derrida mean by atheism? It must be said, firstly, that he does *not* mean a dismissal of the God phenomenon per se. By a-theism Derrida seems to indicate a general openness to an alterity without name, beyond the historical givenness of a specifically revealed deity —for example, Jewish, Christian, Muslim. This basic disposition toward an alterity to come, understood as unforeseeable advent and event, Derrida calls "messianicity"—in contradistinction to any particular "messianism" of positive revelation.[66] Atheism, then, is less a refusal of God as such, for Derrida, than a renunciation of a specific God (or Gods)—a renunciation which could almost be said to serve as condition of possibility of a God still to come, still to be named.

We might recall here Derrida's suggestion in *On the Name* that the "most consequent forms of declared atheism will have always testified to the most intense desire of God."[67] This is a bold suggestion very much in keeping with his observation that "like mysticism, apophatic discourse has always been suspected of atheism" (Derrida cites the example of Angelus Silesius suspected by Leibniz and other rationalistic and scholastic thinkers.)[68] It is, tellingly, on foot of this latter passage that Derrida goes on to ask *who speaks to whom?* in the desire of God. "If atheism, like apophatic theology, testifies to the desire of God . . . in the presence of *whom* does it do this?"[69]

II

But what exactly is this desire of God which Derrida speaks of? Let's begin by stating what it is not. It differs, most obviously, from the "desire of the proper" operating within a thematics of identity and possession.[70] It transcends the desire to have, to know, to see (*avoir, savoir, voir*). And, more specifically, it goes beyond the "fratricidal desire" of rivalry and *ressentiment* invoked by Augustine in the *Confessions* in his discussion of sibling rivals at their mother's breast (or by Derrida himself in his allusion to coveting his brother's drawing in *Memoirs of the Blind*).[71]

Desiring God is, Derrida avows, not just an insatiable human questing but another voice of apophasis foreign to every "anthropotheomorphic form of desire"—a desire which carries with it "its own proper suspension, the death or the phantom of desire." "To go toward the absolute other," writes Derrida, "isn't that the extreme tension of a desire that tries thereby to renounce its own proper momentum . . . of appropriation?"[72]

This seems very close to what Levinas called *eschatological* desire: that messianic disposition of attention and vigilance which, as noted above, surpasses the onto-theological nostalgia for original causes and first foundations. Indeed Derrida appears to deepen this parallel in his analysis of *"désir et trouble"* in *Archive Fever,*[73] where he deconstructs the archaeological desire which burns feverishly for the trace of the primordial beginning—that is, the archive, the arche, the aboriginal origin, the inaugural source. This is the oldest drive, he claims, not only of archival history but of metaphysics itself—to know, for once and for all, how it was in the beginning, *in principio, en arche.* This archaeological-archival lust ultimately spells trouble and confusion. It provokes another kind of fever, turning passion to malady and mania, "for we are thereby driven beyond the archive to the *arche,* pushed past the slow labor of working with traces, of patiently reconstructing competing versions of memory, in order to displace the trace with *la chose même,* to displace the general archive with living memory and pure presence."[74] Something deconstruction sets its face against.

But Derrida goes further. Where Levinas could be said to have exempted certain forms of metaphysical and theological desire from his critique of presence, Derrida is uncompromising. For deconstructionists, Levinas is still *too metaphysical.* At strategic junctures, Levinas lapses back into the most classical (Neoplatonic and mystical) metaphysics, to that negative theology of "loving desire" (*eros*) which Derrida explicitly identifies with Dionysius's theory of the "erotic" power of the Good in the *Divine Names* (IV, I, 708–709, 712, 716). All too often, Levinas's God of desire approximates to the "ecstatic" desire of God, through which, Derrida notes, "erotics leads or leads back to the Good."[75] And it is this kind of approximating to the old apophatic theologians which prompts Caputo to comment that "Levinas is vulnerable to all of the criticisms that beset metaphysics, for this is metaphysics indeed, a metaphysics of the Good not the true, a metaphysical ethics, not a deontology, but metaphysics still."[76] So Caputo (like Derrida) deconstructs Levinas by taking the metaphysics out of him.

Even negative theology, which shares the same passion for the impossible as deconstruction, is too specific here in closing down options of alterity.[77] For Derrida, negative theologies are not immune to archive fever; they simply replace the theistic essentialism of onto-theology with a higher and more rarefied form of hyper-essentialism. Whereas negative theologians—from Dionysius to Meister Eckhart and Marion—desire the *tout autre* in the name of a biblical-monotheistic God, deconstructionists construe this wholly other as *every* other, regardless of its theistic pedigree. An all-inclusiveness summed up in the claim—*tout autre est tout autre.*

It is in virtue of this radicalization, this unconditional openness to *every* other regardless of its identity, that Derrida speaks of a "desire beyond desire," an atheistic eros in the "other voice," gesturing toward an "absolute other," a *tout autre* irreducible to the language and limits of anthropo-theo-morphism. So if Derrida continues to speak of a "desire of God"—as he does—he has in mind an impossible God of such indeterminate and undefined alterity that it always remains to be invented. This *à-Dieu* of pure invention is what Derrida calls the "messianic": a non-lieu of absolute passion and passivity, of incessant waiting and welcome, preceding and exceeding every historical revelation of a specific messiah (e.g., the "messianisms" of Judaism, Christianity, Islam, and so on).

III

In *The Prayers and Tears of Jacques Derrida* (1997), John Caputo equates this non-locatable "desire beyond desire," this messianic beyond messianism, with deconstruction itself. Deconstruction is the desire for the impossible as impossible, that is, for what is beyond all our intentional horizons of possibility. Indeed Caputo implies that this messianic inventiveness may be just that bit *more* respectful of radical alterity than any of our revealed religious eschatologies. Desire beyond desire is, after all, precisely beyond the "desire of the proper," which, he argues, draws the Gift "back into the circle of a proper or identifiable Giver which gives us a proper or identifiable Gift."[78] That is why desire beyond desire remains desire for a Godless God—a God still to be invented.[79]

The desire beyond desire is divested, it seems therefore, of all *specific* "horizons of waiting."[80] It keeps its options open. The time to cast your die, make your wager, nail your colors to the mast, choose your specific faith, never seems to arrive. Deconstruction is like waiting for Godot, not just in two acts but forever (*go deo*). And here again, we are well beyond negative theology. For if it is true that certain negative theologians and mystics—notably Eckhart—prayed God to rid them of God, they had no doubt that it was the God of Judeo-Christian revelation that they were praying to. Not so with deconstruction. Deconstructive faith is a leap into radical atheism.

But in not wishing to exclude any other-to-come is not deconstruction opening itself to the risk of indiscrimination? In *On the Name*, Derrida puts us to the pins of our collars on this vexed question. He writes: "The other, that is, God or no matter who, precisely, any singularity whatsoever, as soon as every other is wholly other. For the most difficult, indeed the impossible, dwells there: there where the other loses his name or is able to change it in order to become no matter what other."[81] But here precisely is the problem, as I see it: the metamorphosis of the messianic other into "every other . . . no matter what other." If every other is wholly other, does it still *matter* who or what exactly the other is? Derrida deepens the dilemma at this point, injecting theology with a dose of teratology: "One should say of *no matter what* or *no matter whom* what one says of God or *some other thing*" (my italics).[82] And this "some other thing," as we learn in *Given Time*, also includes things neither divine nor human. This is a "wholly other form of alterity," explains Derrida, "one or other persons but *just as well places, animals, language*" (my italics).[83]

If we thought Kierkegaard was making the question of identifying "who speaks when God speaks" difficult in *Fear and Trembling*, we hadn't yet read Derrida! Caputo offers a characteristically lucid gloss on this difficulty, countering that what might *appear* like indifference—every other is the same as every other—is in fact its opposite: a scrupulous attention to the singularity of each other before me in flesh and blood, here and now. "The wholly other is any singularity whatever, whoever, whose this-ness we cannot lift up, cannot generalize, cannot universalize, cannot formalize, any singularity which fixes us in this place so that we cannot look away." Which means, he concludes, that "every singularity is a wholly other whose alterity should be respected, not assimilated to the same, not subsumed under the universal."[84]

But can the problem be put to bed so quickly? In rightly resisting the temptation to reduce the alterity of every other to the rubric of species and genus, to the identifiable features or fingerprints of a nameable being, is deconstruction (or Caputo's version of it) not, in spite of itself, removing the very criteria whereby we distinguish one kind of other from another—divine from human, good from the evil, true from false? Are we not in fact confounding the otherness of God with everything and everyone that is not-God, thereby compromising God's unique transcendence? In the name of a God of desire beyond desire, do we not perhaps lose something of the God of love who takes on very definite names, shapes, and actions at specific points in time, the God of *caritas* and *kenosis* who heals specific cripples and tells specific parables, who comes to bring life here and now and bring it more abundantly?[85]

At this juncture, we might recall those figures in sacred history who received a call from God, insisted on some kind of sign, and were granted one. So it was with Gideon who said to the Angel of God who appeared to him under the oak of Oprah: "show me a sign that it is you who speaks with me" (and he was shown one). So it was with Jacob who wrestled with God's angel through the night until he received the name of Israel. So it was too with Moses and the burning bush; with Elijah and the "thin, small, voice"; even with Abraham (*pace* Kierkegaard) on Mount Moriah—for the sign that it was the God of goodness who summoned Abraham, and not some evil impostor, was that God intervened and commanded Abraham to *replace* Isaac with a sacrificial lamb.

And so it was with Christ who, while refusing to convert stone to bread, nonetheless revealed himself as a son of God through acts of healing and love. Even after his death, the resurrected Messiah acknowledged the human need for "signs" of recognition—making himself known to Magdalene as "teacher" (*rabounai*), to Thomas as wounded, to Peter on Lake Tiberias as fisherman, to the disciples on the road to Emmaus as eucharistic sharer of bread. The passage in Luke is telling here: "They *recognized* him in the breaking of the bread . . . their eyes opened and they *recognized* him." And it is only on foot of this sign that they realized, retrospectively, that "their hearts had been burning inside them while he had spoken to them on the road, explaining the Scriptures" (Luke 24:30–35). In other words, it is through a specific epiphany of broken bread that the Messiah appears and, at the same time, reveals to the disciples their own desire, the passion in their hearts for something still beyond them. It is through the *identifiable* sign of sharing bread that the desire of God is made manifest—*shown* even if it cannot be *said.*

What I find telling in these incidents is that God needs to be *recognized* for us to be able to say that it is indeed God we desire (and not some idol, simulacrum, or false prophet). That is, presumably, why it is not sufficient for the bride in the *Song of Songs* to aimlessly wander the streets at night, seeking and desiring any other whatsoever: she can find whom she is seeking only when God's sentinels *find her* and respond to her burning question "have you seen him whom my soul loves?" It is because our desire is human that we have to see to believe, that we need signposts and signals on our night journey, sentinels to guard and guide us on our undecidable way toward the absolute other. For without such spiritual guides, without such mentors of wisdom, story, and interpretation, how are we to practice what Ignatius calls "discernment of spirits"—discriminating between good and evil specters, between those thieves that come in the night to violate and those who come to heal and redeem?[86]

IV

By releasing the "desire of God" from any particular tradition of revelation and narrative, does deconstruction not make it difficult for us to address the human need to identify divinity, to look for at least *some* sort of credentials before taking it in—or being taken in? In prizing God free from both onto-theology (where idols abound) and from the biblical messianism with which Levinas and the negative theologians still affiliate themselves, does deconstruction not leave us open to *all* comers?

Derrida acknowledges the terrifying riskiness of undecidable "newcomers" when he concedes that we have no way of telling the difference between the demonic and divine other. "For pure hospitality or pure gift to occur there must be absolute surprise . . . an opening without horizon of expectation . . . to the newcomer whoever that may be. The newcomer may be good or evil, but if you exclude the possibility that the newcomer is coming to destroy your house, if you want to control this and exclude this terrible possibility in advance, there is no hospitality. . . . The other, like the Messiah, must arrive whenever he or she wants."[87] Indeed, for Derrida it is precisely because we do not see or recognize who the other is that *faith* exists. "If we refer to faith, it is to the extent that we *don't see*. Faith is needed when perception is lacking. . . . I don't *see* the other, I don't *see* what he or she has in mind, or whether he or she wants to deceive me. So I have to trust the other, that is faith. Faith is blind."[88] This God of absolute faith would be a God of absolute desire—but also a *"tout autre* without face."[89] A God not just of discretion but of absolute "secrecy." A God not only reserved in terms of its coming but also an "impossible, unimaginable, un-foreseeable, unbelievable ab-solute surprise."[90]

Yet—to repeat—how could we ever recognize a God stripped of every specific horizon of memory and anticipation? How could we give content to a faith devoid of stories and covenants, promises, alliances, and good works, or fully trust a God devoid of all names (Yahweh, Elohim, Jesus, Allah)? If the powers of human vision and imagination are so mortified by the impossible God of deconstruction—leaving us "without vision, without truth, without revelation"—then must not our encounter with the coming of the other *find* itself not only blind but empty? We might be tempted to put to Derrida here the question he put so adroitly to Levinas in "Violence and Metaphysics"— how is alterity to be *experienced* as other if it surpasses all our phenomenal horizons of experience?

Let me try to spell out further the radicality of deconstruction on this point. If *tout autre* is indeed *tout autre*, what is to prevent us saying yes to a malevolent agent as much as to a transcendent God who comes to save and liberate? Is there really no way for deconstruction to discriminate between true and false prophets, between holy and unholy spirits? Surely it is important to tell the difference, even if it's only more or less; and even if we can never *know* for certain, or *see* for sure, or *have* any definite set of criteria? Blindness is all very well for luminary painters and writers, for Homer and Rembrandt, but don't most of the rest of us need just a little moral insight, just a few ethical handrails as we grope through the dark night of postmodern spectrality and simulacritude towards the "absolute other," before we say "yes," "come," "thy will be done"? Is there really no difference, in short, between a living God and a dead one, between Elijah and his "phantom,"[91] between messiahs and monsters?

Caputo has this to say about deconstruction's duty to oblige the undecidable: "The figure of the future is an absolute surprise, and as such, Derrida says, something 'monstrous.' To prepare for the future, were it possible, would be to prepare for a coming species of monster, 'to welcome the monstrous *arrivant*, to welcome it, that is, to accord hospitality to that which is absolutely foreign or strange.' Whatever arrives as an 'event,' as an absolute surprise, first takes 'the form of the unacceptable, or even of the intolerable, of the incomprehensible, that is, of a certain monstrosity'" (*Points*, pp. 386–387).[92] Alterity as absolute surprise is always absolutely unprepared for.[93]

But can we square such unconditional fideism with the messianic cry of Psalm 34: "Taste and *see* the goodness of the Lord"? If it is true, as Caputo claims, that "differance does not love you or even know you are there . . . when you pray, do not say thanks"[94]—if this is true, how can we reconcile Derrida's monstrous *Dieu du désir* with the biblical God who knows every hair on our head and to whom we give thanks for what is given?

To make these monster-matters even more perplexing, I might cite Simon Critchley's disturbing suggestion that the Levinasian model of subjectivity-as-substitution, predicated on an alterity that can be neither comprehended nor refused, is as susceptible to evil as to good, and perhaps even more so. "Does not the trauma occasioned in the subject possessed by evil more adequately describe the ethical subject than possession by the good?" asks Critchley. "Is it not in the excessive experience of evil and horror . . . that the ethical subject first assumes its shape? Does this not begin to explain why the royal road to ethical metaphysics must begin by making Levinas a master of the literature of horror? But if this is the case, why is radical otherness goodness? Why is alterity ethical? Why is it not rather evil or an-ethical or neutral?"[95] Why indeed. These questions find no easy answers, it seems, in the writings of Levinas or the deconstructionists.

V

Derrida is painfully aware of these difficulties of judgment and goes to considerable lengths to address them. He makes it very clear, for example, that the desire beyond desire is a desire for justice.[96] Indeed, having ostensibly released the "desire of God" from the ethical constraints of biblical affiliation, Derrida seems to redress this somewhat by reintroducing a certain complementarity of the messianic and messianism. The messianic needs messianism in the final analysis as much as messianism needs the messianic. Perhaps deconstruction, like the Freudian version of psychoanalysis analyzed by Derrida in *Archive Fever*, is really a form of "Jewish science" after all?[97] Caputo also appears to re-inscribe Derrida within a specific tradition of "messianism"—what he terms a "certain Jewish Augustinianism" extending to those wandering prophets and anchorite desert fathers who desired a God without being, beyond being, otherwise than being. And in response to the objection that deconstruction evacuates God completely of God, Caputo replies that it is precisely the "haze of indefiniteness" which deconstruction's "faith without faith" provokes in us which nourishes "the urgency and passion of decision."[98] But can we be so sure? Can we draw a line in the sand between deconstruction as desertification of God and desertion of God? Can we dance and sing before the God of deconstruction? Can we desire God without *some* recourse to narrative imagination? Without some appeal to tradition(s)? Without some guide for the perplexed?

In *Given Time*, Derrida returns to this abiding dilemma. He explains here that desire beyond desire is always bound to a double injunction—to respond to the gift *and* to the economy of exchange.[99] In other words, desire beyond desire—as precisely that desire for the gift beyond the commerce of daily transactions—both *is* and *is not* outside the circle of exchange; just as the messianic desire of God both is and is not outside the circle of messianism. This confession of double allegiance allows Derrida to concede that the "overrunning of the circle by the gift, if there is any, does not lead to a simple exteriority that would be transcendent and without relation."[100] On the contrary, it is this very exteriority that sets the circle going. Ultimately, the desire of God can never step completely outside of the circle of desire as *vouloir, amour, envie, attente, conatus, concupiscentia*; nor, if we keep Levinas in mind, beyond the carnal circle of *voluptuosity, paternity, fecundity.*[101]

Conclusion

What, one might ask finally, has all this to do with our own postmodern condition? Given the contemporary proliferation of phantoms and false prophets, ranging from the spectral simulacra of the mass media to the virtual realities of the world Web (where some of the most popular Internet sites pertain to extraterrestrial "aliens"), the deconstructionists' puzzling over undecidable others—ghosts, hallucinations, substitutions, simulacra—is timely. "Aliens are everywhere!" a new mass hysteria announces: at the borders of the United States and Europe; landing in wheat fields in Santa Rosa from outer space; or donning all kinds of extraterrestrial masks and makeup on our multiplex silver screens. One only has to recite recent box office hits to realize the exponential extent of this cultural paranoia: *Mars Attacks, Men in Black, The Fifth Element, Independence Day, Contact,* not to mention the ostensibly self-replicating *Alien* and *Star Wars* series. Never, arguably, has it been more necessary to separate mass-media fantasies from real-life others who call us to justice and love.

The deconstructionist response to this postmodern dilemma would seem to be twofold—*believe* and *read!* In spite of our inability to know for sure "who speaks" behind the many voices and visages that float before us, now present now absent, now here now elsewhere, Derrida tells us that we must continue to trust and have faith. "*Je ne sais pas, il faut croire,*" as the refrain of *Memoirs of the Blind* goes. But if our belief is blind, and each moment of faithful decision terrifying, we can always be helped by the vigilant practice of meticulous reading. We must never abandon our responsibility to read between the lines. "In order to overcome hallucination we have to listen to and closely read the other," insists Derrida. Reading, in the broad sense which he attributes to this word, is an "ethical and political responsibility. In attempting to overcome hallucinations we must decipher and interpret the other by reading. We cannot be sure that we are not hallucinating by saying simply 'I see.' 'I see' is, after all, just what the hallucinating person says. No, in order to check that you are not hallucinating you have to read in a certain way." In what way, we might ask? "I have no rule for that," Derrida humbly concedes. "Who can decide what counts as the end of hallucination? It is difficult. I too have difficulties with my own work."[102]

But in spite of these avowed difficulties, Derrida and Caputo have, I believe, done more than most contemporary philosophers—theist or atheist—to make us sensitive to the three calls of God: *donne, pardonne, abandonne*. The problem is that these calls are, for deconstruction, always made in the dark where the need to discern seems so impossible. So my final question is: how do we read in the dark?

One tentative response might be this: we may approach the enigma of sacred eros by inviting various great texts on the subject—from the Song of Songs, and its legacy of religious and secular interpretations, to the contemporary philosophies of the "desire of God" in thinkers like Levinas, Derrida, and Caputo—to confront, cross over, and ignite each other so that the sparks that fly up from their friction may shed some light onto our dark.

Having attempted such a multiple hermeneutic approach, however cursory, in the readings rehearsed above, I conclude with a tentative summary hypothesis. While God's lovers will always continue to seek and desire him whom their soul loves, they have always already been found, because already sought and desired, by him whom their soul loves. Their eros occupies a middle space, a two-way street between action and passion, yearning and welcome, seeking and receptivity. A doubling of desire well captured in the advice given to Nathanaël in Gide's *Nourritures terrestres:* "Let your desire be less expectation than a readiness to receive"—"*Que ton désir soit moins une attente qu'une disposition à l'accueil.*"[103] When it comes to God at any rate, you rarely have one without the other. *Attente* and *accueil* are the two Janus faces of desire. Why? Because desire responds to the double demand of eschaton and eros. God's desire for us—our desire for God.

The Shulamite loves as she is loved.

Possibilizing God

In Mark 10:27, we find Christ and his disciples discussing the question of who can enter the kingdom. In response to the query about how one can be saved, Jesus replies: "For humans it is impossible, but not for God; because for God everything is possible" (*panta gar dunata para to theo*). In this chapter I propose to tease out this web of possibility and impossibility in the light of a number of related scriptural and philosophical texts before proceeding to analyze, in a second section, how these findings may be compared with certain innovative notions of the possible in contemporary thinkers such as Husserl, Bloch, Heidegger, and Derrida. My aim is to suggest how an eschatological reinterpretation of God as "possibility" (*dunamis-posse*), guided by these readings, might help amplify my conjecture that God neither is nor is not but *may be*.

This penultimate chapter prepares the way—both destructively and inventively—for my ultimate contention that it is in fact such an eschatological revision of God which may enable us to retrieve certain neglected texts of our intellectual heritage and offer an account more consonant with the Messianic promise of theism.

The Impossible Made Possible

The eschatological "possible" invoked in Mark 10 suggests that when our finite human powers—of doing, thinking, saying—reach their ultimate limit, an infinite *dunamis* takes over, transfiguring our very incapacity into a new kind of capacity. The reference to the kingdom in this passage of Mark points forward to the Resurrection of the Just "possibilized" (*dia tes dunameos*) by the laws of Moses, to the wisdom of the Prophets, and to the dying and rising of Jesus (1 Corinthians 6:14). It alludes to the possibilizing power of the Spirit (*dunamis pneumatos/pneuma tes dunameos*) which raised Christ from the dead and prepared the disciples for their prophetic mission.[1] As Kittel observes in the *Dictionary of the New Testament*, the "divine possible" (*dunamis theou*)—or what I call the God-who-may-be—"expresses itself as the support or gift of the Spirit which manifests itself in the *personal* rapport between Christ and man . . . accessible through faith."[2]

This is assuredly the same divine *dunamis* which we read of in the prologue to John—the promise of renewed life in the darkest abyss: "The light shone in darkness . . . and to all those who received it was given the possibility of becoming children of God." Several decisive eschatological motifs revolve around this passage. First, we are told that these children are born not "of blood" but "of God." A new category of natality and filiality thus emerges which sees progeny as eschatological rather than merely biological—that is, as pro-created from the future rather than causally engendered by the past. This marks the transition from tribal to cosmopolitan affiliation, so celebrated by Paul, the opening up of a kingdom which includes each human being as son or daughter of the returning God.[3] No longer mere offspring of archaic gods and ancestors, we are now invited to become descendants of a future still to come, strangers reborn as neighbors in the Word, adopted children of the *deus adventurus*—the God of the Possible.

This new category of eschatological filiality epitomizes the vital promise of "Word becoming flesh," described by John (1:1, 18) as the glory of a "father's only son" (or daughter). It is a promise never fully realized until the Kingdom comes—and with it a new heaven and a new earth. We are speaking here again of that messianic time, already analyzed in chapter 1 above, which subverts and supersedes the linear, causal time of history moving ineluctably from past to present to future. The messianic progeniture of the possible is "eternal," not because it refuses time but because it brushes historical time against the grain—anti-clockwise as it were—disclosing a past which unfolds achronically out of the future. Such a-chronic time is neither archaeological nor teleological. It is not preconditioned by some sacred *arche in illo tempore*; nor is it dialectically impelled by some *terminus futurus ad quem*. Resisting all modes of causal determinism—efficient, formal, material, or final—the messianic time of divine *dunamis* constantly surprises us. It operates according to a paradoxical tempo of *hysteron proteron*, or what Levinas calls "future ante-riority." A tempo wherein the Messiah can be now and still to come at one and the same time. This time was before time began, is here and now, and will be after the end of time. It is, paradoxically, already here and not yet here in the eternal now (*Jetzzeit*). Eternal, that is, in the eschatological rather than Platonic-metaphysical sense. Whence the Johannine claim that "He who comes after me ranks ahead of me because he was before me" (John 1:15). This sentiment is echoed in Isaiah's prophesy that the child "born for us" today shall be "father of the world to come"; and it is reiterated in the messianic saying that "before Abraham was I am" (and ever will be). The eschaton, like the *angelus novus* blown backward against time, comes to us from the future to redeem the past. It is *contre temps*.

This messianic tempo relates to my notion of the divine "possible" in that it surprises us with possibilities which would have been impossible to us with-out such grace. It reveals possibles which are beyond both my impossibles and my possibles (as horizonal projections of my existence culminating in the impossibility of any further possibility—viz. my ownmost possibility of death). In much the same way as children are beyond the possibles of parents who beget them, the possibles given to me by the *posse* would be impossible were they not a *gift*. That is what is meant by the biblical sentiment that nothing is impossible to God, even if impossible for me. The possibilities opened up by the eschatological I-am-who-may-be promise a new natality in a new time: rebirth into an advent so infinite it is never final. That is why we are called by the *posse* not only to struggle for justice so that the kingdom may come, but also to give thanks that the kingdom has already come and continues to come. From where? From out of the future into every moment, from beyond time, against time, into time—the Word becoming flesh forever, *sans fin*, without end. That is why, as in Blanchot's story, if ever we meet the Messiah we will ask him, "When will you come?"

"The Holy Spirit will come upon you and the power (*dunamis*) of the Most High will overshadow you," Mary is told by the angel in Luke 1:34–37. "Hence the holy offspring to be born will be called Son of God . . . for nothing is impossible (*a-dunaton*) with God." Although the term *dunamis* is usually translated into English as "power," this gives the mistaken impression of a metaphysical or chronological cause, thereby ignoring the dynamic sense of eschatological possibility inscribed in the conception and nativity of Jesus and John. For what appeared *impossible* (*a-dunaton*) for both Mary and Elizabeth in the Annunciation narrative is made *possible* (*dunaton*) by God. The matrix-womb that *cannot*—from a causal/chronological perspective—bear fruit, sud-denly and surprisingly *can* bear fruit. One of the six joyful mysteries, the Churches tell us. But by any account an extraordinary enigma of the impossi-ble being transfigured into the possible: one powerfully captured in the ap-pellation of Mary, in certain ancient Byzantine churches, as "container of the uncontainable" (*khora tou akhoretou*).[4] The Madonna is *khora* transfigured by the Word.

I believe that such an eschatological notion of the possible can blaze trails to a new understanding of God in our time. By way of trying to consolidate this contention here, I will outline, in the second part of this chapter, what I believe to be four crucial if partial approximations in twentieth-century thought to what I call the "possible God": (1) teleological (Husserl); (2) dialectical (Bloch); (3) ontological (Heidegger); and (4) deconstructive (Derrida). But first a word about the dominant categories of possibility in our mainstream metaphysical tradition.

Metaphysics of the Possible

In standard metaphysics, the category of the possible was generally understood as a dimension of being precontained within reality. Possibility was conceived as a latency or lack in matter to be realized into act. It was a material striving toward fulfillment. Aristotle called this *dunamis* (*Metaphysics* 9.8. 1059). Moving from the *Metaphysics* to his more epistemological treatise, the *De Anima*, Aristotle also recognized the existence of a "potential intellect" (*nous en dunamei*) which he described as a material or receptive faculty which needs to be activated and completed by an eternal or quasi-divine "active intellect" (*nous poetikos*) (*De Anima* 3.5).

Aquinas and the scholastics translated the Aristotelian doublet of *dunamis* and *nous dunamei* as *potentia* and *intellectus possibilis*, respectively. But what all agreed—ancients and medievals alike—was that whatever you called it, it was *not divine*. The Aristotelian and scholastic deity was deemed to be a self-causing, self-thinking Act lacking nothing and so possessing no "potencies" which might later be realized in time. Aquinas states this position succinctly: "God is pure act without any potentiality whatsoever" (*Deus est actus purus non habens aliquid de potentialitate*; *Summa Theologiae* 1.3–4). Indeed Aquinas is quite scathing of someone like David of Dinant who suggested God might be a "potentiality preceding realization" (1.3–8). The potential is the hallmark of human insufficiency, retorts Aquinas: "the possible intellect . . . is inadequate to cause knowledge in us unless we presuppose that there is an agent intellect" (*Quaestiones De Anima* 4).[5]

A second traditional concept of possibility was that of intellectual representation. The rationalists and idealists referred to this as *possibilitas*—an influential example being Leibniz's theory of "possible worlds." But whether this logical category of represented possibility was understood from a metaphysical or nominalist viewpoint, it was invariably contrasted with various notions of "reality." And since almost every theistic metaphysics considered God to be Supreme Reality or Sufficient Reason, it would have been little less than blasphemy to describe the divine in terms of the merely "possible." Possibility, as a category of modal logic, fell far short of a true grasp of God. And this falling short was no less true of dialectical logic, as became clear in Hegel's argument that the possible is that which is actualizable (non-self-contradictory) but not yet actualized.[6] Actuality supersedes possibility by actualizing one possibility rather than its negation and by realizing the internal and absolute necessity of things.

A third metaphysical approach which exerted a profound influence on our Western understanding of the possible was that of evolutionist or vitalist thought. This view was no doubt best outlined by Bergson in the "The Possible and the Real" (1930), a seminal text for the notion of God as "Process" (later advanced by thinkers like Whitehead and Hartshorne).[7] What this vitalist model argued was that the possible is the *retrospective* result of reality as it invents and creates itself. The possible doesn't pre-exist the real in any ontological sense; it post-exists it as precisely that which can be recognized as a possibility *after the event.* The possible exists therefore only as a retroactive image which Spirit projects backward into the past once it has been historically realized! "According as reality creates itself, new and unpredictable, its image reflects itself behind it into an indefinite past," writes Bergson. "The possible is therefore the mirage of the present in the past."[8]

In all three approaches—realist, representationalist, and vitalist—the possible is thought of as a sub-category of the real (understood as substance, being, act, reason, existence, or history). In no way, according to such readings, could the possible be construed as the royal road to a new understanding of the divine. Now it is just this metaphysical opposition between the divinely real and the non-divinely possible that I want to contest here, as throughout this volume. To this end, I propose to rehearse and explore a number of pioneering modern attempts to rethink the whole notion of possibility (to wit, by Husserl, Bloch, Heidegger, and Derrida). My ultimate aim is to see how these preparatory soundings of post-metaphysical notions of the possible may serve as pointers on the path toward a new eschatological understanding which, in light of a hermeneutical retrieval of certain biblical passages, invites us to consider God in a very different fashion: namely, as *posse* rather than *esse.*

Post–Metaphysical Readings of the Possible

Teleological Notion of the Possible (Edmund Husserl)

In his last work, *The Crisis of Transcendental Phenomenology and European Science* (1934–38), Edmund Husserl speaks of the ultimate aim of Western philosophy as a teleological Idea of reason. This telos plays the role of a Kantian limit-Idea which surpasses the categorial intuition of essences toward a horizon of *pure possibility.*[9] As such, it signals a radical openness to the ongoing perfectioning—or as the phenomenologists would say "filling-out"—of meaning. It recognizes the possible as the *future of meaning.*

This Husserlian insistence on the futurity of the possible was to inaugurate a whole series of subsequent studies by phenomenologists into the temporal and historical character of consciousness. Heidegger would talk of the "pre-understanding" of *Dasein*, Levinas of the "otherness" of time, Sartre of our being-toward-our-possibles, and Derrida of *differance*. Various names for the temporalizing transcending of the present toward the possible.

Husserl had already touched on this protentive-projective character of our intentional possibilities in various early works—for example, volume 6 of the *Logical Investigations* and section 129 of *Ideas*—but it was not until the *Crisis*, and especially appendix 13, that Husserl tackled the issue of teleological possibility in both its theoretical and ethical aspects. Identifying philosophy as the conscience of a universal humanity, Husserl declared that "to be human is to have a teleological meaning, to have a duty-to-be."[10] Both our theoretical and ethical consciousness, Husserl insists, are structured according to the teleological possibility of an Idea which is unconditioned and therefore surpasses any determined intuitive fullness (or presence) we may presume to have. Any attempt by our consciousness to grasp the telos as a fixed or complete object fails, for the goal of meaning is forever escaping us, *immer wieder*. The telos is always *beyond* us.

In a sense, Husserl is rehearsing here Kant's claim, in his critique of transcendental illusion, that the highest goal of all human endeavor is the ultimate Good—*die Absichte aufs hochste Gut*.[11] This teleological Good is a "postulate of reason" which expresses itself as a hope in the order of things to come—a hope which is the philosophical equivalent of a "God resurrected from the dead."[12] For both Husserl and Kant such a rational project takes the form of a practical aim (*Absicht*) which transcends all modes of cognitive intuition, manifesting itself instead as a perpetual extension and expansion (*Erweiterung und Zuwachs*) of our experience in the direction of a higher goal.[13] The teleological Good is what Kant, in the third formulation of the categorial imperative in *Foundations of a Metaphysics of Morals*, calls the "possible kingdom of ends." But where Kant crosses over from a strictly philosophical notion of a teleological Good to a Christian notion of a resurrected God (albeit within the limits of reason), Husserl is more reserved—at least up until his final Manuscripts.

Husserl might also be said to differ from Kant in seeing the ultimate telos of Reason as motivating a *historical* striving, that is, a long and progressive trajectory leading from the origin of geometry and mathematics in the ancient Greeks to Newton and Galileo, right up to the transcendental turn in the modern philosophy of Descartes and Kant culminating in phenomenology.[14] For Husserl the perfectioning of philosophical reason is a teleological vocation for all humans, from the genesis of human reason to its end. Indeed from the time he wrote the *Crisis*, a latent Hegelianism appears to modify Husserl's Kantian transcendentalism: "We may understand that everywhere limit-forms are announcing themselves," he now claims, "emerging from the praxis of conceivable perfectioning, and towards which are tending each series of perfectionings, as towards an invariant and inaccessible pole."[15]

This teleological Idea which governs the history of our intellectual-practical endeavors is not subject to intuitive realization (sensible or categorial). It remains a *possibility* which manifests itself to us only in the symbolic mode of the *as-if*. Qua possibility, the Idea announces itself without ever actually appearing in the presence of a present. Derrida offers the following illuminating gloss on Husserl's retrieval of the Kantian notion of teleological Idea: "The Idea in the Kantian sense of the regulating pole of every infinite task, assumes diverse but always analogous and decisive functions at various points in Husserl's itinerary. . . . However, while granting a growing attention to what it conditions, Husserl never made the Idea itself into the theme of a phenomenological account."[16] The ultimate possibility of Husserl's teleology of reason remains irreducible to a finite object or determinate essence; but this does not prevent it from serving as both origin (*Urstiftung*) and end (*Endstiftung*) of all our intellectual-practical labors.

No matter how much Husserl strives to elucidate this teleological possibility in the *Crisis* or elsewhere (e.g., *Ideas*, para. 143, or *Formal and Transcendental Logic*, para. 16), he never manages to offer a full phenomenological description. The teleological possible eludes every knowledge we can have of it. It operates as a pure, prospective intention without intuition.[17] It is an "essential possibility" (*Wesenmöglichkeit*) which transcends the reality of essences (*Ueberwirklichkeit*) while constituting the final meaning (*Zwecksinn*) of all historical reality.[18] For Husserl it is both "innate in humanity" *and* that goal toward which we are "called"—making all thinkers "functionaries of humanity" who must never "abandon faith in the Possibility of philosophy as a task, in the possibility of universal knowledge."[19]

In a striking passage in his late E Manuscripts (III, 4), Husserl identifies this teleological possibility of reason as "God." Again using language more akin to Hegel or Aristotle than to Kant, Husserl speaks of this deity taking the form of an evolving telos-logos whose "hidden meaning" goes beyond the world of actual being in itself (*Ueberwirklich*/*Ueber-an-sichlich*) toward a goal yet to be realized.[20] It is, as Husserl puts it, "teleologico-historical." At a more personal level, he confided to his student Edith Stein in December 1935 that "the life of man is nothing other than a path towards God."[21] But while he leaves such tantalizing hints and guesses, Husserl never chose to elaborate on his understanding of God in his published work.[22]

Several of Husserl's phenomenological followers developed his notion of teleological possibility. None of them, however, with the ambivalent exception of Heidegger, explored the theological character of Husserl's wager. Thus while Sartre described the human desire to be God as our ultimate teleological possibility in *Being and Nothingness* (1943), he deemed this possibility to be both ontologically and logically absurd, and so utterly meaningless.[23] And though Merleau-Ponty was less dogmatic in his pronouncements on the issue, for him even the most "essential possibility" (*Wesenmöglichkeit*) of being remained always an immanent "world possibility" (*Weltmöglichkeit*) which had little or nothing to do with the transcendent God of Revelation.[24]

Finally, Nicolai Hartmann developed Husserl's category of teleological possibility in the direction of a logical ontology devoid of any theological dimension. Resolved to pursue Husserl's insights, Hartmann published a book entitled *Möglichkeit und Wirklichkeit in* 1939, just one year after Husserl's death. But Hartmann remained a captive of the metaphysical priority of the actual over the possible. Dividing the category of the possible into the "real" (an empirical condition of possible existence) and the "ideal" (a principle of logical non-contradiction), Hartman fell back into the traditional dualism between realist *potentia* and idealist *possibilitas*. Thus reinforcing the old dichotomy between historically actualizable possibles (*Real-Möglichkeiten*) and purely essential ones (*Wesensmöglickkeiten*), Hartmann declared a clear preference for the former as candidates for a true ontology. Indeed, he concluded by subordinating ideal and fictional possibilities to a *Realontologie* which discloses the existence of authentic possibles *within* the actual-actualizable order of being: *Was real möglich ist, das ist auch real wirklich*. To say truly of something that it is possible, even as a telos, is tantamount to saying that it is realizable here and now: *Hier-und-jetzt-wirklich-werden-können*. If the conditions for the actualization of something do not or cannot obtain, one is not really entitled to say that it exists as a possibility.[25] In the process, the possible is relegated to a secondary or subjacent category of reality, and any dimension of alterity is denied. For Hartmann, the possible is not beyond the real but beneath it.

In developing the Husserlian notion of teleological possibility in the direction of an unambiguously immanentist ontology, Hartmann might be said to have deprived it of its inchoate potential for theistic transcendence, recasting it instead in the evolutionist categories of the possible enunciated by non-phenomenological thinkers like Whitehead and Bergson.[26] Either way, the intriguing eschatological implications of Husserl's innovation are as neglected by Hartmann as by Sartre and Merleau-Ponty. We will have to wait until Heidegger and Derrida for some of these implications to be retrieved and extrapolated.

Dialectical Notion of the Possible (Ernst Bloch)

A second approach which I believe is conducive to an eschatology of the possible is Ernst Bloch's dialectical utopianism. The notion of God as a dialectical end of historical struggle finds its most explicit religious expression in the theology of liberation (Boff, Guttierez, Cardenal, Moltmann, Metz); but it draws much of its theoretical inspiration from neo-Marxist dialectical thinkers like Ernst Bloch and the critical theorists.

Advancing a singular brand of humanist utopianism, Bloch speaks of a coming kingdom which reveals itself as an "objectively real possible" (*Das objektiv-real Mögliche*).[27] Nicknamed the "theologian of the Revolution," Bloch was determined to show that the pivotal "principle of hope" evinced by all great religious traditions is nothing less than the utopian quest for a future society of revolutionary justice and peace. He thus restores the energies of spiritual striving from a heaven of transcendence and transcendentalism to their proper place in the immanent dialectic of history. Interpreting what he calls the "symbolism of hope" as it expresses itself in the signs and images of a wide variety of cultures, myths, dreams, literatures, and liturgies, Bloch identifies a universal project for the New (*Novum*) precontained in each of them. The *Novum* is the promise of a "renewed nature" implicit in all progressive social expressions. It is the pre-figuration of a materially equal and emancipated society which is "not yet" (*noch nicht*). And in this sense it takes Marx at his word when he said that as soon as we become conscious of what the world has dreamed of up to now, it will be obvious that there is no real "rupture between past and future but rather a realization of the projects of the past" (Marx in a letter to Ruge, 1843).

Spiritual and religious aspiration thus finds its appropriate material correspondent in the revolutionary horizon of history. And in the process, the old Hegelian definition of being as that which has been (*das Wesen ist das Gewesene*) is replaced by the neo-Marxist notion of utopia as a latent possibility of history, as that which has not yet actually been (*noch nie so gewesen*). Yet far from constituting a simple "negation" or "nihilation" of historical reality, as in the manner of Sartre's imaginary possibles, the possibility of utopia takes the form of a "maieutics" which brings the tacit imaginings of history to birth.[28] As such, the revolutionary category of the possible previews the "leap ahead" from present alienation to future peace.[29] Indeed, Bloch will not hesitate to critique fellow humanist Marxists Lukács and Adorno for reducing the "prophetic" potencies of cultural dreams to distorted forms of ideological false-consciousness.[30] He castigates Lukács in particular for wearing "sociological-schematic blinkers" which prevent him from recognizing that works of art can transcend existing ideologies and point toward a "creative cultural surplus" which serves as both a "pre-vision" (*Vor-Schein*) and "pre-figuration" (*Vor-Bildung*) of utopia.[31]

It is, however, in a chapter of his monumental *The Principle of Hope* (1938–47), entitled "The Category of the Possible," that Bloch makes his most detailed contribution to this debate. Here Bloch outlines a notion of "real possibility"—as opposed to a purely ideal, formal, or transcendental one—which shakes up any metaphysical given (*fixum*) in the name of a coming newness (*novum adventurum*). To interpret the world in the light of "real possibility" is to understand it as both "being-according to the possible" (*chata to dunaton*) and "being-in-the-possible" (*to dunamei on*). Bloch thereby intends to re-inject a dose of utopian historicity into the old Aristotelian metaphysics of "potency" (*dunamis*). Indeed he will go so far as to claim that the revolutionary discovery—by Hegel-Marx—of a "concrete theory-praxis" is inextricably linked to the "inquiry of the modality of objectively-real possibility."[32]

So doing Bloch historicizes Aristotle's concept of potency. But this move has nothing to do with a reductive materialism which would dismiss possibility as mere "sub-being." Rather, Bloch rehabilitates the Aristotelian concept of "being-according-to-the-possible" (*chata to dunaton*) as a dynamizing magnet which draws matter toward its future. And he likewise restores the category of "being-in-the-possible" (*to dunamei on*) to an equally active role, serving as a "lap of fertility which gives rise to all the figures of the world . . . the hopeful visage of real possibility."[33] Bloch, in short, dispenses with the metaphysical understanding of potency as inchoate matter awaiting the meaning-giving imprint of form (*morphe*) or act (*entelecheia*) and elevates it to the primary role of a mobilizing catalyst: "the consideration of what is to be achieved in this moment or that depends on the being-according-to-the-possible" of matter.[34] Moreover, it is thanks to this enabling potential that a hermeneutics of utopia can help us critically discriminate between authentically "real" possibilities— capable of historical realization—and mere empty fantasies.

For Bloch, the most effective critique of ideological paralysis stems from a recognition of the correspondence between the goals of historical struggle and the inherent potencies of the material cosmos which surround us. As he puts it in *A Philosophy of the Future*: "The meaning of human history from the start is the building of the commonwealth of Freedom, yet without a positively-possible, possibly-positive meaning in the surrounding cosmology which all historical events ultimately merge with, the progress of this historical process might as well never have happened."[35] This, Bloch believed, was one of the great insights of the heretic Giordano Bruno who, brushing traditional ontology against the grain, discovered the root of divine fecundity in the "potentiality and potency" of history.[36]

The dialectical category of the possible thus serves double duty. In so far as it signals the world according-to-possibility, it plays a critical role regarding the limits of what is possible (almost a Kantian condition of possibility); while as token of the world-in-possibility it mobilizes an unlimited dynamism of meaning, forever extending into the "utopian *novum* of all of history."[37] It would be a mistake, therefore, to construe the *novum* as some kind of ontological *entelecheia*, understood in the sense of a "form of forms" or "self-thinking-thought"—timeless, immutable, devoid of potency. The *novum*, qua end of history, is not a transcendent *actus purus*; nor is it some Supreme Being already accomplished beyond time and awaiting the culmination of history to reveal itself. No, the *novum* is that promise of possibility inscribed in the not-yet-now of time and the not-yet-there of space. And as such, far from being an indifference that leaves us, human agents, indifferent in turn, the *novum* galvanizes our utopian drive toward the kingdom whose realization "here on earth human labour so powerfully helps to accelerate."[38] What connects this distant goal to our everyday earthly labors is, according to Bloch, precisely the intermediary realm of "dream," both aesthetic and religious. For without the "visible pre-appearing" of our images and icons, our struggling toward the *novum* would be blind and directionless. With it, by contrast, we are liberally instructed in the "power-to-be" (*Kann-sein*) of human history.

But if art and religion open up history to utopia, history grounds art and religion in the real. The dialectical category of *Kann-sein* plays a crucial role here as a reminder not only of the still undetermined ends of revolutionary endeavor, but also of the socio-material conditions which can bring such goals about. For utopia, as Bloch insists, "is only possible if it is partially conditioned."[39] Utopian possibility is thus redefined as what is not-yet-realized but realizable. Or to use Bloch's own terms, the "real possibility" of utopia is at once: (a) the measure *of* things (as ultimate goal: *das sachlich-objektiv Mögliche*); and (b) the measure *within* things (as yardstick of feasibility: *das sachhaft-objektgemass Mögliche*).[40] In contrast to Kant, Bloch sees possibility not as an a priori condition of formal knowledge but as a precondition of historical transformation. Utopian possibility is less a power-to-know than a power-to-become-other than what is at present the case. This transmutational capacity reaches its highest expression in Bloch's secularized concept of salvation (*Heilsbegriff*): "Interdependence is here such that without the potentiality of the power-to-become-otherwise, the power-to-make-otherwise of potency would not have the space in which to disclose itself; just as without the power-to-make-otherwise of potency, the power-to-become otherwise of the world would have no mediating meaning with humans. Consequently, the possible reveals itself as being what it is . . . thanks to the activating intervention of humans in the field of the transformable: the concept of salvation."[41]

Far from guaranteeing redemption, therefore, the utopian possible presents itself as a free invitation from history to humanity—an offer which may be rejected or accepted.[42] It is our response to the summons of the possible latent within history that determines its realization or non-realization. This dynamic notion of possibility is directly opposed, in Bloch's view, to the inherited notions of "essence" as something already achieved, to be simply "remembered" (Platonic *anamnesis*) or "recollected" (Hegel's *Erinnerung*). Such metaphysical spiritualism is the kiss of death to true utopia; for it reduces the "possible" to a mere lack of being—a form of negative non-being with no status outside of actuality. In sum, Bloch was uncompromising in his resistance to any metaphysics for which "there is no possibility that is not already realized, no essence that has not already appeared."[43]

Equally vehement, however, is Bloch's critique of rival models of logical possibility. In a polemical section of *The Principle of Hope*, entitled "The Struggle of Static Logic against the Possible," he maintains that all purely logical-positive definitions of possibility, from Duns Scotus to nominalists like Ockham and later Vermeyer, evacuate the radically transformative power of *das Mögliche*, replacing it with a purely abstract category of modality. One could say, Bloch quips ironically, they wrote nothing "very real about the possible."[44] Against, therefore, *both* the metaphysical reduction of the possible to the primacy of form/act/essence *and* its logical reduction to a formal modality of ratiocination, Bloch militates for the retrieval of its radical utopian power. He resolves to reinstate it as the future-oriented determination of history itself (*zukunft-tragende Bestimmtheit*).[45]

Ontological Notion of the Possible (Heidegger)

In the introduction to *Being and Time* (1927), Martin Heidegger makes the arresting claim that for phenomenology "possibility stands higher than actuality." He probably had his mentor, Husserl, in mind; but he also, as would become clear, had thoughts of his own on the matter. Later in the same book—section 76—Heidegger goes on to speak of the "quiet power of the possible" (*die stille Krafte des Möglichen*). This, he suggests, is a privileged way in which Being reveals itself to us as temporal-historical beings. The question we are left with, however, is whether this power of loving possibility is something humans express toward Being or something Being expresses toward humans? In other words, which possibilizes which—Being or man? *Sein* or *Dasein*?

Given Heidegger's phenomenological analysis of *Dasein's* different categories of possibility in *Being and Time—Seinkönnen, Möglichkeit, ermöglichen*—one might be forgiven for supposing that the "power of the possible" refers to an essentially human property.[46] However, in the *Letter on Humanism* (1947), Heidegger claims that such a humanist supposition is in fact mistaken. In a pivotal if much neglected passage in his post-war letter to Jean Beaufret, Heidegger recites this exact reference to the "quiet power of the possible," redefining it this time as an unambiguous gift of Being itself. Theological connotations abound, albeit elusively. And we are tempted to ask: what, if anything, does this "quiet power" of Being have to do with God?

The passage in question opens as follows: "Being as the element is the 'quiet power' of the loving potency (*Vermögens*), i.e., of the possible (*des Möglichen*)." Already the interpolation of the new term *Vermögen*, to qualify the standard term for the possible in *Being and Time*—namely, *das Mögliche*—signals a shift from an existential-transcendental perspective (easily confused with humanism) to a more unequivocally Being-centered one. This new assignation for Being's own power of possibilizing is more topological than anthropological. It marks a clear departure from the logical and metaphysical residues of "possibility" still evident in the existential analytic of *Dasein* in *Being and Time*. Determined to avoid any further humanist misreadings, Heidegger is emphatic on this point. "Our words 'possible' and 'possibility' are," he explains, "under the domination of 'logic' and 'metaphysics', taken only in contrast to 'actuality', i.e., they are conceived with reference to a determined—viz. the metaphysical—interpretation of Being as *actus* and *potentia*, the distinction of which is identified with that of *existentia* and *essentia*." But Heidegger explains that when he speaks of the "quiet power of the possible," he means neither (1) the "possible of a merely represented *possibilitas*" (a Leibnitzian-

Kantian category of modal logic), nor (2) "the *potentia* as *essentia* of an *actus* of the *existentia*" (an Aristotelian-scholastic category of metaphysics). He means, as he states here, "Being itself, which in its loving potency (*das Mögend*) possibilizes (*vermag*) thought and thus also the essence of man, which means in turn his relationship to Being." Heidegger concludes this decisive passage thus: "To possibilize (*vermögen*) something is to sustain it in its essence, to retain it in its element."[47]

The significance of this pronouncement on the "possible" cannot be underestimated. It offers a unique insight into the famous "Turn" in Heidegger's thought from "phenomenology" (with its residual transcendental, existential, *Dasein*-centered idioms) to "thought" (with its shift of emphasis to Being-as-Being, *Sein als Sein*).[48] Heidegger I's humanist-sounding language of Being as temporality and historicality is now replaced with a more sacred-sounding liturgy of love and grace, consistent with Heidegger II's rethinking of Being as Gift (*Es gibt*). Playing on the latent etymological affinities between the German verbs for loving (*mögen*) and making possible (*vermögen*), Heidegger invites us to rethink Being itself as the power that possibilizes the authentic being of things: "It is on the strength of this loving potency or possibilization of love" (*das Vermögen des Mögens*) that something is possibilized (*vermag*) in its authentic (*eigentlich*) being. This possibilization (*Vermögen*) is the authentic "possible" (*das eigentlich "mögliche"*), that whose essence rests on loving."[49]

The proper response of human beings to such loving-possibilizing is, Heidegger suggests, to love-possibilize Being in return by thinking things and selves in their authentic essence. "Thought is . . . to concern oneself about the essence of a 'thing' or a 'person', that means to like or to love them."[50] The possibilizing of Being may thus be understood in terms of a double genitive; it refers to both Being's loving-possibilizing of thought and thought's loving-possibilizing of Being. Thus might we translate Heidegger's phrase—"*Aus diesem Mögen vermag das Sein das Denken*"—as "Being possibilizes thought which possibilizes Being." A translation whose sense is confirmed, it seems, in Heidegger's immediately subsequent sentence: "The one renders the other possible. Being as the loving-possibilizing is the "*posse-*ible" ("*Jenes ermöglichte dieses. Das Sein als Vermögend-Mögende ist das "Mög-liche"*").[51]

By choosing to translate the operative term, "*mög-liche*," as "*posse-*ible," I am suggesting that the shared semantic sense of *mögen* (to love) and *vermögen* (to be able/to make possible) is perhaps best captured by the Latin term *posse*—a term which according to Nicholas of Cusa, lies at the very heart of divine being, qua God's power to love. Cusanus coined the term *possest* to capture this double belonging of possibility and being which he identified with God.[52] But I shall return to this in my conclusion.

Heidegger does not go so far. And there is no mention of Cusanus. Yet much of his language is deeply resonant with the religious language of Christian eschatology. Indeed, in a related passage in the same letter to Beaufret,

Heidegger actually equates the essence of Being with the "sacred" and the "divine."[53] This, in conjunction with his *Der Spiegel* claim that "only a god can save us now" and his *Beiträge* allusion to Schelling's equation of the God of Exodus 3:14 with the "possibility of being" (*Seyn wird/Seyn-könnende*) certainly invites the surmise that *some* rapport might exist between the "possibilizing" power of Being and the *Possest* of God.[54] Moreover, Heidegger's liberal borrowings from Christian mystical theology—for example, Eckhart's *Gelassenheit*, Angelus Silesius's "rose-that-blooms-without-why," or Paul's eschatological *kairos*—all suggest a deep and residual affinity with the author's early fascination with Catholic and Lutheran theology. And even if it is probably more the "god of the poets" (than of revelation) that the later Heidegger has in mind when he invokes a "saving god," one cannot gainsay some kind of relation between ontological and theological readings of the "loving possible." Indeed, in the *Introduction to Metaphysics*, Heidegger had already hinted that the ontology/theology relationship might take the form of an analogy of proper proportionality: the believer is to God what *Dasein* is to Being.[55]

So, when Heidegger speaks of poetic dwelling as an invitation to abide in "that which has a loving for man and therefore needs his presence" (*was selber den Menschen mag und darum sein Wesen braucht*), one has reason to suspect that some kind of deity is hovering in the vicinity.[56] And this suspicion is substantiated when one observes how several of Heidegger's last writings recast the Husserlian notion of teleological possibility in terms of a quasi-eschatological drama. A typical example is *The End of Philosophy*, where Heidegger claims that the "end of philosophy is the place in which the whole of philosophy's history is gathered in its most ultimate possibility"—a final possibility which is also the "first possibility" from which all genuine thought originates.[57] Such a possibility is clearly beyond all human powers of determination, for "its contours remain obscure and its coming uncertain."[58] So we are back once again, it seems, with that possibilizing-appropriating of human thinking by Being itself: a form of happening (*Ereignis*) and giving (*Es gibt*) which remains beyond our ken and control. Being is thus reinterpreted as "that which is capable of being," the *esti gar einai* of Parmenides now being rethought by Heidegger as the "possibility of Being." From a human point of view this suggests, quite simply, letting things be what they *can be*.[59]

But whatever this "possibility of Being" means, it is certainly *not* the mere *potentia* of some metaphysical substance, nor the *possibilitas* of some representational logic (alongside reality and necessity).[60] The loving-possible is for Heidegger something that surpasses the understanding of both metaphysics and logic. It is nothing less than the giving of Being itself.

Deconstructive Notion of the Possible (Derrida)

In an essay entitled "Comme si c'était possible" (1998), Derrida revisits the notion of possibility in terms of what he calls the "irreducible modality of 'Perhaps' (*peut-être*)."[61] Cautioning against all talk of "last words," in philosophy no less than in history, Derrida declares this "perhaps" to be the necessary condition of possibility of every experience—to the extent that every experience is an event which registers that which comes from the unpredictable otherness of the future. Such an experience of the "perhaps" is at once that of the possible *and* the impossible. Or as Derrida puts it, the possible *as* impossible. If what happens is only that which is possible in the sense of what is anticipated and expected, then it is not an event in the true sense. For an event is only possible in so far as it comes from the impossible. An event (*événement*) can only happen, in other words, when and where the "perhaps" lifts all presumptions and assurances about what might be and lets the future come as future (*laisse l'avenir à l'avenir*), that is, as the arrival of the impossible. The "perhaps" thus solicits a "yes" to what is still to come, beyond all plans, programs, and predictions. It keeps the ontological question of "to be or not to be" constantly in question, on its toes, deferring any last word on the matter. But if deconstruction suspends the security of ontological answers, it also, Derrida insists, eschews the levity of a purely *rhetorical* "perhaps" (*peut-être/Vieleicht*). The "perhaps" sustains the survival of the question. But what might such a possible-impossible actually mean?

In *The Politics of Friendship* (1994), Derrida had already ventured some kind of response. Picking up on Nietzsche's talk of a "dangerous perhaps" as the thought of the future, Derrida argues that such a thought is indispensable to friendship precisely as a category of futurity. Distinguishing between the bad possible (of predictability) and the good possible (of impossibility), Derrida affirms that it is only the latter that can safeguard true friendship as a commitment to what is to come. It is also only the good possible (i.e., the impossible possible) which can respect the dual fidelity of friendship to undecidability and decision.[62] Without the openness of a radically indeterminate "possible"—which like the phenomenological reduction brackets our prejudices about the future—there could be no genuine decision. But, equally, no decision could be made without somehow also lifting the "perhaps," while retaining its "living" possibility in a kind of living memory. Consequently if no real decision—ethical, political, juridical—is possible without conjuring the "perhaps" that keeps the present open to the coming event, there could be no decision either—no committing of oneself to one possible rather than others— if there was not some limiting of this opening "perhaps" which serves as condition of the possibility of decision![63]

This circle is what Derrida calls the "lucky aporia of the possible impossible."[64] In "Comme si c'était possible," he expands on this aporia, as first outlined in the *Politics of Friendship*. In the event of decision, he writes here, "only the im-possible takes place; and the unfolding of a potentiality of possibility already there would never constitute an event or invention."[65] Why? Because, explains Derrida, "a decision that I *can* take, the decision *in my power* and which merely manifests the acting out (*passage à l'acte*) or unfolding of what is *already possible* for me, the actualization of my possibility, decision which only derives from me, would it still be a decision?"[66] The answer is no, for genuine decision—like genuine responsibility—is not just about *my* possibles but is also about *others'* possibles intervening which may well represent the impossibility of my own possible. Whence Derrida's preference for a paradoxically *receptive* decision, recalling Levinas's notion of a "*difficile liberté*" which allows for the irruption of the other in the self. He notes: "the responsible decision must be this im-possible possibility of a 'passive' decision, a decision of the other in me which removes none of my liberty or responsibility."[67] Moreover, Derrida insists that every responsibility must traverse this aporia of the impossible-possible which, far from paralyzing us, mobilizes a "new thinking of the possible."[68]

Later in "Comme si c'était possible," Derrida gives further examples of this aporetic logic. He cites, for instance, the fact that an *interpretation* is possible only if it remains to some extent inadequate (i.e., if an adequate interpretation is impossible). For an interpretation without any default—closed therefore to the possibility of misinterpretation—would represent not only the end of interpretation, as an ongoing process of exploring meaning, but also the end of a historical future in any sense whatsoever. Closing off the future, it would make everything impossible.

Derrida notes a similar interplay of possibility and impossibility in the instance of *invention*. Invention is always possible in so far as it is the invention of the possible; but invention is really only possible when it does not invent something new out of itself—in which case it would not be new—but rather allows something *other* to come, occur, happen. Now, given the fact that this otherness that comes to it is not part or parcel of invention's own resources of possibility, it means that the "only possible invention would be the invention of the impossible."[69] Of course, we may object that the invention of the impossible is impossible; but in fact, insists Derrida, it is the only kind possible. "An invention must pronounce itself as invention of what does not appear possible," short of which it would be little more than an explicitation of a "program of possibles in the economy of the same."[70]

A similar logic of impossible-possibility applies to Derrida's analysis of "pardon." Here we cross the threshold from epistemological aporias to ethics. Pardon, Derrida claims, is only possible, as such, when faced with the unpardonable, that is, where it is *impossible*. For pardon—like hospitality, gift, justice, and so on—is an unconditional that has to deal with conditions as soon as it becomes an act or decision. In such instances, the possible "is" impossible. Or to put it in more formal, quasi-transcendental terms, the condition of possibility of pardon (hospitality/gift/justice) is also and at the same time the condition of its impossibility.[71] The possibility of pardon, therefore, requires us to *do the impossible*, to make the impossible possible. But this must occur, says Derrida, without resorting to some sort of morality of rules and prescriptions, of oughts or obligations. Pardon must, by its very unconditional nature, remain unpredictable and gratuitous (*gratuit et imprévisible*).

In all of these examples, Derrida argues that im-possibility is not the mere contrary of possibility but rather its mark of renewal and arrival as event. No event worthy of its name is simply an actualization of some precontained potential program. For an event to be possible it must be both possible (of course) but also impossible (in the sense of an interruption by something singular and exceptional into the regime of pre-existing possibles-powers-potencies). The event happens not just because it is possible, qua ontological acting-out of some inherent *dunamis* or *potentia*, but also because something impossible—hitherto unanticipated and unplanned—comes to pass. It is precisely the impossibility of formerly predictable possibilities which makes new ones announce themselves beyond this very impossibility. The impossible reminds us, therefore, that beyond our powers the impossible is still possible. There are impossible possibles beyond us, never dreamt of in our philosophies. Or as Derrida puts it in *Politics of Friendship*: "Perhaps the impossible is the only possible chance of something new, of some new philosophy of the new. Perhaps; perhaps in truth the *perhaps* still names this chance."[72]

Derrida does not directly engage, it has to be said, with the eschatological implications of this issue. But he does leave us one or two tantalizing hints. In a note which refers to my own notion of the "may-be" in *Poétique du possible* (1984), and to my discussion of Heidegger's "loving possible" (*des mögende Vermögens*), Derrida makes mention of the possible as that which is "more than impossible" (*plus qu'impossible* or *plus impossible*). And he refers us here, tellingly if only in passing, to the mystical maxim of Angelus Silesius: "*das uberunmöglichschste ist möglich.*" The deeply theological connotations of this claim are not addressed by Derrida here, alas. But he does allude to his discussion of the "name of God" in "Sauf le nom." And he adds, furthermore, this sentence—recalling the opening claims about the "desire of God" in that essay—"All the aporias of the possible-impossible or of the more-than-impossible would thus be 'lodged' but also dislodging 'within' (*au-de-dans*) what one might calmly call the desire, love or movement towards the Good etc."[73]

The "etc." resists any temptation to pronounce a "last word" and leaves open, in my view, the option of adding a "possible God"—a God whom we might now be inclined to refer to, along with Silesius, as a "more than impossible" God. Indeed, it might be noted that Derrida himself does advert here to a certain connection between the possible-impossible aporia and the undecidable aporia of who/what which he relates to the question of *khora* (which precedes the distinction who/what). And this question of *khora*, as I have had occasion to remark elsewhere, is deeply linked in Derrida's work, as in Caputo's, to the question of God.[74] But such an eschatological possibility is not, it must be said, explored or extrapolated by Derrida himself.

What Derrida is trying to do, it seems to me, is to think a post-metaphysical category of the possible by rethinking the category of the im-possible in a way that is not simply negative or disabling. The impossible needs to be affirmed because, as I have noted above, it is precisely im-possibility which opens up possibility and makes it possible. Strangely, however, this can occur only when my power of possibility undergoes its own death as "my" possibility—acknowledging in mourning, passion, suffering, and anxiety that it is this very impossibility which allows a new possible, another possible, another's possible, an im-possible possible, to come, or to come back. This "other" possible returns, says Derrida, as a specter. It assumes the guise of a *revenant*, rising up from the grave of my own possible in the form of an in-coming other. And we experience this as surprise, gift, openness, grace, resurrection.[75]

In one especially charged passage, Derrida departs somewhat from his characteristic elusiveness and offers a more explicitly phenomenological take on this moment. Here he endeavors to describe the more affective dimension of the impossible-possible aporia: "It names a suffering or passion, an affect at once sad and joyous, the instability of disquietude (*inquiétude*) proper to every possibilization. This latter would allow itself to be haunted by the specter of its impossibility, by its mourning for itself: the mourning of the self carried in itself, but which also gives it its life or survival, its very possibility. For this *im*-possibility opens its possibility, it leaves a trace, at once an opportunity and a threat, *in* what it renders possible. The torment would signal this scar, the trace of this trace. . . . All this recurs with respect to Freud's concept of *Bemachtigung*, of the limit or the paradoxes of the possible as power."[76]

Derrida even goes so far as to identify this paradox of the impossible-possible with the experience of *faith* itself. For how is it, he asks, that that which makes possible makes impossible the very thing it makes possible? How is it that promise is so related to ruin, affirmation to death, renewal to deprivation? "The *in*-of the im-possible is no doubt radical, implacable, undeniable," he replies. "But it is not simply negative or dialectical; it *introduces* to the possible. . . . [I]t makes it come, it makes it revolve according to an anachronistic temporality or incredible filiality—a filiality which is also, he avows, the *origin of faith*" (my italics).[77]

But why, we may ask, should Derrida introduce the question of faith at this juncture? Because, he explains, such incredible filiality both "exceeds knowledge and conditions the address to the other, inscribing every theorem in the time and space of a testimony ('I talk to you, believe me')."[78] But, we may further ask, why testimony? Why attestation? Because we can only possess and practice faith in a possibility never adequately or fully *present*, but always already anachronistic (remembered) or still to come (promised). In this sense, Derrida's relating of "virtuality" to "the origin of faith" alludes, one suspects, to a general "spectral" structure of *all* human experience rather than to any *specially religious* experience of a loving God.[79] As such, it may have as much to teach us about the postmodern phenomenon of virtual reality—simulations, simulacra, cyborgs, and so on—as about the revealed reality of Yahweh or Jesus. For Derrida, in sum, the aporia of the impossible-possible may be said to be another name for deconstruction: "the beating pulse of the possible impossible, of the impossible as condition of the possible." From within the very heartbeat of the impossible, writes Derrida, "one could thus hear the pulse or pulsion of deconstruction."[80]

For me, the impossible-made-possible signals the promise of new thinking about the "possible God." Resurrection rather than deconstruction. (Though I would not deny that the former traverses the later and has constant need of its purging powers). There is not opposition here, in my view, but difference. And the difference is one of emphasis as much as of substance. Derrida sees in the play of impossible-possible a structure of "experience in general." (Indeed at one point Derrida admits that his entire reflection on the impossible-possible may be little more than a gloss on his early exegesis of Husserl's phenomenology of the possible as a never-adequate intuition; see his *Introduction à "L'Origine de la géométrie" de Husserl*).[81] By contrast, I would want to claim it marks a specifically *religious* experience of God. And I would want to suggest that this is a difference not only of language games but also of "reference." *Differance* and God, as Derrida is the first to remind us, are *not* the same thing.

While Derrida's reflections on this subject do open up new ways of thinking about faith and eschatology, it does not particularly interest Derrida—a self-confessed atheist—to pursue these issues in a specifically theological or theistic manner. It would appear that Derrida admires and applauds thinkers like Caputo and others who do this, but it is not his thing. Yes, he will go so far as to declare the impossible-possible paradox of pardon/gift/justice/hospitality as a general "messianic" structure of all experience; but he does not, I believe, see it as his business to pronounce on the authentically theistic or atheistic import of any given *messianism*. The closest Derrida's reflection comes to religion is in the guise of a "messianicity without messianism," a form of vigilant openness to the incoming events of *all our experiences*—secular, sacred, or profane; good or evil; loving or violent. Derrida, in short, is more concerned with the everyday (every moment) incoming of events than in the truth or otherwise of some divine advent. The other that leaps toward us from this incoming moment may be a "monster slouching towards Bethlehem to be born" or a lamb who lays down its life for love of mankind. There is no way of knowing.

It is for this reason, I suspect, that Derrida refrains from responding one way or another to any particular God-claim. He speaks of the "spectral" rather than "revealed" structure of such incoming. But what his deconstructive reading of the impossible-possible certainly does help us to perform is a thoroughgoing purge of all "purist" or "dogmatic" notions of possibility as an immanently unfolding power blind to the invention of otherness which makes events happen. And this deconstructive critique of inherited onto-theological notions of both potentiality and presence marks, I think, an invaluable opening to a new eschatological understanding of God as *posse*. Derrida points to such possible paths but he does not choose to walk them. In the heel of the hunt, he prefers ghosts to gods. He prefers, as is his wont and right, to leave matters open. He reserves judgment.

This is where we part company. But I would add that, on this matter, anyone concerned with tolerance—religious or otherwise—would do well to take Derrida very seriously indeed. The indispensable lessons to be learned from deconstruction here are vigilance, patience, and humility.

Conclusion: Toward an Eschatological Notion of the Possible

All of the above "post-metaphysical" readings offer pointers to a properly *eschatological* understanding of the Possible God. But each, I suggest, has its limits.

Husserl discloses the teleological idea of possibility which motivates the development of reason toward a universal goal—but there always remains some ambiguity in Husserl's phenomenology as to whether this telos is transcendent of history or immanent in it.[82] There is always a lingering suspicion that his elusive notion of "God" may slip back into some kind of rationalist or idealist theodicy where the possible is predetermined from the outset.

Bloch, for his part, grounds the possible firmly in the dialectical history of striving toward utopia; but his neutral position on the eschatological status of the *noch-nicht* leaves this "theologian of the revolution" uncommitted at a theological level. One cannot avoid the surmise that the Utopian Possible in question is at times nothing other than the dream-projection of a universalist humanism.

Heidegger's notion of the "loving possible" clearly goes beyond both the transcendental idealism of Husserl and the dialectical humanism of Bloch. It stops short, however, of identifying this "possibilizing power" (*das Vermögen des Mögens*), with a theistic or theological God. Heidegger is more interested in Being than in God; and the curious "saving god" he invokes in his final days is probably more akin to the God of Apollo and the poets than to Yahweh or Jesus.

Finally, Derrida exposes the intriguing enigma of the impossible-possible, and even links this to the "origin of faith"; but the faith in question is a deconstructive belief in the undecidable and unpredictable character of in-coming everyday events (what he calls "experience in general") rather than in some special advent of the divine as such.

Despite their respective reservations on the religious front, however, these approaches proffer crucial critical signposts for a new eschatology of God—what I term the God-who-may-be. What all four thinkers teach us is that the conventional metaphysical concepts of the possible—as *dunamis, potentia*, or *possibilitas*—fail to appreciate its force as something higher rather than lower than the actual. We may read them accordingly as suggesting, even if they do not pursue this suggestion, that since onto-theology defined God as the absolute priority of actuality over possibility, it may now be timely to reverse that priority. The consequences are far reaching and I have attempted to explore them elsewhere in some detail.[83] Suffice it to note here, in summary, the following crucial implications of such a Possible God, understood as the eschatological May-be:

(1) It is radically transcendent—guaranteed by the mark of its "impossible-possibility."

(2) It is "possible" in so far as we have faith in the promise of advent—the scandal of "impossible" incarnation and resurrection!—but also equally reveals itself as what "possibilizes" such messianic events in the first place.

(3) It calls and solicits us—where are you? who are you? who do you say that I am? why did you not give me to drink or eat?—in the form of an engaging personal summons (unlike Husserl's Telos, Bloch's Utopia, Heidegger's *Vermögen*, or Derrida's Perhaps);

(4) And, finally, the eschatological May-be unfolds not just as can-be (*Kann-sein*) but as should-be (*Sollen-sein*)—in short, less as a power of immanent potency driving toward fulfillment than as a power of the powerless which bids us remain open to the possible divinity whose gratuitous coming—already, now, and not yet—is always a surprise and never without grace.

Poetics of the
Possible God

How do we describe the infinite May-be? What metaphors or figures, what images or intimations from our religious or philosophical heritages, might we deploy to speak of this unspeakable enigma?

Taking some pointers from the above sketches of an eschatology of the possible, I explore here in conclusion (a) a hermeneutic retrieval of certain key, if all too often neglected, readings of possibility to be found in the Western heritage of thought (e.g., Aristotle, Cusanus, Schelling); and (b) a reinterpretation of these in light of the paradigm of God-play. My aim here, as throughout this volume, is to break open new sites and sightings of the God-who-may-be.

Hermeneutic Retrievals

(1) The Aristotelian reading of *dunamis* which has informed most philosophical and onto-theological concepts of the possible has, as noted, been considered as a subjugation of potentiality to actuality. Now while this is certainly true in the case of material *dunamis* being subordinated to formal act (*morphe, energeia, entelecheia*), it is not necessarily the only reading of *duna-*

mis available in Aristotle. Might it not be possible, for instance, to re-read the Aristotelian doctrine of the *nous poetikos* (*De Anima* 3.5) in the light of an eschatological perspective? And might such a perspective not prompt us to reinterpret the "making mind" as a divine power which empowers, in the sense of enabling and transfiguring, the latent capacities within the human mind? If the human intellect is indeed, as Aristotle holds, a material "capacity to become all things," then might we not reconstrue the *nous poetikos* as a making God who "brings all things about . . . in just the way that a state, like light, does."[1] We could thus invoke later theistic commentaries of the *nous poetikos* by the likes of Avicenna or Suarez to the effect that this "light" is a metaphor for the transcendent separate power of the divine creator without which all human thought or meaning would remain impossible, that is, in the dark. When Aristotle tells us accordingly that the light of the "eternal and immortal" *nous poetikos* makes the latent color quality of things visible, is this not at least conceivably analogous to the transfiguring power of the Creator, as outlined in Genesis, Exodus, the *Sefer Yetzirah*, or the eschatological writings of Paul and the early patristic commentators? Going beyond a narrow metaphysical dualism of potency versus act, we might then be in a position to say that for the eschatological God possibilizing is actualizing and actualizing is possibilizing— indeed that that is precisely what divine transfiguring means. Or, again, to put it in terms of Mark 10, what remains impossible for our passive mind is made possible by the divine "maker mind." This puts quite a different spin on the concluding claim of *De Anima* 3.5 that the material human intellect "thinks nothing without the other" (*nous poetikos*). Both need each other. Creatures need a Creator and a Creator needs creatures.

Certain Christian and Arab commentators, in particular Averroës, went so far as to suggest that the human mind can, through ongoing contemplation of truth, enter a sort of intimate mystical communion with the divine *nous poetikos*. So doing, we may eventually approximate to a condition of beatific and blissful transfiguration, becoming more and more like the divine Maker in whose image we are made. So fearful was Thomas Aquinas of the powerful influence such teaching was having on the Christian West that he made a point of vehemently denouncing Averroës as a "depraver of philosophy" (*philosophiae depravator*).[2]

In a commentary entitled "What Does the Maker Mind Make?," L. A. Kosman poses this intriguing question: "does the maker mind make the potentially thinkable actually thinkable or does it make the already actually thinkable actually thought"?[3] In other words, does *nous poetikos* possibilize thought by making us really capable of thought or does it do the thinking for us by determining our actual thoughts as well? My eschatological reading is more inclined to the former reading in that it sees the divine Creator as transfiguring our being into a can-be—a being capable of creating and recreating new meanings in our world—without determining the actual content of our creating or doing the actual creating for us. This seems to be what Alexander

Aphrodisieus was hinting at when he spoke of the divine mind producing in us the "power to think" (*hexis noetike*). A position which would appear to suggest that Aristotle's famous light metaphor in *De Anima* 3.5 might be taken to mean that the illuminating-enabling power of the *nous poetikos* "makes what it shines upon actually visible, and thus potentially seen."[4] In short, the divine *nous* transfigures our capacity *for* seeing into a capacity *of* seeing; it makes us *able-to-think* at the same time as it makes the world *think-able*.[5] Might this not also be what Averroës himself had in mind when he saw the realizing of the creative-productive power of the *nous poetikos* as a goal rather than a cause, an aim rather than an acquisition, an end to be achieved rather than something given from the beginning?

(2) Nicholas of Cusa goes further than any of his predecessors in the monotheistic tradition by explicitly equating the divine with the "possibility-to-be" (*posse esse*, or as he coins the compound term, *possest*). In a three-way exchange between a cardinal and his two friends, John and Bernard, entitled *Trialogus de Possest*, Cusanus goes so far as to claim that *possest* is the most appropriate "approximate" name we can find for God according to our human concept of him. It is at once "no name," the "name of each distinct name," and the very "name of names" revealed by God in Exodus 3:14.[6] But the fact that *possest* is both the name of names and no name means, in turn, that it surpasses the limits of all human understanding. "The name ('*possest*')," writes Cusanus, "leads the one who is speculating beyond all the senses, all reason, and all intellect unto a mystical vision, where there is an end to all cognitive powers and . . . the beginning of the revelation of the unknown God."[7]

So how does Cusanus arrive at the conclusion that *posse est* or *possest* is the best name we can have for God? *Possest* means that possibility itself exists. And since the fact that what exists exists actually, the "possibility-to-be exists insofar as the possibility-to-be is actual." Hence all things are enfolded in this "actualized-possibility" (*possest*) which is none other than the proximate (if never adequate) term for God himself. But if the divine *possest* is indeed beyond the limits of human reason, it nonetheless lets itself be witnessed indirectly, through a glass darkly, in a poetics of creation where the Son is the perfect "Image" of God, "as art in a master or light in the sun."[8]

In the opening pages of the *Trialogus* Cusanus argues that absolute possibility is neither prior nor posterior to actuality, but co-exists with actuality in what he calls a co-eternal union. Absolute possibility and actuality are so eternally identical that "they are Eternity itself."[9] It is only in God, however, who is the Beginning of the world, that the two co-exist in this way. Rejecting the conventional metaphysical view that the possible is secondary or derivative vis-à-vis the actual, Cusanus claims accordingly that God himself combines the two in a miraculous identity. For God is everything which he is able-to-be (*posse esse*). "God exists before actuality that is distinct from possibility and before possibility that is distinct from actuality. But all things that exist after

Him exist with their possibility and their actuality distinct. And hence God alone is what (He) is able to be (*solus deus id sit quod esse potest*); but no creature whatsoever (is what it is able to be), since possibility and actuality are identical only in the Beginning."[10] Everything that exists already exists, Cusanus insists, from the Beginning *enfolded* in God (*complicite in deo*). And the whole process of creation in time and history must be seen consequently as a universe *unfolded* into the created world (*explicite in creatura mundi*).[11] Unlike us creatures, therefore, the divine Creator is everything that he is able to be (*est omne id quod esse potest*).

Responding to the question of one of the interlocutors (John) as to how all things can be enfolded in the *possest*, understood as "Actualized-Possibility," another (Bernard) replies that it is so because *posse* in this unqualified sense means *every* possibility. If we are to understand that every possibility is actual, we would have to conclude that "nothing more would be left over."[12]

However, does such reasoning inevitably imply some form of theodicy? Is not everything that happens in the world—good or evil—not precontained and predetermined in the mind of God from the beginning of time? Cusanus seems to confirm as much in the following passage: "if the possibility-to-be does exist, then all things are-what-they-are in it, and nothing (remains) outside it. Therefore, necessarily, all created things have existed in it from eternity. For what-was-created always existed in the possibility-to-be, in whose absence nothing was created. Clearly, Actualized-Possibility (*possest*) is all things and includes all things; for nothing which is not included in it either exists or is able to be made. Therefore, in it all things exist and have their movement and are what they are (regardless of what they are) (*id sunt quod sunt quicquid sunt*)."[13] This last qualifier (*quicquid sunt*) is particularly worrying. For it suggests, does it not, that anything and everything that occurs in the created world—including war, pestilence, famine, disease, torture—is all part of the eternal Godhead. Moreover, since there is nothing other than God, anything that appears to be different or distinct from him—such as non-being or otherness—is in fact really already contained within him. Even evil itself, it seems, is intrinsic to God. Outlining the famous mystical principle of *coincidentia oppositorum*, beyond the limit of all human understanding, Cusanus declares finally that God is above all opposition. "For in Him there cannot be otherness, since He is prior to not-being. For if He were posterior to non-being, He would not be the Creator but would be a creature, brought forth from not-being. Therefore in Him not-being is everything which is possible to be (*omne quod esse potest*). And so, He creates not from any other, but from Himself; for he is everything which is possible to be . . . in Him all things and nothing are Himself."[14]

In response to this ostensible lapse into mystical pantheism, I would invoke the Augustinian argument that evil is a *lack* or *absence* of God—a *privatio boni* which removes misery and mayhem from the eternal design of divine volition. Cusanus ends up embracing a version, however sophisticated, of theodicy not altogether different from that later espoused by Hegel or Leibniz. The question, so central in this volume, of human freedom and creativity as a way of participating in the transfiguring play of creation is thus foreclosed. By allowing *posse* to ultimately collapse back into an ontological system of necessity, Cusanus recoils from the original daring of his *possest* hypothesis and conforms once again to the scholastic concept of God as *necessitas*—a being that cannot but exist as it exists qua uncaused self-existence.[15] The notion of the God-who-may-be I am endeavoring to adumbrate is an effort to re-inject an eschatological radicality into the idea of a possibilizing God. Hermeneutically retrieving Cusanus's idea of God as absolute possibility (*absoluta potentia*),[16] I hold firm to the view that such *potentia* cannot be reduced to a totalizing necessity where every possible is ineluctably actualized from the beginning of time—history being reduced, by extension, to a slow-release "unfolding" of some pre-established plan. On the contrary, from an eschatological perspective, divinity is reconceived as that *posse* or *possest* which calls and invites us to actualize its proffered possibles by our poetical and ethical actions, contributing to the transfiguration of the world to the extent that we respond to this invitation, but refusing this transfiguring task every time we do evil or injustice or commit ourselves to non-being. In short, while Nicholas of Cusa's initial bold challenge to the traditional priority of actuality over possibility is a welcome contribution to the rethinking of God as *posse*, it does not go far enough.

(3) As a third brief example of hermeneutic retrieval, we might consider Schelling's comments on Exodus 3:15, in his *Philosophy of Mythology*, as the capacity to-be (*Seyn wird*). Rendering the famously elusive "name" of God as "I will be what I will be,"[17] Schelling argues that God is here revealing himself not as being *in strictu sensu* but as the general possibility of being. Or as he puts it in the language of more traditional metaphysics, the "essence" of God is disclosing itself as the capacity to-be or to-become his "existence." In this sense, God is defined as the "can-be" (*Seyn-könnende*). In the final analysis, Schelling deems this potentiality of essence inferior to the free actualized existence of God insofar as the latter overcomes the ground or nature of God (which Schelling equates with his "dark side"). Thus while Schelling interprets the ground of God as an "immediate can-be" (*unmittelbar Seyn-könnende*), identifying it with Spirit conceived as the "can-be of the divine ground as the beginning of its being," he subordinates this to Christ as a mediating cosmic potency (*kosmische Potenz*); and more importantly still, he subordinates the "can-be" of Spirit to the Father as Being itself (*Seyn*) qua ultimate source (*fons et principium divinitatis*).[18]

What my hermeneutic revision of Schelling's trinitarian paradigm might offer is a re-reading of the paternal primacy of being to allow for an eschatological revisioning of the Father from the perspective of the eschatological Son and Spirit. Thus rather than associating the possibilizing Spirit and Son with the dark ground or essence to be ultimately overcome in order that divine existence and freedom be achieved, we could see them rather as figures of the eschatological Kingdom which promises to fulfill the pledge of the Father in Exodus 3:14 (I shall be with you) and in Mathew 10 (Everything is possible to God). The Father might thus be re-envisaged as the loving-possible which transfigures the Son and Spirit and is transfigured by them in turn. That, admittedly, is a long way from the standard German idealist reading, from Hegel to Heidegger, but it is, I suggest, one more attentive to the hidden eschatological potencies latent within Schelling's own texts if all too distorted by their onto-theological and Gnostic baggage.

Godplay

But there is another path which a deconstructive-eschatological reading might explore. If we follow Heidegger's suggestion in *An Introduction to Metaphysics* that we rethink the relation between Being and God in terms of proportional analogy, we might apply this in turn to the construal of the "power of the possible" in terms of *play*: the play of Being and the play of God.[19] In a number of later texts, Heidegger describes the interrelationship between mortals and gods within the fourfold of Being as a mirror-game (*Spiegel-Spiel*). Citing a pair of peasant shoes painted by Van Gogh or a meal of bread and wine epiphanized in Trakl's poem "A Winter Evening," Heidegger seeks to demonstrate how even the most simple things may participate in the ontological "play of the world" once transfigured by the poet or artist. Through art the "thing things" and the "world worlds"—a ludic tautology which discloses the "loving power" (*das mögende des Vermögen*) of Being itself. Thinkers and poets, says Heidegger, bear witness to such disclosure.[20] But we might also take some additional direction from Derrida's own intriguing allusions to ontological and theological play—and in particular his commentary on Angelus Silesius's statement:

> God plays with creation.
> All that is play that the deity gives itself:
> It has imagined the creature for its pleasure.[21]

Our concluding question is therefore: how might such an ontological model of play relate, analogously, to the eschatology of the possible? As always with analogy there are differences as well as proximities. The first difference is that whereas ontological play refers to the "power" of the Same returning to itself, eschatological play refers to the powerlessness of the other, summoning us beyond the Same. Unlike a destiny of Being unfolding itself with ineluctable *Vermögen*, the eschatological possible invites us to freely realize its promises and prophesies. Here we find various metaphors of the possible God as a *deus ludens* who creates and dances before its own creation. In Proverbs 8:30, we read that divine Wisdom "plays" before the face of the Creator: "I was his joy all those days, playing always before him." This creative play of *sophia* is the pre-figuration of the world's genesis which itself serves as prelude (*praeludium*) to the eschatological kingdom still to come.[22]

Each human being is a *homo ludens* transfiguring the world to the extent that God is a *deus ludens* who possibilizes the world in the first place. Biblically interpreted, the possibilizing play of the world is a "may-be" dependent upon humans for its coming to be, a fragile promise symbolized in Judeo-Christian-Islamic mysticism by the naked playful child. Think here of Meister Eckhart's *nackter Knabe* or the "little child" in Proverbs which "enchants the sons of man" as it creates the cosmos (8:28–31). David rehearses this motif when he declares that he will "dance and play" before his Creator. For as 2 Samuel tells us, "David and the house of Israel danced before the Lord with all their heart" (2 Samuel 6:5, 21). And pursuing this motif, Saint Jerome describes the messianic age prophesied in Zachariah 8:5 as "a play between young men and women" where the "joy of the Spirit will manifest itself in the harmonious gestures of its children who dance together, repeating David's boast that he will dance and play before the face of the Lord."[23]

This eschatological vision of a kingdom of play is reiterated by many of the early church fathers and later mystics. Origen interprets the image of Wisdom playing before the Creator as a *praefiguratio* of the divine-human interplay of the New Creation (*De Principiis* I, 4,4). Gregory of Nyssa describes the eschatological God as one who "always plays as he turns the world to and fro" (*Carmina* 1, 2,2). While Clement of Alexandria elaborates on this idea when he affirms that those who bear witness to the messiah "participate in the mystical play of children (*mustike paidia*)" (*Paedagogus* I, 5, 22,1). And, finally, Maximus the Confessor goes further still when he explains that the game of Genesis reveals each human person as a *homo ludens* formed in the image of the divine player himself. "Truly," he writes, "we should consider our life as a game played by children before God"; adding that this game is nothing other than the Incarnation itself which surpasses all the limits of nature (*Ambigua* 261–262a). This leads on to the idea, so dear to many mystics, that the Word becoming flesh in the history of creation constitutes a "Trinitarian play" in which the "spirit plays freely before the Father so that he becomes fecund and creative" through the coming into being of his Son.[24]

This recurring motif of Creation as "child play" epitomizes, I believe, the eschatological *posse* as both promise and powerlessness, fecundity and fragility. For the God of the possible is like child play to the extent that it opens up a realm of free possibles but is unable to actualize those possibles without the help of other human beings. Etty Hillesum offers one of the most vivid testimonies to the childlike helplessness of God in her extraordinary book *An Interrupted Life*: "If God does not help me to go on, then I shall have to help God. . . . I shall merely try to help God as best I can, and if I succeed in doing that, then I shall be of use to others as well."[25] Or as she puts it, addressing God directly about his inability to intervene to save the Jews from the Holocaust: "You cannot help us, but we must help You and defend Your dwelling place inside us to the last."[26]

By choosing to be a player rather than an emperor of creation, God chooses powerlessness. This choice expresses itself as self-emptying, *kenosis*, letting go. God thus empowers our human powerlessness by giving away his power, by possibilizing us and our good actions—so that we may supplement and co-accomplish creation.[27] To be made in God's image is therefore, paradoxically, to be powerless; but with the possibility of receiving power from God to overcome our powerlessness, by responding to the call of creation with the words, "I am able." To God's "I may be" each one of us is invited to reply "I can." Just as to each "I can," God replies "I may be." In this eschatological play of power and powerlessness, the human self becomes the capable self. *L'homme faillible*, to use Ricoeur's terms, becomes *l'homme capable*. Or to borrow another startling thought from the Holocaust witness, Etty Hillesum, it is when stripped of all external illusions and supports that we find the strength of God within. Faced with the certainty of imminent dispatch to Westerbork concentration camp, and the collapse of European civilization all around her, Hillesum could still write: "I have been feeling strong . . . so free of fears and anxieties. . . . Perhaps I shall walk right across Russia one day, who knows? . . . [W]e are lost permanently and for all time unless we provide an alternative, a dazzling and dynamic alternative with which to start afresh somewhere."[28]

It is then the dis-possessed self, emptied of ego and naked as a child, that becomes a "lodging" for the "in-dwelling" of God. Or to put it another way, it is in the renunciation of my will-to-power, and even in my refusal to rest satisfied with my ownmost totality as a being-toward-death, that I open myself to the infinite empowering-possibilizing of God. Abandoning ego, I allow the infinite to beget itself in my persona. This was the essence of Hillesum's extraordinary testimony. And an echo of Eckhart's teaching that the "pure of heart knows no bounds to its capabilities."[29]

The metaphor of eschatological play also reveals the dispossessive nature of the kingdom. The kingdom is precisely that which can never be fully possessed in the here and now, but always directs us toward an advent still to come—an alternative site from which to rebegin afresh." Indeed we can only ever find the kingdom by losing it, by renouncing the illusion that we possess it here and now. If we think we have the kingdom, it can only be in the mode of the "as if," as imaginary, a play of images. At best, such images may serve as icons of something beyond our grasp, ciphers of a transcendence which eye has not (literally) seen nor ear (literally) heard. But images nonetheless which promise a better world, carrying the ethical imperative that things must change. This is the role of art and more especially of religious art. At worst, such kingdom-images degenerate into idols which harbor the illusion of immediate possession, of total and totalizing power (Hitler's Third Reich, Stalin's New Soviet Man). The ancient prophets called this idolatry. Today it goes by the more colloquial names of fetishism and ideology—false fantasies peddled by consumer and propaganda industries. The danger of play, in short, is when the players *forget* they are players: when they deny they are dealing with images and mistake the figural for the literal, the possible for the actual. The virtue of play, by contrast, is when we do not take ourselves, or our world, or our God *literally*. When we learn the humility and humor of participating in a game without emperors. Like a child playing in sand by the edge of the sea. Not idle play. Sacred play upon which the future of our world reposes.

The ludic possible comports, for humans as for God, a double movement of engagement and detachment. It reminds us that we are in the world but not wholly of the world. Committed to action yet never a mere thing in the midst of things. Preoccupied for our neighbor's good but never submerged in mindless busyness. Or as Rahner puts it in *Man at Play*: "The internal gaiety of the person who plays, and for whom honesty and humor are sisters, is ultimately a religious matter, for this quality can only be attained by those who participate in heaven *and* in earth."[30] The mystical metaphorics of play teaches us to become *ioculatores domini*—players in the world who are at once iconoclasts and lovers of the earth. Disciples of a gaiety that transfigures dread.

Perichoresis

It is telling in this regard that one of the most powerful figures of the Trinity in the Oriental Church is that of a sacred dance-play between three persons. As remarked in chapter 1 above, this God-play was known as *perichoresis* in Greek and as *circumincessio* in Latin. Meaning literally "dance (*choros*) around (*peri*)," it referred to a circular movement where Father, Son, and Spirit gave place to each other in a gesture of reciprocal dispossession rather than fusing into a single substance. The Latin spells this out intriguingly by punning on the dual phonetic connotations of *circum-in-sessio* (from *sedo*, to sit or assume a position) and *circum-in-cession* (from *cedo*, to cede, give way or dis-position). So what emerges is an image of the three distinct persons moving *toward* each other in a gesture of immanence and *away from* each other in a gesture of transcendence. At once belonging and distance. Moving in and out of position. An interplay of loving and letting go.

This Trinitarian play includes humanity, of course, to the extent that the second person becomes incarnate and enters history. "God sent his own son, born of woman, so that we could be adopted as his sons" (Galatians 4:4). Here the Son becomes the famous "Lord of the Dance" inviting all believers in the kingdom to join in the "great dance of creation and rebirth," as Lucian put it (*De Saltatione* 7). To accept this invitation is to join the dance-play of the possible that began in Genesis, before we ever came to be, and that continues on beyond our death until the kingdom comes. We thus find ourselves players in an eschatological game of which we are neither the initiators nor the culminators, a game which we cannot master since its possibles are always beyond our possibles, refiguring the play of genesis, prefiguring the play of eschaton, a game that knows no end-game, no stalemate, whose ultimate move is always still to come. But if we cannot master the divine play of the possible, we can partake of it as a gift given to us, a grace that heals and enables, a love that comes to us from the future summoning us toward the other beyond ourselves. This is surely what Gregory of Nyssa had in mind when he spoke of our eschatological vocation to transfigure the world into a new creation by form- ing a "dancing choir which looks forever forward to the Lord who leads the dance."[31] In this sense we might describe the new creation as a pro-creation, for it is not something we invent out of ourselves, a possible projected by our subjective dreams and imaginings alone; no, it is a creation *for* the other, *on behalf of* the other. If God has created the world for us, we recreate the world for God. We carry each other within; we give birth to each other. And when we do, we cannot tell the dancer from the dance.

This play of mutual rebirth promises more, it seems, than the *Spiegel-Spiel* of the Destiny of Being which happens when it happens, come what may and irrespective of our actions. If the play of eschatological possibility may indeed "save us," it is only to the extent that we choose to respond to it by acting to bring the coming Kingdom closer, making it more possible, as it were, by each of our actions, while acknowledging that its ultimate realization is impossible to us alone. That's what we mean when we say "God may be." The Kingdom is possible but we may decide not to accept the invitation. The Gospel of Matthew acknowledges this freedom to respond or refuse when it says, "we sang for you but you did not dance" (Matthew 11:17). We don't *have* to dance. And the eschatological dance cannot be danced without two part- ners. To respond to the song of the Creator is to hear the Word which promises a possible world to come, a second creation or recreation of justice and peace, a world which the divine *posse* is always ready to offer but which can come about only when humanity says yes by joining the dance, entering the play of ongoing genesis, transfiguring the earth. God cannot become fully God, nor the Word fully flesh, until creation becomes a "new heaven and a new earth."[32]

Epilogue

So how, if at all, does the play of God relate to the play of Being? Are we condemned to yet another dualism? We do not believe so. Some kind of nuptial chiasm is possible between them. For if the God of the possible is indeed *possest*, this is not a matter of opposing *posse* to *esse* in some binary division. On the contrary, the *possest* contains the possibility (though not the necessity, as Cusanus held) of *esse* within itself. Unlike the old metaphysical *esse*, conceived as "presence," or in Cusanus's case as the necessary unfolding of a pre-existing identity, the eschatological *possest* I have been endeavoring to sketch out in this volume promises something radically new and adventurous. For *possest* may now be seen as advent rather than arche, as eschaton rather than *principium*. The realization of *possest*'s divine *esse*, if and when it occurs, if and when the kingdom comes, will no doubt be a new *esse*, refigured and transfigured in a mirror-play where it recognizes its other and not just the image of itself returning to itself. In this way, *posse* may bring being beyond being into new being, other-being. It promises a new heaven and a new earth.

Is such a thing possible? Not for us alone. But it is not impossible to God—if we help God to become God. How? By opening ourselves to the "loving possible," by acting each moment to make the impossible that bit more possible.

NOTES

INTRODUCTION

1. Etty Hillesum, *An Interrupted Life* (New York: Owl Books, 1996), p. 176. On this question of God's "powerless power," see also Hans Jonas, "The Concept of God after Auschwitz: A Jewish Voice," in *Mortality and Morality: A Search for the Good after Auschwitz*, ed. Lawrence Vogel (Evanston, Ill.: Northwestern University Press, 1996), pp. 138–142.

2. See my 1982 exchange with Derrida, "Deconstruction and the Other," in Richard Kearney, *Dialogues with Contemporary Continental Thinkers* (Manchester: Manchester University Press, 1984), pp. 105–125; reprinted in Richard Kearney, *States of Mind: Dialogues with Contemporary Thinkers* (New York: New York University Press, 1995), pp. 156–176.

3. See the published proceedings of the first two Villanova conferences: *God, the Gift, and Postmodernism*, edited by John D. Caputo and Michael J. Scanlon (Bloomington: Indiana University Press, 1999); and *Questioning God*, edited by John D. Caputo and Michael J. Scanlon (Bloomington: Indiana University Press, 2001).

4. Richard Kearney, *Poétique du possible: Phénoménologie herméneutique de la figuration* (Paris: Beauchesne, 1984), and Richard Kearney and Joseph S. O'Leary, eds., *Heidegger et la question de Dieu* (Paris: Grasset, 1981).

5. John Caputo in correspondence with the author; see also John D. Caputo on the relationship of the possible and the impossible in *The Prayers and Tears of Jacques Derrida* (Bloomington: Indiana University Press, 1997), especially pp. 20–26, and (with Michael Scanlon) "Apology for the Impossible: Religion and Postmodernism," in *God, the Gift, and Postmodernism*, pp. 1–20. See also "The Becoming Possible of the Impossible: An Interview with Jacques Derrida by Mark Dooley," in *From Aquinas to Derrida: John D. Caputo in Focus* (forthcoming, 2002). In this exchange, Derrida makes the characteristic deconstructive claim that God is a "useless but indispensable name."

6. Hans Jonas, "The Concept of God after Auschwitz," p. 134. Jonas's notion of divine possibility is, however, much more indebted to metaphysical and dialectical notions of being and causality than my own.

7. Nicholas of Cusa, *Trialogus de Possest*, translated into English as *On Actualized-Possibility* by Jasper Hopkins, in *A Concise Introduction to the Philosophy of Nicholas of Cusa* (Minneapolis: University of Minnesota Press, 1980), pp. 62–153. I am indebted to Dermot Moran for bringing this text to my attention.

8. Charles Taylor, *A Catholic Modernity?* (Dayton, Ohio: University of Dayton Press, 1996), pp. 17–18.

9. William Desmond, *Being and the Between* (Albany: SUNY Press, 1995).

10. See, for example, Emmanuel Levinas, *Totality and Infinity*, trans. Alphonso Lingis (Pittsburgh: Duquesne University Press, 1969); Jacques Derrida, "How to Avoid Speaking: Denials," trans. Ken Frieden, in *Derrida and Negative Theology*, ed. Harold Coward and Toby Foshay (Albany: SUNY Press, 1992), pp. 73–142; and Jean-Luc Marion, *L'Idôle et la distance* (Paris: Grasset, 1977).

11. Paul Ricoeur, "The Nuptial Metaphor," in Paul Ricoeur and André LaCocque, *Thinking Biblically: Exegetical and Hermeneutic Studies*, trans. David Pellauer (Chicago: University of Chicago Press, 1998), p. 297.

12. Ibid., pp. 302–303.

13. Ibid. For an illuminating commentary on Ricoeur's radical use of a hermeneutics of narrative and metaphor to interpret religious texts, see Jean Greisch, "Penser la Bible: L'Herméneutique philosophique à l'école de l'exégèse biblique," *Revue biblique*, no. I (January 2000): 81–103. See also my analysis of the crucial role played by narrative in attempting to say the unsayable in my related companion volumes *On Stories* and *Strangers, Gods, and Monsters*.

14. See, for example, the Pseudo-Dionysius, who claimed that God was so hyperessential as to be utterly transcendent of being and so "unknowable" as to be totally beyond the "reach of mind" ("The Divine Names," VII, III, 869, in *Pseudo-Dionysius: The Complete Works*, trans. Colm Luibheid [London: SPCK, 1987]). See also Clement of Alexander, who argued that God is that first principle of things who resides "above both time and space and name and conception" (*The Writings of Clement of Alexandria*, trans. William Wilson [Edinburgh: T. & T. Clark, 1867], ii, 264). God is "above all speech and thought," Clement concludes, and "can never be committed to writing" (ibid., ii, 260).

1. TOWARD A PHENOMENOLOGY OF THE *PERSONA*

1. I first attempted a sketch of such a project in chapter 8 of *Poétique du possible*. Entitled "La Transfiguration de la personne," this chapter was deeply influenced by both Emmanuel Levinas's notion of the "trace" developed in *Totality and Infinity* (1969) and Jacques Derrida's notion of "alterity" outlined in *Writing and Difference* (1967) and *Of Grammatology* (1967).

2. Julia Kristeva, *Strangers to Ourselves*, trans. Leon S. Roudiez (London: Harvester Press, 1991).

3. Jean-Luc Marion, *L'Idole et la distance* (Paris: Grasset, 1977).

4. See Paul Ricoeur's *Lectures on Ideology and Utopia*, ed. George H. Taylor (New York: Columbia University Press, 1986).

5. Emmanuel Levinas, *Le Temps et l'autre* (Paris: Arthaud, 1984), p. 64.

6. Ibid., p. 185.

7. Kearney, *Poétique du possible*, p. 161.

8. See here Paul Ricoeur's notion of the irreducible "surplus" in each person—what I call their *persona*—which he takes to be their irreplaceable singularity or quasidivine *thisness* or *whoness*. "J'appelle quelque fois l'incognito du pardon la considération, le respect de ce qu'il y a d'insubstituable dans chaque personne. Les personnes peuvent être socialement relativement substituables, pourtant il y a en elles le fond d'une sorte de fraternité . . . dont la source est la singularité de chaque *imago dei*" ("Paul Ricoeur: Un parcours philosophique," Interview with François Ewald, *Magazine lit-*

téraire, no. 390 [2000]: p. 26). See also Jacques Derrida's intriguing analysis of the Messianic (which he contrasts to messianism) in, for example, *Specters of Marx*, trans. Peggy Kamuf (New York: Routledge, 1994).

9. See Edmund Husserl's Fifth Meditation, in *Cartesian Meditations*, trans. Dorion Cairns (The Hague: Nijhoff, 1960).

10. Maurice Merleau-Ponty, *The Phenomenology of Perception*, trans. Colin Smith (London: Routledge, 1962).

11. For a lucid account of Jacques Lacan's difficult theories of the object "petit a" and "le sujet supposé savoir," see John P. Muller and William J. Richardson, *Lacan and Language* (New York: International Universities Press, 1982), and Richard Boothby, *Death and Desire: Psychoanalytic Theory in Lacan's Return to Freud* (New York: Routledge, 1991).

12. See William J. Richardson on the vexed question of the "ethics of psychoanalysis" in a number of studies, notably "In the Name of the Father: The Law," in *Questioning Ethics*, ed. Richard Kearney and Mark Dooley (London: Routledge, 1998), pp. 201–220.

13. Julia Kristeva, *Tales of Love* (New York: Columbia University Press, 1987), p. 111.

14. Ibid., p. 113.

15. Levinas, *Le Temps et l'autre*, p. 88.

16. Ibid., p. 88.

17. I am indebted to Stanislas Breton for bringing this distinction to my attention. See also John Manoussakis, "From Exodus to Eschaton: On the God Who May Be," in *Modern Theology*, Book Symposium on Richard Kearney's "God Who May Be," October 2001; and also "I-M-Possible: Contrapunctus et Augmentationem" (in *Traversing the Imaginary*, ed. John Manoussakis and Peter Gratton [Evanston, Ill.: Northwestern University Press, forthcoming]): "John Damascene (c. 749) speaks of the Trinitarian perichoresis using a language loaded with dance metaphors: the three persons 'hold each other' as in a cyclical dance—'the Son with the Father and Spirit, the Spirit with the Father and Son, the Father with the Son and Spirit in one and the same movement, in one jump, in one movement of the three hypostases' (*De Fide Orthodoxa*, 1000b). An earlier source, a fragment by Amphilochios of Iconium (c. 394), affirms and reinforces the point that all we can speak and know about God is not His *whatness* but rather His *howness*, and this is as 'Father, Son and Spirit' which reveals the *way* that God exists but not *what* He is. In another ancient text we read that God exists only by virtue of this loving interplay with the other Persons (the Father begetting the Son and processing the Spirit). That is why His existence is not subject to any causality, but it is finally 'of any necessity free' (see Theodoretos of Cyrene (c. 458), *Expositiones Rectae Confessionis*, ed. J.-P. Migne, vol. 6, 1212a). This figure of *perichoresis/circumincessio* offers interesting possibilities, in turn, for reading the Chalcedonian formula of the divine-human relation as 'without division and without confusion.'"

18. Levinas: "Le prochain m'assigne avant que je ne le désigne—ce qui est une modalité non pas d'un savoir mais d'une obsession (. . .) la conscience ne vient pas s'interposer entre moi et le prochain; ou, du moins, elle ne surgit déjà que sur le fond de cette relation préalable de l'obsession qu'aucune conscience ne saurait annuler—et dont la conscience même est une modification"(*Autrement qu'être; ou, Au-delà de l'essence* [The Hague: Nijhoff, 1974], p. 100).

19. Ibid., p. 112.

20. Franz Rosenzweig, "The Eternal" (1929), in Martin Buber and Franz Rosenzweig, *Scripture and Translation*, trans. Lawrence Rosenwald and Everett Fox (Bloomington: Indiana University Press), p. 108.

21. See Merleau-Ponty's *Phenomenology of Perception* and *The Visible and the Invisible*, ed. Claude Lefort, trans. Alphonso Lingis (Evanston, Ill.: Northwestern University Press, 1968). See also in this regard Robert Magliola, *On Deconstructing Life-Worlds: Buddhism, Christianity, Culture* (Atlanta: Scholars Press, 1997), pp. 127–128. Magliola cites here Derrida's rendition of the Mosaic God of Edmond Jabes: "God himself is, and appears as what he is, within difference, that is to say, as difference and within dissimulation"; and he goes on to quote, in this connection, Derrida's reflections in *The Post Card* on the two-in-one nature of the biblical God—"this double bind is firstly that of YHVH."

22. Levinas: "Autrui m'apparaissant comme étant dans sa plasticité d'image, je suis en relation avec le multipliable qui, malgré l'infinité des reproductions que j'en prends, reste *intact* et je peux, à son égard, me payer des mots à la mesure de ces images sans me livrer à un dire. La proximité n'entre pas dans le temps commun des horloges qui rend possible les rendez-vous. Elle est dérangement"(*Autrement qu'être*, pp. 112–113).

23. I am greatly indebted to my colleague John Manoussakis for bringing the theological debates on the Greek term *prosopon* to my attention and pointing out that the *prosopon* is, in original usage, that aspect of the human face which is always *related* to others—the human person in front of, before, vis-à-vis others. He also informed me how *prosopon* was translated by Latin fathers like Tertullian as *persona*. See also Pascal Quignard's discussion of *prosopon* in ancient Greek aesthetics as that aspect of the human visage which expresses the inner psychic character (*to tes psyches ethos*) or moral feelings and dispositions usually invisible to the human eye. In theater it referred more specifically to the "face-mask" which expresses secret and inexpressible things, marking off each one as a distinct person (I/you/he/she) and making manifest in figural or imagistic-mimetic terms some inner meaning or script. See, for example, the following passage from Xenophon (*Memorables* III, 10, 1, cited by Quignard in *Le Sexe et l'effroi* [Paris: Gallimard, 1994], pp. 52–53): "Le grand air et l'apparence noble, l'humilité et l'apparence servile, la modération et la juste mesure, l'excès ainsi que ce qui n'a aucune idée de la beauté, c'est grâce au visage (*prosopou*) et c'est au travers des attitudes dont les hommes usent dans leur façon de se tenir et de se mouvoir que cela transparaît." Quignard goes on to offer this illuminating gloss: "Comment représenter l'invisible dans le visible? Comment saisir l'expression à l'instant crucial du mythe (comment montrer *l'éthos* du *muthos* arrêté sur image)? . . . Le mot de *prosopon* veut dire en grec à la fois le visage vu de face et le masque de théâtre (il veut dire encore les personnes grammaticales; 'je,' 'tu,' sont des *prosopa* grecs . . . des *personae* latines: des 'visages-masques' pour les hommes qui parlent). Dans la *Poétique*, Aristote dit: 'Le regard devant la conséquence de l'acte, tel est le meilleur *éthos*.' . . . En d'autres termes, derrière une peinture ancienne, il y a toujours un livre—ou du moins un récit condensé en instant éthique" (pp. 53–54). He concludes his analysis of Greek aesthetics accordingly: "La grand peintre était celui qui rendait sensible à l'intérieur du personnage figuré la lutte entre le caractère et l'émotion. . . . La peinture ancienne est un récit de poète condensé en image. . . . Les images-actions font que les hommes entrent dans la mémoire des hommes en se condensant en *éthos* (en devenant Dieu). . . . La question de la peinture est: comment apparaître comme un dieu apparaissant dans son instant éternel" (pp. 60–61).

24. See Manoussakis, "I-M-Possible." Manoussakis spells out the implications of the term as follows: "To be a *pros-opon* means to be on your way towards the other being. This also situates the being into a perpetual ek-sistence, a stepping-out-of-yourself and a being-towards-the-other. Being-towards-the-other means also to present yourself, to make yourself present in the other's presence (*-opos*). Prosopon strongly implies reciprocity of gaze through which the self is interpellated by the other, and ultimately, 'othered.' The antonym of a prosopon is again described in the Greek language by the term *atomon*. Prosopon and atomon are the only two existential possibilities open to a human being. However, to be an atomon means to be in fragmentation (*a*- and *temno*, to cut; therefore, the a-tomic is that which cannot be cut any further). As in the English language, the in-dividual is he who has been 'divided' so many times that he has reached this point where no further split is possible. The individual stands in sharp opposition to the prosopon. Where the latter gathers and unites, there the former cuts off, separates, alienates. Where, then, does the individual belong? One would say to Hades. Hades, for the Greeks is the place of non-being, the underworld, the place where there is no *seeing*. *A-ides* means the place where there is neither gaze nor face, where the possibility to see the other, face to face, has disappeared and along with it the dynamics of being a prosopon and of being as such. Hades is surrounded by the river *Lethe*—truth or *a-letheia*, therefore, has no place there; this is the reign of existential death."

25. See Procopius of Gaza, *Commentary on Genesis*, Patrologiæ Cursus Completus: Series Græca, ed. J.-P. Migne, vol. 87 (Paris: 1851), p. 361a. See also Jean-Luc Marion, *L'Idole et la distance*, pp. 255–293; "L'Idole et l'icône," *Revue de métaphysique et de morale*, no. 4 (1979): 433–445; and *Etant donné: Essai d'une phénoménologie de la donation* (Paris: Presses Universitaires de France, 1997), pp. 323ff., where Marion speaks of the icon as "irrégardable"—since the icon-face for Marion is the saturated phenomenon which looks at us rather than being looked at by us. However, Marion's attempt to advance a phenomenology of pure donation fails to sufficiently acknowledge the need for a supplementary hermeneutic grafting which would allow for interpretation as well as description, intuition, and worship. Saturation, I would argue, also "gives rise to thought," to borrow Ricoeur's expression. See here Jean Greisch's insightful critique of Marion in *Le Cogito herméneutique* (Paris: Vrin, 2000), pp. 49–50.

2. I AM WHO MAY BE

1. *New Jerusalem Bible* (New York: Doubleday, 1990).

2. Most of the Western translations and interpretations have been deeply influenced by Greek ontology and particularly the metaphysical emphasis on presence and identity. This is surely one of the main reasons why the non-Hebrew versions of Exodus 3:15 take the form of the present tense of the verb to be—"I am he who is" (New Jerusalem Bible) or "I am that I am" (King James Bible).

3. Emilie Zumbrunn, "L'exégèse augustinienne de 'Ego sum qui sum' et la 'Métaphysique de l'Exode,'" in *Dieu et l'être*, pp. 246–272.

4. Quoted by Dominique Dubarle in his chapter "La Nomination ontologique de Dieu," in *L'Ontologie de Thomas D'Aquin* (Paris: Éditions du Cerf, 1996), p. 45. Dubarle suggests that this equation of the God of Exodus with the "Is" of Parmenides and Greek ontology prefigures "la locution nominale de saint Thomas disant Dieu *'ipsum esse per se subsistens.'*"

5. Dubarle considers this Augustinian equation of Greek being qua "substantia/essentia" with the biblical God of Exodus 3:14 to be a decisive determination for subsequent Christian theology, influencing not only Aquinas but also the whole scholastic tradition. Commenting on the above text from the *De Trinitate*, he writes: "Le texte fondamental de l'Exode y sert de base à l'édifice entier. Le *sum* de L'Ecriture y est identifié à l'*essentia* pure et simple qui, à son tour, est identifiée à l'immutabilité. Au-dessous de cet *Est* absolu, s'ordonnent hiérarchiquement les autres *essentiae* selon qu'elles sont 'plus ou moins,' mais elles lui doivent toutes ce qu'elles ont d'être. Enfin l'*essentia* latine déclare ouvertement la filiation qui la relie à *l'ousia* grecque. Tout se passe comme si le Dieu chrétien assumait ici l'héritage de l'*auto kat'auto* de Platon. . . . Le Dieu-Etre augustinien est une positivité de plénitude absolue de l'être" (Dubarle, "La Nomination ontologique de Dieu," pp. 48–50). Extending this reading beyond Augustine, Dubarle points out that the same God of Exodus—le "Qui est"—is also for Aquinas and scholasticism "la nomination la plus propre de Dieu lui même" (*Summa Theologiae* 1.13.11). For a more elaborate development of this thesis, see Dubarle, "La Nomination ontologique de Dieu," pp. 51ff., and *Dieu avec l'être: De Parmenide à saint Thomas, essai d'ontologie théologale* (Paris: Beauchesne, 1986), especially pp. 245–253. In this latter text, Dubarle argues that Augustine must not be reduced, as so often in the Christian speculative tradition, to a purely onto-theological God: "On peut aussi penser à une signification bien plus existentielle de Moïse et de son peuple, sans qu'il s'agisse d'un enseignement de Dieu sur lui-même et sur sa propre nature: 'Je serai avec toi, je serai ce que je serai, ferai ce que j'entends faire, et on verra bien ce que je ferai.' De même 'Qui est' dénomme celui qui agit avec Moïse, son envoyé. . . . Dieu ne se fait pas professeur de théologie, ni d'ontologie" (p. 247). For another post-metaphysical reading of Augustine's formative interpretation of Exodus 3:14, see Goulven Madec, *Le Dieu d'Augustin* (Paris: Éditions du Cerf, 1998), pp. 104, 117–118, 127ff., 147ff. (For Madec, Augustine's God of Exodus 3:14 is a biblical-ethical God of the living more than a God of ontology per se.)

6. See Paul Ricoeur, "From Interpretation to Translation," in *Thinking Biblically*, p. 350. Ricoeur's text offers here an illuminating summary of the main metaphysical readings of Exodus 3:14 from Augustine and the Pseudo-Dionysius to Bonaventure and Thomas, pp. 341–355.

7. Ibid., p. 353.

8. Etienne Gilson, *The Spirit of Mediæval Philosophy* (Paris: Vrin, 1941), p. 51. See also Gilson's neo-Thomist reading of Exodus 3:14 in the section entitled "HE WHO IS" in *The Elements of Christian Philosophy* (New York: New American Library, 1960) pp. 135–145.

9. Although the term "onto-theology" originally came from Heidegger's critique of metaphysics, it has been increasingly invoked by contemporary Christian thinkers (Jean-Luc Marion, Joseph O'Leary, Kevin Hart, John Caputo, Jean Greisch, David Tracey) eager to dissociate themselves from the substantialist metaphysics of scholastic philosophy. The danger they denounce is that of conceptual idolatry. For a daring post-Heideggerian reading of the onto-theological interpretations of Exodus 3:14, see Joseph S. O'Leary, *Questioning Back: The Overcoming of Metaphysics in Christian Tradition* (Minneapolis: Winston Press, 1985), pp. 178–191, and *La Vérité chrétienne à l'âge du pluralisme religieux* (Paris: Éditions du Cerf, 1994), pp. 219–227 (Eng. trans., *Religious Pluralism and Christian Truth* [Edinburgh: Edinburgh University Press, 1996], pp. 159–165). O'Leary claims, in his reading of Augustine for instance, that "despite the

ultimate irreducibility of the divine 'Thou' to metaphysics, Augustine's God remains nine-tenths a metaphysical construction" (*Questioning Back*, p.186). O'Leary does not deny, however, the radical deconstructive import of the remaining one-tenth: "To draw out the more primordial biblical sense of God from the prevailing metaphysical discourse about God, great attention to the tone and narrative movement of the text is required . . . [for] even if biblical elements irreducible to metaphysics are marginalized in the text, they can constitute a quintessential instance of the treacherous margin, calling in question the entire metaphysical order which seeks in vain to integrate them" (pp. 186, 182). In the later book, *La Vérité chrétienne*, O'Leary develops his radical thesis thus: "'Dieu' n'est jamais un terme neutre; il signifie un choix; un jugement polémique. . . . Il 'déconstruit' non pas en tant que pur absolu mettant en évidence la faiblesse et la complexité de nos langages, mais en tant qu'il se nomme. Ce n'est pas par son silence, mais quand il parle, que ce Dieu nous déroute. . . . Le nom qui signifiait la réponse ultime à toutes nos questions . . . est devenu le chiffre d'une question insondable" (pp. 220–221).

10. Quoted by Stanislas Breton in "'Je Suis (celui) qui Suis' (Ontologie et Métaphysique)," in *Libres Commentaires* (Paris: Éditions du Cerf, 1990), p. 64.

11. Cited and commented on by Gabriel Marcel in *Coleridge et Schelling* (Paris: Aubier-Montaigne, 1971). This Schellingian equation of the Exodic God with the transcendental "I am" is what the romantic critic Samuel Coleridge will call "primary imagination"—that is, "the repetition in the finite mind of the eternal act of creation in the infinite 'I AM'" (*Biographia Literaria*, xiii). It might also be noted here that Heidegger's ontology of *Dasein* is itself greatly influenced by the German mystical-romantic-idealist theory of the "I am" and "imagination" (*Einbildungskraft*). See John Caputo's illuminating analysis of the Heidegger-Eckhart connection in *The Mystical Element in Heidegger's Thought* (New York: Fordham University Press, 1982); and also the recent critical genealogies of Heidegger's mystical notion of Being by Theodore Kisiel, *The Genesis of Heidegger's Being and Time* (Berkeley: University of California Press, 1993), and John van Buren, *The Young Heidegger: Rumor of the Hidden King* (Bloomington: Indiana University Press, 1994); also Theodore Kisiel and John van Buren, eds., *Reading Heidegger from the Start* (Albany: SUNY Press, 1994). For a somewhat contrasting account of Heidegger's theory of the "I am," see Paul Ricoeur, "Heidegger et la question du sujet," in *Le Conflit des interprétations* (Paris: Éditions du Seuil, 1969), pp. 222ff. Just to take one example of how deep an echo exists between the I-am-who-am and Heidegger's definition of authentic *Dasein*, see his definition of *Dasein* in *Being and Time* as the Being who has for its end its own Being, or his cryptic rendition of Being in the "Letter on Humanism": Being is its own Being (*"Doch das Sein—was ist das Sein? Es ist Es selbst"*). Here Heidegger betrays a debt not only to Judeo-Christian theology but also, and perhaps more fundamentally, to the notion of the "I am" as transcendental ego/imagination in German idealism and romanticism—a notion of which Derrida writes: "L'essence interne de l'absolu est une éternelle *In-Eins-Bildung* qui se répand à profusion; son émanation (*Ausfluss*) traverse le monde des phénomènes à travers la raison et l'imagination. On ne peut donc séparer philosophie et poésie, affirmation sans cesse répétée par Schelling" (Derrida, "Théologie de la traduction," in *Qu'est-ce que Dieu?* [Brussels: Publications des Facultés Universitaires Saint-Louis, 1985], pp. 170–171ff.). I might also mention here, finally, the intriguing use which Heidegger makes in the *Beiträge* of Schelling's notion of a "last God" (see the third example under "Hermeneutic Retrievals" in the conclusion to the present volume and notes 17–18 of the

conclusion, and the chapter "Last Gods and Final Things" in my *Strangers, Gods, and Monsters*).

12. This New Age mysticism is often an eclectic mix of Eastern Zen Buddhism, Jungian parapsychology, neo-Gnostic esotericism, ecological neo-paganism, comparative mythology à la Joseph Campbell, and even a certain strand of Christian mysticism drawn (often liberally) from such figures as Thomas Merton, Teilhard de Chardin, and Thomas Moore. The following reading of Exodus 3:14 by Thomas Merton is a case in point: "When Moses saw the bush in flames, burning in the desert but not consumed, You did not answer his question with a definition. You said, '*I AM.*' How shall we begin to know You who are if we do not *begin ourselves to be something of what You are?* . . . We come to live in Him alone" (*No Man Is an Island* [Kent: Burns and Oates, 1997], pp. 212, 226).

13. I might also mention here the radical, if frequently misunderstood, influence of Meister Eckhart's interpretation of Exodus 3:14 on the Christian mystical readings of the divine name. Writing in the fourteenth century, Eckhart deployed the onto-theological terms inherited from Bonaventure and Thomas to render Exodus 3:14, but he pushed the metaphysical language to its limits, and some would argue beyond. Let us take the following commentary on the Tetragrammaton from Eckhart's *In Exodum 3:14, Lateinische Werke* II, 20: "First the three words: 'I,' 'am,' 'who,' belong, in their most strict and proper sense, to God. The pronoun 'I' is of the first person. This pronoun, as a separator (*discretivum*) signifies pure substance; pure, I say, without anything accidental or alien, substance without quality, without this form or that, without any addition of this or that. Now all this pertains to God and to Him only, who is beyond all accidents, kinds and genres. . . . Similarly, the 'who' is an infinite (or indefinite) name. Such infinite and immense being can belong only to God. And likewise the verb 'am' (sum) is of the order of pure substance. It is a word: 'and the word is God': a substantive verb: 'carrying all things by virtue of its word,' as it is written in the first letter to the Hebrews" (quoted Breton, "'Je Suis (celui) qui Suis' (Ontologie et Métaphysique)"). In another text, *Von der Abgeschiedenheit*—"About Disinterest"— Meister Eckhart offers a more mystical variation on Exodus 3:14. He glosses the self-revelation as follows: "We might say: The unchanging One hath sent me!" Eckhart goes on to explain how this represents a privileged self-manifestation of God as "unmoved disinterest." To illustrate this he claims that Christ partook of this disinterest even as he cried out "My soul is sorrowful unto death." As did Mary, his mother, standing beneath the Cross. "Whatever about the lamentations of our Lady, inwardly she was still un-moved and disinterested." Moreover, Eckhart is prepared to extend this analogy to human beings. While their outer agents and actions are subject to change and move-ment, the internal soul can partake of eternity. The outward man, or sensual person operating with the five senses, is only one part of us; the inner self lives in unmoved disinterestedness and disengagement. "A man may be ever so active outwardly and still leave the inner man unmoved and passive." The inner person is the divine "word of Eternity" giving birth to itself in us. Using the illustration of the swinging door, he explains: "A door swings to and fro through an angle. I compare the breadth of the door to the outward man and the hinge to the inner person. When the door swings to and fro, the breadth of the door moves back and forth, but the hinge is still unmoved and unchanged" ("About Disinterest," in *Meister Eckhart*, ed. and trans. Raymond Bernard Blakney [New York: Harper and Row, 1941], pp. 86–87). On this theme, see Oliver Davies' very insightful commentary in *Meister Eckhart: Mystical Theologian* (London:

SPCK, 1991), pp. 162–176. The most curious thing about this passage is, arguably, that while God seems identical with Himself as "*he-who-is*," this does not, as we might expect, rule out the possibility of human beings identifying with God by attaining to this same inner point of silent, still disinterest. On the contrary, it secures it. "God became man," suggests Eckhart, "so that I might be born to be God—yes, identically God" (Blakney, *Meister Eckhart*, p. 194). Or, more explicit still, "Between the Son and the soul there is no distinction" (p. 213). "The eye by which I see God and the eye by which God sees me are one and the same" (p. 206). "God's isness (*Istigkeit*) is my isness" (p. 180). We encounter here a startling paradox. For while most orthodox theologies read the Exodus passage as the mark of absolute *separateness* between a transcendent God (the divine *a-se-esse*) and transient humans eager to grasp his name, Eckhart appears to claim a radical *identity* between the two. The human person who abandons its own outer will and enters fully into the desert of its own emptiness becomes one with the Godhead of God. "When both God and you have forsaken self, what remains between you is an indivisible union. It is in this unity that the Father begets his Son in the secret spring of your nature" (p. 127). Just as "life is only to live," so God is only to be (p. 127). God's being is without why. "In him there is neither idea nor form" (p. 180). Such divine Being "ranks higher than life or knowledge. . . . Being is a name above all names" (p. 171). It is beyond all opposites (good and evil etc.) and even beyond all our notions of "God and Godhead" (pp. 172–173). God is pure Being, isness, *esse*, substance, I am.

14. Paul Ricoeur, "From Interpretation to Translation," p. 334. See also Ricoeur's suggestive reading of Exodus 3:14 in terms of a hermeneutic of narrative mission and prescription, "D'un testament à l'autre: Essai d'herméneutique biblique," in *La Mémoire et le temps: Mélanges offerts à Pierre Bonnard*, ed. Daniel Marguerat and Jean Zumstein (Geneva: Labor et Fides, 1991), pp. 299–309. See in particular, pp. 300–301, where Ricoeur insists that the ontological predication of the divine I-am-who-am be framed within a narrative and prescriptive context, made clear in Exodus 20:1: "'C'est moi Jahvé, ton Dieu, qui t'ai fait sortir du pays d'Egypte, de la maison de servitude; tu n'auras pas d'autre Dieu que moi' (Exodus 20). La proposition relative de forme narrative—'c'est moi qui . . . t'ai fait sortir'—et le grand commandement qui suit immédiatement, constituent ensemble ce qu'on peut appeler la *nomination prédicative* de Dieu, laquelle explique, déploie le nom purement *appellatif* contenu dans la clause d'autoprésentation: 'Je (suis) Jahvé.' Sous sa forme narrative, ce nom prédicatif résume toute l'histoire de l'Exode; sous sa forme prescriptive, il résume toute la révélation sinaïque de la Torah" (p. 300). Ricoeur adds: "La proclamation de l'unicité de Dieu ne se laisse pas décomposer en deux énoncés: premièrement 'Dieu existe,' deuxièmement, 'il est un (seul).' Les prédicats éthico-narratifs, qui expliquent la *shema* ('écoute!') équivalent à un acte de confiance dans l'efficacité historique et dans l'efficacité éthique du nom, rend superflue toute assertion prétendument distincte d'existence" (p. 301). The ethico-narrative character of the Exodus revelation is rooted, for Ricoeur, in the fact that the actual moment—when God says "I am who am" and Moses replies "Here I am"—is intrinsically related to past and future, to memory and promise, to ancestry and eschatology. That is why what Gilson calls the "metaphysics of Exodus" needs to be checked and challenged by both the narrative character of the call and the indeterminate-repetitive-excessive character of Yahweh's triple use of the verb *'ehyeh*—a verb translated by Rosenzweig and Buber in terms of "becoming" (*werden*) rather than "being" (*sein*). As Ricoeur writes: "le cadre même du récit de vocation empêche de surestimer et d'hypostasier le triple 'Je suis,' culminant dans le nom 'Jahvé'" (p. 302).

Likewise, this triple use of *'ehyeh* engenders a surplus of meaning, opening up a history of multiple interpretation and constantly renewed fidelity to action (*wirken*): "Cet *excès* . . . n'engendre-t-il pas une situation herméneutique d'un genre unique, à savoir l'ouverture, la signification d'Exode 3:14 ne peut plus être séparée de l'histoire de ses effets, de sa *Wirkungsgeschichte*" (p. 302). On the relation between narrativity and unsayability, see my *On Stories*.

15. Rashi, *The Torah: With Rashi's Commentary*, trans. Rabbi Yisrael Isser Zvi Herczeg, The Sapirstein Edition, 4th ed. (New York: Mesorah Publications, 1997), pp. 24ff. I am greatly indebted to Professor Zeev Harvey of the University of Jerusalem for bringing this passage in Rashi's commentary to my attention.

16. Ibid., p. 24.

17. Ibid., p 26.

18. Ibid., p. 27.

19. On this point, see Paul Ricoeur, "From Interpetation to Translation," pp. 337ff., and Joseph O'Leary, "God Deconstructs," in *Religious Pluralism and Christian Truth*, pp. 159–204.

20. At times, it must be admitted, the Neoplatonic Christian tradition of negative theology did equate the God beyond being with the God per se. And even Aquinas, who favored an analogical rather than apophatic approach to the naming of God, recognized that Being is not as good as Yahweh as a name for God! The scholastic tradition, inaugurated by Albert the Great and Thomas, sought to grant speculative theology the status of a science, but true to a certain Neoplatonic influence it never denied the transcendence of divine being as such. We can never know, as Aquinas admitted, *what* God is. As the Neoplatonist tradition in Christian theology frequently repeated, we can speak of God only *as* or *as-if* (*sicut/quasi/quatenus*) he was this or that kind of being—which, taken literally or nonfigurally, he is not. See Bernard Dupuy, "Heidegger et Le Dieu inconnu," and Stanislas Breton, "La quérelle des dénominations," in *Heidegger et la question de Dieu*, ed. Kearney and O'Leary. Dupuy argues, for example, that "the attempts to harmonise the revelation of Sinai with Greek ontology have long obscured the sense of the disclosure of the divine name. It entails the rejection of all anthropomorphism, the relativisation of all the figures used to apprehend Him who is beyond being and non-being and thus 'without analogy'" (p. 119). For a contrasting reading, see Fran O'Rourke, *Pseudo-Dionysius and the Metaphysics of Thomas Aquinas* (Leiden: Brill, 1992).

21. Gese translates Exodus 3:14 as "*ich erweise mich, als der ich mich erweisen werde*," "I am as I shall show myself" (Gese, "Der Name Gottes," quoted by André LaCocque, "The Revelation of Revelations," in *Thinking Biblically*, p. 312).

22. André LaCocque, "The Revelation of Revelations," p. 312. For other postmetaphysical readings of Exodus 3:14, see also Joseph S. O'Leary, *Religious Pluralism and Christian Truth*, especially the section "The Name of God" in part 6, "God Deconstructs," pp. 159–165.

23. Rosenzweig, "The Eternal," pp. 102–104, 107–108. Rosenzweig argues here that the Holy Name calling out from the burning bush "forges the Bible into a unity in the divine name" and marks the "essence of Judaism" as a "uniting of the distant God with the near, the 'whole' with 'one's own'" (p. 108). Rosenzweig refers to various translations of Exodus 3:14 from Calvin and Luther to Mendelssohn—e.g., "I shall be who I shall be," "I shall be it eternally," "I will be that sent me to you"—as attempts to go beyond the Platonist, Aristotelian, and Alexandrian versions of the Vulgate *qui est* to the

"genuine, unhellenic, Jewish meaning" which "connects the name to the moment of its revelation in Exodus" (pp. 107–108). I am grateful to Robin Gibbs for bringing this scholarly text to my attention. On Rosenzweig's translation of Exodus 3:14, see also Paul Ricoeur, "From Interpretation to Translation," pp. 360–361.

24. Martin Buber, *Moses: The Revelation and the Covenant* (New York: Harper, 1958), p. 49. Buber develops this point as follows: "As replay to his question about the name, Moses is told: *Ehyeh asher ehyeh.* This is usually understood to mean: 'I am that I am' in the sense that YHVH describes himself as the being One or even the Everlasting One, the one unalterably persisting in his being. But that would be abstraction of a kind which does not usually come about in periods of increasing religious vitality; while in addition the verb in the Biblical language does not carry this particular shade of meaning of pure existence. It means: happening, coming into being, being there, being present, being thus and thus; but not being in an abstract sense. 'I am that I am' could only be understood as an avoiding of the question, as a statement that unfolds without any information. Should we, however, really assume that in the view of the narrator the God who came to inform his people of their liberation wishes, at that hour of all hours, merely to secure his distance, and not to grant and warrant proximity as well? This concept is certainly discouraged by the twofold *ehyeh*, 'I shall be present,' which precedes and follows the statement with unmistakable intention, and in which God promises to be present with those chosen by him, to remain present with them, to assist them. This promise is given unconditional validity in the first part of the statement: 'I shall be present.' . . . 'I am and remain present.' Behind it stands the implied reply to those influenced by the magical practices of Egypt, those infected by technical magic: it is superfluous for you to wish to invoke me; in accordance with my character I again and again stand by those whom I befriend. . . . In the revelation at the Burning Bush religion is demagicized. . . . YHVH is 'He who will be present' . . . he who is present here; not merely some time and some where but in every now and in every here. Now the name expresses his character and assures the faithful of the richly protective presence of their Lord" (pp. 51–53). Buber alerts us here to the presence-absence enigma of the Exodic God, an enigma which provokes us to rethink God not as a *deus absconditus* but as a *deus adventurus.*

25. Because the indicative imperfect of the root, *hyh*—as used in Exodus 3:12 *'ehyeh*—suggests the futural sense of "I shall be with thee," it points to a "transitional" meaning of the verb. It prefigures future alteration in present circumstances. That is, *hyh* has the force of a "temporal indicator" opening up the ancestral past toward an *eschaton* yet to be realized. It is this kind of exegesis which tempers any hasty attempts to convert the Exodic Name into an ontological abstraction or ecclesiastical icon, particularly under the influence of speculative thinking from the West (e.g., the translation of *'ehyeh* as *ho on* or "the one who is" in the Septuagint). See here the analysis of the grammar of the Exodic formula by G. S. Ogden cited by LaCocque in "The Revelation of Revelations," p. 313.

26. LaCocque, "The Revelation of Revelations," p. 314.

27. Ibid.

28. Ibid., p. 315.

29. Ibid. A similar shift of emphasis onto the futural potentiality of God is found in Moltmann and the theology of liberation, as well as in Whitehead and process theology (cf. in particular Whitehead's notion of God's "consequent nature," comprising a reservoir of possibilities to be creatively realized as world in *Process and Reality* [New York:

Free Press, 1978]); see also John B. Cobb, "A Whiteheadian Doctrine of God," in *Process Philosophy and Christian Thought*, ed. Delwin Brown, Ralph James, Jr., and Gene Reeves (Indianapolis: Bobbs-Merrill, 1971), pp. 215–243; William Dean, "Deconstruction and Process Theology," *The Journal of Religion* 64 (1984): 1–19; and David Ray Griffin, "Postmodern Theology and A/Theology," in *Varieties of Postmodern Theology*, ed. David Ray Griffin, William A. Beardslee, and Joe Holland (Albany: SUNY Press, 1989), pp. 29–61.

30. LaCocque writes: "It elicits recognition and worship as the recipients are not just made privy to a divine secret but are the objects of an action of salvation. "It is I who am Yhwh" goes far beyond a rhetorical statement—it reveals the ultimate meaning of the redeeming event. Thus we see why the Name is no atemporal, ahistorical, abstract axiom about divine self-sufficiency (*aseitas*). God says *'ehyeh* and the unaccomplished tense helps us see the action as a process. It is not a question of divine essence, but it is a promissory statement that God, as it were, 'stands or falls' with his people, and in the first place with Moses about to return to Egypt where a price is set upon his head" ("The Revelation of Revelations," p. 316). See also here Erich Fromm, *You Shall Be as Gods: A Radical Interpretation of the Old Testament* (New York: Fawcett, 1966), and Martin Buber, *Moses: The Revelation and the Covenant* (New York: Harper, 1958), pp. 48–54.

31. Jacques Derrida, *Memoirs of the Blind: The Self-Portrait and Other Ruins*, trans. Pascale-Anne Brault and Michael Naas (Chicago: University of Chicago Press, 1993), p. 54. Derrida returns to the "I Am" revelation of Exodus 3 on a number of suggestive, if characteristically allusive, occasions, e.g., his discussion of "Jahweh spricht nur immer 'Ja'" in "Nombre de Oui," in *Psyché: Inventions de l'autre* (Paris: Galilée, 1987), pp. 639ff.; his reference to Yahweh as "I am he who is . . ." in relation to James Joyce's use of HE WAR in *Finnegans Wake*, in "Two Words for Joyce," in *Poststructuralist Joyce*, ed. Derek Attridge and Daniel Ferrer (New York: Cambridge University Press, 1984), pp. 145–146, 151, and in *The Post Card* (Chicago: University of Chicago Press, 1987), pp. 141–142; the commentary on "the Eternal speaking face to face with Moses" in his essay on Levinas, "Violence and Metaphysics," in *Writing and Difference*, trans. Alan Bass (New York: Routledge, 1981), pp. 108–109; the analysis of the "unpronounceable name" of the Jewish God in "Shibboleth for Paul Celan," in *Word Traces: Readings of Paul Celan*, ed. Aris Fioretos (Baltimore: Johns Hopkins University Press, 1994), p. 54–55; and in the passage cited from *Memoirs of the Blind* above in the text where Derrida offers a description of God-memory in terms of "desseins-d'aveugles" and the eschatological temporal tension within the disclosure of the unnameable name in Exodus 3:15: "It is theological through and through, to the point, sometimes included, sometimes excluded, where the self-eclipsing *trait* cannot even say itself in the present, since it is not gathered, since it does not gather itself, into any present, 'I am who I am' (a formula whose original grammatical form, as we know, implies the future)" (p. 54). Finally I might refer to Derrida's allusion to the radical alterity of the burning-bush God when he refers to Moses' removal of his sandals before the thornbush as a typically Jewish mark of respect toward the transcendence of the Holy as witnessed in the Mishnah prohibiting the wearing of shoes on the Sabbath (*The Truth in Painting* [Chicago: University of Chicago Press, 1987], pp. 350–351).

32. See Derrida's announcement of the deconstructive God in "Comment ne pas parler," in *Psyché*: "La guerre qu'il déclare, elle a d'abord fait rage au-dedans de son nom: divisé, bifide, ambivalent, polysémique: Dieu déconstruit" (p. 207). See also some of Derrida's other intriguing comments on the possibility of a hyper-ethical

God/Gift/alterity beyond the "proper names" of ontology in "Sauf le nom," in *On the Name*, trans. John P. Leavey, Jr. (Stanford, Calif.: Stanford University Press, 1995), pp. 33–85; *The Gift of Death*, trans. David Willis (Chicago: University of Chicago Press, 1995), p. 71; *Jacques Derrida: Circonfession/Derridabase*, by Geoffrey Bennington and Jacques Derrida (Paris: Éditions du Seuil, 1991), especially pp. 103ff. and p. 91, where Derrida calls himself "l'eschatologiste le plus avancé." Elsewhere again, Derrida insists that the alterity that precedes and exceeds us cannot be "seen" as a primal object or "read" as a proper name, here and now, but calls for another kind of seeing—a "seeing beyond," a "vision-beyond-vision," a "sur-vision"; see Jacques Derrida, "Living On: Border Lines," in *Deconstruction and Criticism* (London: Routledge, 1979), pp. 90–91ff.

33. Yahweh thus comes, as LaCocque notes, to "promise a history of merciful guidance whose onset, namely the Exodus, constitutes both its beginning and its end, its apex and the figure of things to come at the *eschaton*, because the Event in question is paradigmatic *kat'exochen*" (LaCocque, "The Revelation of Revelations," p. 317). One possible objection to this post-sacrificial reading of Exodus 3:14—and one actually put to me after my presentation of this chapter as a paper in the Villanova conference on religion and postmodernism in October 1999 by Professor Tod Linafelt of Georgetown University—is the following: how does one explain the fact that shortly after the burning bush summons, God actually tries to kill Moses and that this murder attempt is only averted by a blood ritual (Exodus 4:24–26)? Is this episode not placed here, Linafelt asked, to balance the overly merciful portrayal of God in Exodus 3–4, suggesting that unleashed holiness and sacred power are not as easily contained or channeled as one might think. This puzzling episode, Linafelt argued, represents the "deep untamed side of God" that conforms to the angry, vengeful, jealous, sacrificial face of Yahweh. A possible response to Linafelt might be that God's threat to Moses as he crosses over to Egypt (Exodus 4:24–26) is a reminder that he has forgotten his mission—hence the rite of circumcision (on his son by his wife and the spreading of the blood on Moses' own genitals) which is a mark of *remembrance* that we are bound to God, and that the transmission of the seed of the people is mere tribalism unless it constantly recalls the burning bush call to justice. The fact that God's reminder to Moses, just before he crosses back into the land of bondage, involves an act of quasi-sacrifice may be read (à la Girard) as a therapeutic re-enactment of the old sacrificial cults which the Mosaic revelation on Mount Horeb is summoned to go beyond—as it opens onto an ethical mandate to emancipate the people from slavery. In other words, the blood ransom idioms of this ostensibly disturbing episode may be read as a deconstructive replay of sacrificial murder—as Girard reads Abraham's "sacrifice" of Isaac on Mount Moriah or Christ's "sacrifice" on the cross of Calvary: a retrieving-surpassing of the old tribal religion which is now being superceded. By means of such a hermeneutic "post-sacrificial" reading, we could release the more affirmative kernel of the overall Exodus narrative, seeing the episode on the Egyptian border as a circumcisionary recall to Moses that he belongs to God and not to the fleshpots of Egypt (which threaten his promise of liberation and remembrance). The fact that the original authors/redactors of this episode may have been confused and ambiguous about such dramatic matters is perfectly normal; but that should not prevent us—unless we confine ourselves to literalist/fundamentalist readings—from reinterpreting the text in a post-sacrificial light. (By sacrifice I mean human blood sacrifice.) Either way, I am deeply grateful to Tod Linafelt for bringing this subject to my attention.

34. Here we are confronted with what Zimmerli describes as a "mystery without a definition," a mystery whose "potency" (*Wirkung*) goes beyond conceptual speculation and imagistic fixation in favor of a divine "calling for decision on the part of Moses and his people—the recipients of the self-revelation" (Walter Zimmerli, *I Am Yahweh* [Atlanta: John Knox, 1982], p. 153, cited in LaCocque, "The Revelation of Revelations," p. 322). The fact that the revelation of Exodus is given in terms of a "word" rather than an "image" is perfectly consistent with the Hebraic interdiction of divine figuration and iconography. God does not here propose some divine icon in contradistinction to an anthropocentric idol (as Christian thinkers like Marion or Von Balthasar might like to believe). "The revelation of the Name is granted by an imageless God who desires to be accessible and known": see LaCocque, "The Revelation of Revelations," p. 319; Gerhard von Rad, *Old Testament Theology* (New York: Harper, 1962); and Gese, "Der Name Gottes," p. 86. Mediated relationships with God through visual representation (third person) are here replaced by the more immediate relationship of the one to one (second person). But as the Decalogue makes plain, God can be fully honored and respected only by refusing both *objectification*—through the mediation of images and idols—and *identification*—through the inordinately immediate.

35. LaCocque is adamant on this point, arguing that "recognition of the lordship of God is no metaphysical knowledge" and that the Tetragrammaton is "no invitation to speculation upon the aseity of God." It does not refer to a divine *causa sui* but takes place within very concrete events (LaCocque, "The Revelation of Revelations," p. 323).

36. Even his judgment over, and his condemnation of, his people may be seen from the perspective of God's personal commitment. See LaCocque, "The Revelation of Revelations," pp. 322–323.

37. Emmanuel Levinas, *Beyond the Verse: Talmudic Readings and Lectures*, trans. Gary D. Mole (London: Athlone Press, 1994), pp. 102–107. On this biblical enigma of human-divine interdependency, interlocution, and co-responsibility, see Levinas, *Totality and Infinity*, as well as Jacques Derrida's tantalizing commentary on Levinas's notion of the "face of God" in "Violence and Metaphysics," in *Writing and Difference*, pp. 108–109: "The foundation of metaphysics—in Levinas's sense—is to be encountered in the return to things themselves, where we find the common root of humanism and theology: the resemblance between man and God, man's visage and the Face of God. 'The Other resembles God.' Via the passageway of this resemblance, man's speech can be lifted up toward God, an almost unheard of *analogy* which is the very movement of Levinas's discourse on discourse. Analogy as dialogue with God: 'Discourse is discourse with God. . . . Metaphysics is the essence of this language with God.' Discourse with God, and not in God as *participation*. Discourse with God, and not discourse on God and his attributes as *theology*. And the dissymmetry of my relation to the other, this 'curvature of inter-subjective space signifies the divine intention of all truth.' It 'is, perhaps, the very presence of God.' Presence as separation, presence-absence—again the break with Parmenides, Spinoza, Hegel, which only 'the idea of creation *ex nihilo*' can consummate. . . . A resemblance which can be understood neither in terms of communion or knowledge, nor in terms of participation and incarnation. A resemblance which is neither a sign nor an effect of God. Neither the sign nor the effect exceeds the same. We are 'in the Trace of God.' A proposition which risks incompatibility with every allusion to the 'very presence of God.' A proposition readily converted into atheism; and if God was *an effect of the trace*? If the idea of divine presence (life, existence, parousia, etc.), if the name of God was but the movement of

erasure of the trace in presence? Here it is a question of knowing whether the trace permits us to think presence in its system, or whether the reverse order is the true one.... The face of God disappears forever in showing itself. Thus are reassembled in the unity of their metaphysical signification, at the very heart of the experience denuded by Levinas, the diverse evocations of the Face of Yahweh.... The face of Yahweh is the *total* person and the *total* presence of the 'Eternal speaking face to face with Moses,' but saying to him also: 'Thou canst not see my face: for there shall be no man see me and live . . . thou shalt stand upon a rock; and it shall come to pass, while my glory passeth by, that I will put thee in a cleft of the rock, and will cover thee with my hand while I pass by: And I will take away mine hand, and thou shalt see my back parts: but my face shall not be seen' (Exodus 33:20–23). The face of God which commands while hiding itself is at once more and less a face than all faces. Whence, perhaps, despite all Levinas's precautions, the equivocal complicity of theology and metaphysics in *Totality and Infinity.* Would Levinas subscribe to this infinitely ambiguous sentence from the *Book of Questions* by Edmond Jabes: 'All faces are His; this is why He has no face?'" The tensive relationship between Levinas's eschatology of divine transcendence and his phenomenological humanism of the face is underlined here in dramatic fashion. The reference of the Eternal speaking face to face with Moses bears a telling allusion to Exodus 33:11 and to the Burning Bush episode. It is also worth bearing in mind here that in verse 6 Moses hides his face, in contrast to Exodus 33:11 where Moses speaks "face to face" (though God's face remains hidden, v. 20). Opher Kutner has pointed out to me that Levinas reads the term "ahorai" (Exodus 23) as "trace" while it actually means "backside."

38. LaCocque, "The Revelation of Revelations," p. 324: "Praise is the proper human response to revelation, rather than speculation on how it is that God made himself dependent on the human to be Yhwh, as the human is dependent on the divine to be the *imago Dei.*"

39. Ibid. A late midrash on this verse reads "I am that I am—just as you are with me so I am with you." I am grateful to Opher Kutner of the University of Jerusalem for bringing this midrash (quoted in Nachmanides' commentary) to my attention.

40. LaCocque, "The Revelation of Revelations," p. 325.

41. Ibid.: "Justice triumphs in the prayer, faith, hope, and love, of those who seek justice. God is God only through the proclamation of his people. *Yhwh malakh! (God reigns!* cf. Psalm 93:1, 96:10, 97:1, 99:1, etc). In this acclamation is redeemed the human abandonment of God reported in the myth of Genesis 2–3. God's risky wager, which he lost from the outset of creation, is now salvaged in Israel's liturgy celebrated in the temple."

42. *Sifre Deuteronomy* 346 (ed. Finkelstein), cited in LaCocque, "The Revelation of Revelations," p. 325.

43. "I posits another person, the one who, being as he is, completely external to me, becomes my echo to whom I say you and who says you to me" (Emile Benveniste, *Problems in General Linguistics* [Coral Gables, Fla.: University of Miami Press, 1971], p. 224). Cited in LaCocque, "The Revelation of Revelations," p. 326. See also ibid.: "Within Israel's consciousness, the Exodus inaugurates not only its history as a people . . . but also the world's redemption. The exodus from Egypt is toward the Promised Land, the microcosm and 'bridge-head' from where the whole of creation has started its transfiguration into the Kingdom of God. The Exodus is thus *the* event par excellence, the 'V-Day' of history, the day when the world is changed into itself by eter-

nity." See also Moses Hess's ethico-political reading of Exodus 3:15 in *Der Hebraische Gottesname* (1862) (Jerusalem, 1954), pp. 173–174. His concluding sentence reads: "As God has redeemed the people from Egypt, so he will be the redeemer from every social slavery (whether material or spiritual, bodily or moral) in the future."

44. It is this temporal, historical, dynamic God-in-process who is evoked again and again in the Jewish Agadic tradition. The *Midrash Agadah*, for instance, renders Exodus 3:14 as "I who used to be the One is I who shall be the One"; while Mekhita Bahodesh 5 offers this variation: "I was in Egypt, I was at the sea, I was at Sinai, I was in the past, I will be in the future" (cited in LaCocque, "The Revelation of Revelations," p. 327). In a similar vein, *Targum Yerushalmi I* reads: "I who was, who am and who shall be, sends me to you." Or again: "The one who says to the world—be! and it is; and who will say to it—be! and it is. . . . It is He who sent me to you." Here again the emphasis is not so much on the magic or essence denoted by the Name itself but the *invocation* of the Name—an invocation that is at the same time a *vocation*: "This will you tell the child of Israel: *'ehyeh* sent me to you" (cited in LaCocque, "The Revelation of Revelations," p. 328). In his 1992 Cambridge lecture, "The Great Tautology," Steiner adds an interesting semantic inflection to the hermeneutic tradition of Exodus 3:14. Confirming this Exodic text to be one of the most foundational and seminal passages of Western and Middle Eastern religion, Steiner remarks how the untensed Hebrew wordplay disturbs the various attempted translations into the Indo-European language systems and injects ambiguity into the very heart of theological reflection, from the post-Exodic books of the Bible down to the fourth gospel and beyond. The recurrent question becomes: who speaks in the burning bush? Is it being or non-being? Is it radical absence or real presence? Steiner identifies this voice as one of "spiritual and existential duplicity." Only by wagering on transcendence, he says, on an ultimate mystery beyond ourselves, can we begin to hear the voice of the burning bush. This Exodic passage calls for a conversion from the "symmetries of immanence" to a new theology of *transcendence.* (See R. P. Carroll, "On Steiner the Theologian," in *Reading George Steiner*, ed. Nathan A. Scott, Jr., and Ronald A. Sharp [Baltimore: Johns Hopkins University Press, 1994], p. 271.)

45. Jean-Luc Marion, *God without Being*, trans. Thomas A. Carlson (Chicago: University of Chicago Press, 1991), p. 123. Marion is greatly indebted here to Levinas's discussion of transcendence in *Totality and Infinity*, in *Otherwise Than Being* (The Hague: Nijhoff, 1981), and in *De Dieu qui vient à l'idée* (Paris: Vrin, 1982).

46. Ibid., p.152.

47. Ibid., p. 153.

48. Ibid., pp. 156–158.

49. Ibid., p. 155.

50. Ibid.

51. Jean-Luc Marion, "In The Name: How to Avoid Speaking of Negative Theology," in *God, the Gift, and Postmodernism.* The title and theme of this paper critically echoes Derrida's "Comment ne pas parler" in *Psyché.* For the most pioneering and illuminating treatment of Derrida and Levinas on the God question and negative theology, see John D. Caputo, *The Prayers and Tears of Jacques Derrida.*

52. Ibid. Marion offers a more critical and discriminating account of the phenomenology of mystical manifestation and intuition in his essay "The Saturated Phenomenon," in *Phenomenology and the "Theological Turn,"* by Dominique Janicaud et al. (New York: Fordham University Press, 2000), pp. 176–216.

53. John D. Caputo, "Roundtable on the Gift," discussion on the phenomenology of the gift with Jacques Derrida, Jean-Luc Marion, and Richard Kearney, with response by John D. Caputo, Villanova University, in *God, the Gift, and Postmodernism.*

54. Joseph Campbell, *The Power of Myth* (New York: Doubleday, 1988), p. 22.

55. See Friedrich Schelling, *Of Human Freedom,* trans. James Gutmann (Chicago: Open Court, 1936); see George Seidel, "Heidegger's Last God and the Schelling Connection," in *Laval théologique et philosophique* 55, no. I (February 1999): 85–98, pp. 91ff. See also the section on Heidegger in chapter 5 and the conclusion below; and the chapter on Heidegger's "Last Gods" in my *Strangers, Gods, and Monsters.* I am grateful to John Manoussakis for bringing this text to my attention.

56. Slavoj Zizek, *On Belief* (London: Routledge, 2001).

57. Ibid.

58. See Simon Critchley, *Very Little . . . Almost Nothing: Death, Philosophy, Literature* (London: Routledge, 1997), p. 80. See also Paul Ricoeur's suspicion of a certain masochism in Levinas's ethics, *Autrement* (Paris: Presses Universitaires de France, 1997).

59. Moses Hess, *Rome and Jerusalem* (New York: Bloch, 1943).

60. Paul Ricoeur, "From Interpretation to Translation," p. 341: "This resonance would already have at least a double sense: the enigma of a positive revelation giving rise to thought (about existence, efficacity, faithfulness, accompanying through history), and of a negative revelation dissociating the Name from those utilitarian and magical values concerning power that were ordinarily associated with it. And perhaps the even greater enigma of a revelation, in the usual sense of a theophany, or a non-revelation, in the sense of a withdrawal into the incognito."

61. Ibid., p. 341.

62. Breton, "'Je Suis (celui) qui Suis,'" p. 59.

63. Ibid., p. 60.

64. Ibid., p. 64. See Derrida's subtle and suggestive reading of Eckhart's negative theology in "Comment ne pas parler," from *Psyché,* trans. Ken Frieden, in *Languages of the Unsayable: The Play of Negativity in Literature and Literary Theory,* ed. Sanford Budick and Wolfgang Iser (New York: Columbia University Press, 1989), pp. 3–70.

65. Eckhart, *In Exodum 3:14, Lateinische Werke* II, 21. Cited in Breton, "'Je Suis (celui) qui Suis,'" pp. 61–62. See Breton's suggestive gloss on this in ibid., p. 62: "L'acte d'être, sous la flamme du buisson ardent, devient flamme à son tour, élan de vie, feu originel, déployé en un groupe d'opérations, de mouvements et de relations qu'entretient une énergie bouillonnante qui se répand au-dedans comme au-dehors. Le mot *ferveur* est ici décisif. Il projette sur l'abstrait dynamisme de la *causa sui* l'irradiation d'une source de lumière et de chaleur qui entraîne, en son tourbillon, le monde et la divinité elle-même. L'univers est un buisson d'étincelles. Ephémères ou durables, ces 'fleurs du feu' naissent d'un espace festif qui n'est autre que la surabondance de l'acte pur." On this metaphor of the God of Exodus 3:14 as an overspilling, bubbling, super-abundant source, see also Adolph Gesché, "Apprendre de Dieu ce qu'il est," in *Qu'est-ce que Dieu?* (Brussels: Publications des Facultés Universitaires Saint-Louis, 1985), p. 743: "La tradition chrétienne parle de Dieu comme *pègè,* Source intarissable. C'est sans doute parce que Dieu est source débordante qu'il peut ainsi 'se vider' (Ph. 2,7) et donner sans rien perdre, se perdre sans rien perdre. Qu'il peut même donner 'ce qu'il n'est pas,' si l'on peut se permettre d'exprimer ainsi ce qu'est la création, position et surgissement d'une véritable alterité. La surabondance divine explique cette priorité de

Dieu, d'un Dieu toujours en avance, jamais en retard sur l'être. 'Je suis qui je suis' (*Ex* 3,14). Superbe tautologie, qui signifie que Dieu n'est pas déterminé par une antériorité qui le limiterait, comme il en est des Idées éternelles incréées de Platon. Surtout, il n'est pas précédé par *nos* définitions. Dieu *est* 'dès-avant' (*prior*), il est *Sur-Sum*. Non pas, comme l'être précédé ('cogito/ergo sum'), mais le précédant, puisqu'il y a infiniment plus dans le mot Dieu que dans le mot être.' Seigneur, ainsi que nous l'avons vu plus haut,—termes plus adéquats que celui de personne,—que Dieu peut ainsi prendre l'initiative d'une priorité et le risque d'un premier pas, qui chez tout autre serait faux pas?"

66. Eckhart, *Meister Eckhart*, pp. 208 and 206.

67. One might usefully compare and contrast this Eckhartian reading of Exodus 3:14 with Franz Rosenzweig's radical reading from a more Jewish perspective; see "The Eternal," p. 108.

68. Meister Eckhart, *Meister Eckhart*, "The Sermons, 16," p. 171. This notion of a self-giving God in turn echoes Eriugena's view of the divine as a self-othering self-creation—a form of *kenosis-poesis-dunamis* whereby the world is created by God in and through the human. See Wayne Hankey, "Theoria versus Poesis: Neoplatonism and Trinitarian Difference in Aquinas, John Milbank, Jean-Luc Marion, and John Zizioulas," *Modern Theology* 15, no. 4 (1999): 387–415.

69. Breton, "'Je Suis (celui) qui Suis,'" p. 66. He adds: "Having divinised being one must go beyond it by passing through it."

70. Ibid., p. 67.

71. Nicholas of Cusa, *Trialogus de Possest*, translated into English as *On Actualized-Possibility* by Jasper Hopkins, in *A Concise Introduction to the Philosophy of Nicholas of Cusa*, by Jasper Hopkins, pp. 120, 69. See also my commentary on Nicholas of Cusa's discussion of God as *possest* in *The Wake of Imagination* (London: Routledge, 1994), pp. 75–78.

72. Jacques Derrida, "Loving in Friendship: Perhaps—the Noun and the Adverb," in *The Politics of Friendship*, trans. George Collins (London: Verso, 1997), pp. 28–29. See also Derrida's development of this notion of the "perhaps" as "impossible possibility" in "Comme si c'était possible, 'Within such Limits' . . . ," *Revue internationale de philosophie* 3, no. 205 (1998): 497–529; and John Caputo's illuminating "Apology for the Impossible," in *God, the Gift, and Postmodernism*. Cf. my development of this theme in the fourth and final part of "Eschatology of the Possible God" in *The Religious: Blackwell Readings in Continental Philosophy*, ed. John D. Caputo (Oxford: Blackwell, 2001), and ch. 5 below.

73. See my development of this notion of God as *possest*/possibility/may-be—in comparison and contrast with Heidegger's notion of Being as *Vermögen*/power/can-be—in *Poétique du possible* (in particular part 4, where I adumbrate a new eschatological hermeneutic of God as *posse* in critical comparison and contrast with Heidegger's ontological hermeneutic of being as *Vermögend-Mögende* in his "Letter on Humanism" and elsewhere). See also my development of this critical rapport in "Eschatology of the Possible God," in *The Religious*, and ch. 5 below.

3. TRANSFIGURING GOD

1. See *Le Dictionnaire de la Bible*, vol. 50 (Paris, 1912); see also *Le Dictionaire théologique* (Desclée, Belgium, 1963), p. 628; and *Dictionnaire encyclopédique de la Bible* (Valence-sur-Rhône, 1973), vol. 1, p. 793.

2. Jean-Luc Marion misreads this passage, it seems, when he takes it to mean that Peter and the disciples kept silence because they didn't know what else to say. See *God, the Gift, and Postmodernism*, ed. Caputo and Scanlon, p. 69.

3. See homilies on the Transfiguration by Saint John Damascene and Saint Anastasius of Sinai in Roselyne de Feraudy, *L'Icône et la Transfiguration*, special issue of *Spiritualité orientale*, no. 23 (1978): 172.

4. Ibid., p. 173.

5. Ibid., p. 156.

6. Herman Melville, *Moby Dick* (New York: Modern Library, 1930), p. 282.

7. Robert Magliola, *On Deconstructing Life-Worlds*, pp. 127ff. I am indebted here once again to John Manoussakis for his scholarly comments on the multilayered implications of the terms *persona/prosopon* as human and divine. See also Paulo Goncalves's provocative and insightful article "Vital Necrographies: Deconstruction, God, and Arche-Idolatry," *Scottish Journal of Religious Studies* 19, no. 1 (1999): 83–100. Goncalves explores the "question of Christ, the ambiguous supplementary *Logos* essential to bridging the divide between God and the world. He is in the paradoxical position of being an image of the imageless or unrepresentable God, while also being fully human" (p. 91). One attempted theological solution to this paradox was to suppose with Origen that the incarnate Christ possesses a human soul which is the image of the *Logos* (which is in turn the image of God), thereby divinizing Christ's human nature (a process which Origen compares to iron being melted into the fire of the *Logos*). The temptation here was, of course, to ultimately deny Christ's humanity altogether, reducing Jesus to a mere ventriloquist's dummy (the monophysite or Sabellian heresy). Origen, for example, ends up speaking of Christ as the "invisible image of the invisible God" (cited in Goncalves, p. 93)—the next step being the denial of any visible, carnal, or even figural role to Christ whatsoever. We find a more extreme version of this position in Clement of Alexandria's claim that Christ was entirely "impassible (*apathes*), inaccessible to any movement of feeling—either pleasure or pain," adding that when "He ate, [it was] not for the sake of the body which was kept together by a holy energy" (Clement, *Miscellanies*, bk. 6, ch. 9, p. 496 [cited in Goncalves, p. 92]). The other extreme was to humanize the *persona* to the point where one is left with only a literal, positivist or "historical Jesus."

The problem with these polarizations of Christ into the wholly divine or wholly human is that the paradox of figuration is itself betrayed, resulting in puritanical and dogmatic oppositions between the sensible/visible/contingent images of paganism and atheism (demonized as "idols") and the suprasensible/invisible/celestial images "perceived by the mind" (Clement) and ultimately canonized as "icons." One even finds the absurd theory of divinely produced images—*acheiropoietos* (not made by human hands)—to explain how we can have non-human replications of God's non-human manifestation as Christ. This demonizing of all human-made images as idolatrous itself cultivated a notion of the divine as impassive to the point of "indifference" (see Derrida, *Of Grammatology*, p. 71).

The Council of Chalcedon in 451 was an attempt to overcome such theological extremes by declaring that Christ had two separate natures, one fully divine and one fully human—a position which gave considerable support to those who wished to retain a role for images and art within the Christian religion (cf. for example, John of Damascus's appeal to Christ's incarnation to justify his claim "I boldly draw an image of the invisible God") (cited in Goncalves, p. 94).

Goncalves's own position is that Christian theology ultimately ignored the paradoxical injunction of the two-in-one when it came to religious art and images, privileging reason over imagination to the point that the theologians themselves came to "ignore their own metaphors and images," thereby seeking to guarantee for God "the innocence and universality of the self-evident" (p. 98), that is, the status of a purely divine *Logos* totally exempt from the supplementarity of *figuration* (with its inevitable corollaries of time, space, movement, desire, differance). This internal repression of its own figurative mediations and dependencies was to have disastrous consequences for the more dogmatic Christian churches and sects: "This simultaneously facilitated their attack on what they saw as the moral corruption and vice caused by the imagination in idolatry, and legitimized the intolerance which marked Christian attitudes towards other religions" (p. 98). Unable to face up to the deconstructive consequences of the "incoherent image of absolute transcendence" at the very heart of Christianity, several centuries of doctrinaire and puritanical theologians practiced an apartheid of holy "icon" versus unholy "idol." Goncalves's conclusion is quintessentially Derridean: "The transcendent and independent realm of divinity comes to depend, *even for the formulation of its very concept*, on the mimetic realm of images and representations which it allegedly excludes. This dependence undermines the attributes usually ascribed to God. It would be impossible, *a priori*, to conceptualise a God defined in terms of transcendent unity, formlessness, independence, and impassibility, together with all the other attributes which these imply, except by means of supplements. . . . I would propose that this arche-idolatry obliges us to recognise the positive and necessary role which idolatry plays as constitutive of all theology. . . . In Derrida's words, 'the other cannot be absolutely exterior to the same without ceasing to be other' (*Writing and Difference*, p. 126)" (Goncalves, pp. 96–97).

I consider Goncalves's deconstruction of the icon/idol polarization a valid critique of the puritanical and intolerant excesses of Christian onto-theology. By neglecting, however, to leave room for any critical differentiation between emancipating and fetishizing images (whether we call them icons, idols, or simply "figures"), Goncalves's deconstructive reading runs the risk of a certain neutral indifferentism which ignores the need for *some* kind of judgment and discernment when it comes to the realm of images—religious, commercial, ideological, or political. Goncalves does call for a new kind of religious "responsibility" but he does not offer any hints as to how we might critically and responsibly *judge* between different kinds of images.

8. "Homilie de Damascène" in Feraudy, *L'Icône de la Transfiguration*, p. 177.

9. Ibid., p. 152. See also the brilliant analyses of this topic in Christos Sidiropoulos, "L'Homme Jesus et le principe trinitaire" (Ph.D thesis, University of Strasbourg, 1978), pp. 116–232. This mystery of "union without confusion" also recalls the presence-absence/universal-singular doubleness of the living divine in *Wisdom of Solomon* 7:22–8:1: "For wisdom is more mobile than any motion; because of her pureness she pervades and penetrates all things. For she is a breath of the power of God, and a pure emanation of the glory of the Almighty; therefore nothing defiled gains entrance into her. For she is a reflection of eternal light, a spotless mirror of the working of God, and an image of his goodness. Although she is but one, she can do all things; in every generation she passes into holy souls and makes them friends of God, and prophets; for God loves nothing so much as the person who lives with wisdom."

10. On the necessity, and impossibility, of translating the "messianic" import of Mount Thabor, see my *Poétique du possible*, pp. 168.

11. Feraudy, *L'Icône de la Transfiguration*, pp. 130, 175.

12. Ibid., p. 128.

13. Tertullian, *Adversus Prazean (Against Praxeas)*, Patrologia Cursus Completus: Series Latina, ed. J.-P. Migne, vol. 2 (Paris: 1878). Once again I am indebted to John Manoussakis for bringing this text to my attention.

14. Manoussakis, "I-M-Possible."

15. See my *Poétique du possible*, p. 160.

16. On the pre-figuring/re-figuring temporality of the transfiguration, see my analysis of Anastasius's homily in *Poétique du possible*, pp. 170–171: "Anastase annonce qu'avec la transfiguration du Christ sa 'nature adamique, jadis créée semblable à Dieu, mais obscurcie par les figures informes des idoles, a été transfigurée en l'ancienne beauté de l'homme créé à l'image et à la ressemblance de Dieu" (*Homilie d'Anastase, L'Icône de la Transfiguration*, pp. 128, aussi 138, 149, 152–4, 150). Autrement dit, la Transfiguration est à la fois une *préfiguration* de la nouvelle création à faire (ce qu'Anastase nomme 'la terre de promesse') et une *refiguration* de la création originelle de l'homme selon l'image de Dieu. Le sens eschatologique de la Transfiguration du Christ nous renvoie ainsi à la création du commencement et de la fin. C'est pour cela qu'Anastase appelle Moïse et Elie 'les célestes *préfigures* du Christ' (pp. 135, 138), et affirme que le Christ en tant que 'potentialité divine dans la figure d'un homme,' doit être compris à son tour comme 'préfigure de la parousie': 'Tout esquissait et préfigurait là les mystères de la seconde parousie . . . le Royaume des cieux à venir" (p. 142).

17. On this complex notion of "Messianic time," see Emmanuel Levinas, *Totality and Infinity*, and Jacques Derrida, *Specters of Marx*. A key passage in Luke (17:20–25) where the Christian paradox of Messianic time is found reads as follows: "The kingdom of God is not coming with things that can be observed: nor will they say, 'Look, here it is!' or 'There it is!' For in fact the kingdom of God is among you." The passage continues, combining several of the motifs observed in the above analysis of the transfigured Christ—the whiteness of light, the refusal of immediate presence (literalism), the resurrection following the passion and brokenness of Christ: "Then Jesus said to the disciples, 'The days are coming when you will long to see one of the days of the Son of Man, and you will not see it. They will say to you, "Look there!" or "Look here!" Do not go, do not set off in pursuit. For as the lightning flashes and lights up the sky from one side to the other, so will the Son of Man be in his day. But first he must endure much suffering and be rejected by this generation.'"

18. Cited in *Poétique du possible*, p. 172.

19. *L'Icône de la Transfiguration*, pp. 168–169.

20. Ibid., p. 170.

21. Ibid., p. 143.

22. Ibid., p. 132.

23. Levinas in conversation with me during the Levinas Colloquium at Cerisy-La-Salle, Normandy, August 1987. But in extending the Christian reference to include the Jewish, I do not mean to replace a Christo-centric bias with a Judeo-Christo-centric one. Messianic time (as variously outlined by Levinas, Benjamin, Derrida, Marion, and even Heidegger in his pre–*Being and Time* period) marks a universal quasi-transcendental condition which may include all religious experience of some sacred "other" time, be it monotheistic or otherwise.

24. This ethical choice between our transfiguring and disfiguring acts corresponds broadly with the Talmudic distinction between the Good and Evil *yezer* as two opposing

drives—namely, to re-create the world according to the design of God or to reduce it to our own ego-image. See *The Encyclopaedia Judaica* (London: Macmillan, 1971–72), vol. 8, p. 1319; see also my chapter on the "Hebraic Imagination" in Kearney, *Wake of Imagination*, pp. 39–53.

25. See Slavoj Zizek *The Ticklish Subject* (London: Verso, 1999), p. 331: "Christianity proper—the belief in Christ's Resurrection—is the highest religious expression of the power of symbolic fiction as the medium of universality: the death of the 'real' Christ is 'sublated' in the Holy Spirit, that is, in the spiritual community of believers. This authentic kernel of Christianity, first articulated by St. Paul, is under attack today: the danger comes in the guise of the New Age Gnostic/dualist (mis)reading, which reduces the Resurrection to a metaphor of the 'inner' spiritual growth of the individual soul."

26. Zizek, ibid., pp. 331–332, beginning "these narratives endeavour to supplant the diminishing power of the *symbolic function* of the Holy Spirit (the community of believers) with the *bodily real* of Christ and/or his descendants. And again, the fact that Christ left his body or bodily descendants behind serves the purpose of undermining the Christian-Pauline narrative of Resurrection: Christ's body was not actually resurrected; 'the true message of Jesus was lost with the Resurrection.' This 'true message' allegedly lies in promoting 'the path of self-determination, as distinct from obedience to the written word': redemption results from the soul's inner journey, not from an act of pardon coming from outside; that is, 'Resurrection' is to be understood as the inner renewal/rebirth of the soul on its journey of self-purification. Although the advocates of this 'return of/in the Real' promote their discovery as the unearthing of the heretic and subversive secret long repressed by the Church as Institution, one could counter this claim with the question: what if this very unearthing of the 'secret' is in the service of 'undoing,' or getting rid of the truly traumatic, subversive core of Christian teaching, the *skandalon* of Resurrection and the retroactive forgiveness of sins—that is, the unique character of the Event of Resurrection?"

27. Ibid., p. 331: "the crucial point is that this New Beginning is possible only through Divine Grace—its impetus must come from *outside*; it is not the result of man's inner effort to overcome his/her limitations and elevate his/her soul above egotistic material interests; in this precise sense, the properly Christian New Beginning is absolutely incompatible with the pagan Gnostic problematic of the 'purification of the soul.' So what is actually at stake in recent New Age pop-Gnostic endeavours to reassert a kind of 'Christ's secret teaching' beneath the official Pauline dogma is the effort to undo the 'Event-Christ,' reducing it to a continuation of the preceding Gnostic lineage."

28. In terms of the above controversy, I would side with Zizek against the neo-Gnostics. But I also have my differences with Zizek, for whom the symbolic order is in fact an empty void. For Zizek, it is precisely the non-existence and emptiness of God that makes him function as the "big Other" in the symbolic chain, although this function begins to wane (as in our postmodern times) when the religious belief system starts to collapse. I do not think Zizek's atheist reading is compatible with my theistic interpretation of this Pauline Christ. I also disagree with Zizek's attempt to evacuate Christ of any carnal or corporeal character, reducing the notion of the "body" to the purely empirical, material order of the historical Jesus. As our examples below of Christ's post-paschal apparitions seek to suggest, the body can take on a more significant "transubstantiated" sense in the context of a resurrected-transfigured Christ. Once

again I find most suggestive here Merleau-Ponty's model of the body-subject as chiasmic crossing-over between visible carnality and invisible transcendence: as double but indivisible. It certainly points to a third way beyond the Zizek-Gnostic alternative extremes: either all spirit or all body! For me, as for the Chalcedonian theologians, the two natures are in one person (*hypostasis*).

29. On this notion of Christ-bread as "monstrance" see Robert Magliola, *On Deconstructing Life-Worlds*, p. 128: "In the Benediction rite, the 'host' of consecrated Bread (through which form God dissimulates)—the *shechinah* of the New Covenant—is 'exposed' and 'exhibited' in a golden receptacle (called the 'monstrance,' from L. *monstrare*, to show). That is, Christ is concealed/revealed: He is self-concealed under the form of Bread, and thus *dissimulates*; yet He is really the Bread, and thus self-reveals. Raising the monstrance on high, the priest moves the host in a giant 'sign of the Cross' over the adoring faithful, blessing them, *marking* them, in and into God's Chiasm." There follows Magliola's own profession of faith in the Chiasmic God: "I am called to Christ's differential way" (p. 129).

4. DESIRING GOD

1. Rabbi Hayyhim de Volozhyn, *Nefesh Hahayyim*, trans. into French as *L'Ame de la vie*, with an introduction by Emmanuel Levinas (Paris: Verdier, 1986), pp. 51–52.

2. Ibid., p. 77. This approximates in some respects to the three parts of Rosenzweig's *Star of Redemption*—Creation, Revelation, Redemption—and to Levinas's related schema of immemorial beginning, ethical relation, and eschatological-messianic peace. In his preface to the French translation of Volozhyn's book, Levinas hails it as an "exceptional" work from one of "the most eminent Talmudists of our epoch and founder of a school which formed the greatest Talmudic masters up to the present time." He goes on to praise it as expressing "the intimate thinking of a rabbinical authority . . . who devoted his days to what he deemed to be the kernel of all Jewish existence: study" (pp. vii–x). Levinas sums up what he considers to be Volozhyn's main thesis as follows: "Voici qu'un livre extraordinaire, attestant une culture rabbinique intégrale et parfaite, consacré à un Dieu qui se veut dépendant des humains, et à des hommes qui, dès lors infiniment responsables, supportent l'univers. Intrigue invraisemblable du religieux. . . . L'être des mondes, l'être des autres que moi, ne pourrait subsister que si Dieu s'associe à cet être, qu'il crée et le récrée. Si Dieu s'en retire, les êtres tombent en néant. Et cependant Dieu tout-puissant—c'est là la grande thèse de Rabbi Hayyim—ne pourrait s'associer à l'être des mondes que si, moi humain, je me conforme aux exigences de la Thora. . . . *Je* répond de l'univers! . . . L'homme est l'âme de tous les 'mondes,' de tous les êtres, de toute vie, comme le Créateur lui-même . . . par la volonté de Dieu lui-même qui n'a pas reculé devant cette égalité avec l'Humain et même devant une certaine subordination à l'Humain. . . . Le règne de Dieu dépend de moi. . . . Le monde est, non pas parce qu'il persévère dans l'être . . . mais parce que, par l'entremise de *l'humain* il peut être justifié dans son être" (pp. viii–x).

3. Ibid., p. 110.

4. Ibid., p. 52.

5. Ibid., pp. 294, 322–325, 363. On the relationship between cosmology, anthropology, and eschatology in the Book of Creation, see Volozhyn, pp. 363, 322, 294. See

also Levinas's interpretation of this relationship as a mark of the primacy of the ethical, in ibid., p. 292 note, citing Levinas, *L'au-delà du verset: Lectures et discours talmudiques* (Paris: Éditions du Minuit, 1982), p. 194.

6. See André LaCocque's argument that the Song of Songs is a subversion of the social, legal, and matrimonial establishment: "The Shulamite," in *Thinking Biblically*, pp. 236ff. See also Karl Barth's eschatological reading of the Song, as interpreted by Ricoeur, in Paul Ricoeur, "The Nuptial Metaphor," p. 298: "Ought we then, in order to bind the poem of innocent love more closely to the myth of a good creation, assign to the Song of Songs an eschatological significance, following Karl Barth, the innocence sung by the Song anticipating the Kingdom to come, like the eschatological banquet? This interpretation clearly stems from a theology . . . where the song of beginning and that of fulfilment frame the history that this theology calls the 'history of salvation.' But one must be wary of reducing such an eschatological reading to some overarching systematic theology whose Grand Narrative would risk depriving the Song of its powerful resolve to 'sing the innocence of love within the heart of everyday life'" (p. 299). For Karl Barth's reading of the Song of Songs in the light of Genesis 2, see his *Church Dogmatics*, vol. 3, pt. 2, trans. G. W. Bromiley (Edinburgh: T. & T. Clark, 1960). My own eschatological reading would be one which rereads the poem hermeneutically, with Ricoeur, such that the good of eros is not totally abolished by the Fall (Genesis 2:23) but lives on as a potential within human creatures which can be revived and celebrated whenever it recovers its human-divine dimension as in the Song. The epithalamium may thus be read, in the light of the face-to-face love of the last days (still to come), as a singing of "on-going rebirth at the very heart of profane everyday existence . . . despite the history of evil and of victimization" (p. 299). But the eschatological reading of the Song is by no means confined to Christian interpretations of the Kingdom; one also finds interesting commentaries by Rabbi Hayyim de Volozhyn (a major influence on Levinas) which go in this direction. See, for example, his suggestion that verse 2:3, comparing the lover/Israel to the "apple tree" of Genesis, be read in terms of the primacy of ethical action (fruit) which transforms the universe into a future kingdom, over mere epistemological understanding (leaves) which is content to interpret the world rather than to change it (*Nefesh Hahayyim*, p. 33 note). See also Rabbi Volozhyn's reading of Song 5:15 as referring to that activity of reading the Torah to the point where our eyes go dark but only to be illuminated in the eschatological kingdom of the future: "Quiconque accepte d'être ténébreux dans ce monde à cause de la Torah!, le Saint béni soit-il l'éclaire de sa splendeur dans le monde futur" (p. 33). The Rabbi goes on to celebrate the holy "flame" or "spark" by means of which we work toward the creation of the eschatological "future world" (p. 39).

7. See Ricoeur's account of certain allegorical readings of the Song of Songs, in "The Nuptial Metaphor," pp. 287–290. The allegorist interpretation sees the beloved either as the people of Israel returning to Yahweh or, in the Christian tradition, as the bride of Christ returning to Christ. Several Talmudic commentaries tend to see the Song as an allegory for the Shepherd leading his lost flock back from Exile to Palestine. According to this reading, the breasts of the beloved symbolize the tribes of the North and South, the "bed of green" symbolizes Palestine covered with olive and fig trees, and the "bed at night" is the bed of Jerusalem. See, for example, A. Robert and R. Tournay, *Le Cantique des Cantiques, traduction et commentaire* (Paris: Gabalda, 1963), pp. 75, 89, 130. By contrast, a rabbinical scholar like Volozhyn reads the Song more in terms of a return to the Torah as a way of enlightenment and revelation. Thus, for instance, he

reads verse 1:4—"The King led me to his chambers"—as referring to the act of being led into the different chambers of the Torah where we may find wisdom (*Nefesh Hahayyim*, p. 201). At the opposite pole, we have "naturalist" readings which reduce the text to a literalist, realist, or fundamentalist account of the songs as an account of "what actually happened." The hermeneutic reading I propose is one which seeks to chart a middle course between these two poles of allegorism and naturalism.

8. Brevard Childs, *Introduction to the Old Testament as Scripture* (Philadelphia: Fortress Press, 1979), p. 575, cited in LaCocque, "The Shulamite," p. 238. By contrast, LaCocque claims that the "entire Song strums on the chord of 'free love,' neither recognized, nor institutionalised" (p. 238). LaCocque argues, for example, that the declaration by the "fiancée" in 8:1–3 would make no sense if the lovers were *already* "legitimately" married; any more than would the discussion in 8:8–12 regarding what should be done when the Shulamite girl "will be of an age to marry" (p. 238). Carnal love, says LaCocque, is not being sung here as a utilitarian means toward some allegorical end, nor as some "mimetic duplication of a primordial divine archetype" (p. 247), nor even as some moralizing marriage hymn. He insists that the Song obstinately "resists any allegorisation" (p. 250). Indeed, so iconoclastic are the songs' references to nature, courtship, eroticism, and luxury—things generally frowned upon by the prophets and sages—that LaCocque surmises that the author penned a romance which became an "embarrassment for her fellow Jews (and, later, for Christians)" (p. 251). We are in a setting of "total irreverence," he concludes, where the poetess speaks in a "naturalistic" language of an erotic passion "untamed" and "clandestine" between a man and a woman (p. 262). Nothing more and nothing less. Far from being an allegory or moral exhortation—where the erotic serves as rhetorical ploy or pretext—this poetess wanted to shock her audience even to the point of alluding to banned Canaanite deities, playfully mocking "divine names" and parodying "sacrosanct oath formulations . . . in the form of conjurations invoking wild animals" (pp. 253, 256, 262). We are even quoted the view that the "flame of Yahweh" is really a reference to a male organ ("the flame symbol represents the penis") (p. 262). But in concluding that this is an utterly irreligious and unbiblical poem, LaCocque tends at times, I believe, toward an excessive literalism almost to the point of an inverse dogmatism. By declaring, for example, that the famous "return" of the Shulamite has "totally lost" its "spiritual meaning" (p. 259), he risks undermining the rich eschatological implications of the Song when reread hermeneutically in the light of Genesis, the Prophets (Isaiah, for example), or the later Christian promise of a "redeemed eros." Indeed, it is hard to see how LaCocque's exegetical "naturalist" commentary can be squared with Ricoeur's hermeneutic reading which follows in the same volume (see "The Nuptial Metaphor," pp. 296–303).

9. LaCocque, "The Shulamite," p. 243. See also Michael Fox, *The Song of Songs and the Ancient Egyptian Love Songs* (Madison: University of Wisconsin Press, 1985), p. 309: "All events are narrated from her point of view, though not always in her voice, whereas from the boy's angle of vision we know little besides how he sees her."

10. See Michael Fox, *The Song of Songs and the Ancient Egyptian Love Songs*, and LaCocque, "The Shulamite," pp. 243ff. Neither Fox nor LaCocque reads this passage, as I do, in the eschatological light of an ultimate nuptial reconciliation between traditional enemies, Israel and Egypt, Jew and Gentile, and other adversarial brothers. This is, of course, only one of many readings possible within the semantic surplus of this text as hermeneutically re-read and "re-used" throughout the history of its constant reinterpretation and re-enactment. See Ricoeur, "The Nuptial Metaphor," pp. 291ff.

11. LaCocque, "The Shulamite," p. 245.

12. Ibid., 253.

13. Ibid., pp. 259–262.

14. See Paul Ricoeur, "From 'I am who I am' to 'God is love': An Essay in Biblical Hermeneutics," cited in LaCocque, "The Shulamite," p. 263. Here Ricoeur suggests that the claim in 1 John that "God is love" provokes a "surplus of meaning" in both the terms God and love. By virtue of this statement "we think more about God and about love." In "The Nuptial Metaphor," Ricoeur makes much of the hermeneutic-linguistic-semantic role of the Song as a poetic reworking and augmentation of meaning, opening the poem up to multiple intertextual possibilities of recital and indeed re-enactment (in liturgy, baptismal rites, and sexual acts). "The poetic sublimation at the very heart of the erotic removes the need for contortions meant to desexualize the reference. That it should be poetically displaced is sufficient. And it is in this way that the same meta-phorical network, once freed of every realist attachment through the unique virtue of the song, is made available for other investments and disinvestments" (p. 274). And so Ricoeur goes on to ask why what is "demetaphorized" cannot be "remetaphorized" on the basis of a "general metaphorization of the nuptial": for example, in terms of an intertexual interpretation of the Song in dialogue with other texts of the biblical and scriptural traditions (p. 276). This is precisely what Ricoeur himself proposes in the third part of his essay "The Nuptial Metaphor" (pp. 295–303). Rabbi Volozhyn appears to propose something rather similar when he suggests that the metaphors of fecundity, fruition, and flourishing in the Song refer not only to the richness of human-divine love but also to the multiple levels of meaning which flourish and proliferate within the sacred texts themselves, especially when read intertextually or rabbinically, in terms of one another (pp. 191–196). On this hermeneutic function of metaphorical multiplicity and multiplication, see also note 15 immediately below.

15. Rabbi Aquiba, *Tosephta Sanhedrin* 12:10, cited in LaCocque, "The Shula-mite," p. 263. See also LaCocque, p. 262: "Love, love 'pure and simple,' love faithful and wholly integrated, is a reflection of the covenant between the divine and the human. It is probably in this sense that we should read Song 8:6 where love is compared to a 'flame of Yah (weh).' The expression is ambiguous. It can just indicate a superlative, but in the subversive language of the author, it indicates precisely that human love reflects divine love." It is in this context that LaCocque quotes Andrew Greeley's claim that the woman author is speaking of the "(always potent) male organ of Yhwh (the flame symbol represents the penis), but, as it were, appropriating it for herself" (Andrew Greeley and Jacob Neusner, *The Bible and Us: A Priest and a Rabbi Read Scripture Together* [New York: Warner Books, 1990], p. 35). See also A. S. Herbert 's claim that the Song suggests that natural love, once freed from its sinful inclinations, can be hailed as the "least inadequate type of love of man for God and God for man" ("The Song of Songs," in *Peake's Commentary on the Bible*, ed. Matthew Black and H. H. Rowley [London: T. Nelson, 1962], p. 469). See equally radical readings of the Song of Songs by Levinas's spiritual mentor, Rabbi Hayyim de Volozhyn, in *Nefesh Hahayyim*, espe-cially pp. 50–53, 77, 92–93, 191–195, 110, 152, 201, 217, 291: for example: "le rapport idéal entre le mâle et la femelle est compris comme une quête de la fraternité, c-à-d un amour parfaitement reciproque: unité essentielle, sans aucune sujetion." Cf. Robert and Tournay, *Le Cantique des Cantiques*, 4:9, 12; 5:1; 8:1. See also Ricoeur's brilliant reading of this Song of Eros in terms of an "intersecting metaphor," which contrary to

the anti-carnal and anti-phenomenological readings of "Platonizing allegorism" (which reduce the sensible to the spiritual-intelligible) celebrates divine and human desire in terms of a "mutual belonging of equal partners to each other" (pp. 301–302). It is, he states, "the power of love to be able to move in both senses along the ascending and descending spiral of metaphor, allowing in this way for every level of the emotional investment of love to signify, to intersignify every other level" (p. 302). For metaphor is precisely that power of "seeing as" and "saying as" which enables us to suggest that human desire both *is* and *is not* like divine desire. It is also one of the virtues of metaphorical language—this metaphorical function of seeing-saying-as produces multiple layers of equivalences and correspondences throughout the text, evident in the Song's various comparisons between, for example, amorous bodies and landscapes, fruits, and animals; the Shulamite and censored fiancée, shepherdess, or Israel itself; the male lover and shepherd, king, or Yahweh. And we may extrapolate from these in turn different kinds of proportional analogy, most obviously: the shepherdess is to the shepherd as Israel is to Yahweh or (according to some Christian commentators) as the Church is to Christ and so on. It is, moreover, one of the key virtues of such metaphorical language to keep open the possibility of different hermeneutic reinterpretations of the Song's various "figures of love" down through the ages. These might range from those readings of the Song in the light of Genesis, Exodus, or the Prophets to those stemming from later rabbinical debates, patristic commentaries, and medieval or mystical theologies, not to mention modern or postmodern readings from a feminist, critical-historical, liberationist, psychoanalytic, or deconstructive perspective. Ricoeur wonders finally if what he calls the "nuptial" is not the "virtual or real point of intersection where these figures of love all cross?" And he concludes that if this indeed be the case, "may we not then also say that the nuptial as such is an effect of reading, issuing from the intersecting of texts, only because it is the hidden root, the forgotten root of the great metaphorical play that makes all the figures of love refer to one another? . . . Let us gather those sparks of meaning that fly up at their points of friction" (p. 303). I borrow this suggestive image of intersecting texts igniting each other in my own concluding paragraph to this chapter below.

16. Julia Kristeva, *Tales of Love*, trans. Leon S. Roudiez (New York: Columbia University Press, 1987), p. 80.

17. Ibid.

18. Ibid.

19. Ibid.

20. Ibid., pp. 94–95.

21. Ibid., p. 95. See also Paul Ricoeur, "The Nuptial Metaphor," p. 272: "When the nuptial is invested in the erotic, the flesh is soul and the soul is flesh." And he adds that the "inclusion of the body itself within the overall metaphorical play of the poem" (p. 274) makes for a constant "double entendre," requiring an equally double or multiple reading.

22. See Ricoeur on the indetermination and proliferation of metaphorical meaning in the Song, in "The Nuptial Metaphor," pp. 268–270.

23. Ricoeur, "The Nuptial Metaphor," p. 269: "Is it a question, for example, in 1:6–8 of shepherd and a shepherdess, or in 1:4 and 3:2 and 11 of a king and a woman who might be a townswoman, or of a peasant in 1:12–14 and 7:6 and 13? What is more, the dialogue is rendered even more complex by internal explicit and implicit quota-

tions. Nor is it sure that certain scenes are not dreamed or that they might consist of dreams. . . . These features of indetermination are incontestably favorable to the freeing of the nuptial held in reserve within the erotic."

24. Ibid., p. 270.

25. Ibid., pp. 271 and 274–275.

26. Kristeva, *Tales of Love*, p. 97.

27. Ibid., p. 96.

28. Ibid., p. 98.

29. Ibid., p. 98.

30. Emmanuel Levinas, *Totality and Infinity*; Jacques Derrida, "Sauf le nom," in *On the Name*, originally published as *Sauf le nom* (Paris: Galilée, 1993).

31. See my analysis of the *yezer hara* and its relation to desire in the first chapter of *The Wake of Imagination*, pp. 37–53, and in Richard Kearney and Ghislain Lafont, *Il Desiderio e Dio* (Milan: San Paolo, 1997), pp. 2–10.

32. Augustine, *Confessions*, trans. R. Pine-Coffin (New York: Penguin, 1961), 174–180/245–247. See commentary by Garry Wills, *Saint Augustine* (New York: Viking, 1999), p. 21: "*Amicitia* comes from the verb for love (*amo*), and Augustine always referred back to Cicero's definition of it: 'A union at the divine and human level effected by benevolence and love' (*Answer to Skeptics* 3.13). . . . '[L]oving love' is not a dismissive term for adolescent infatuation. It is the very definition of God, and 'whoever loves God must also love love' (Trin 8.12)." Or again, p. 93: "His trinitarian theology would be built on an understanding of God's free will as 'loving love' (*amans amorem*): 'Love is the act of a lover *and* the love given the loved person. It is a trinity: the lover, the loved person, and love itself' (Trin 8.14)."

33. See John van Buren, *The Young Heidegger*, pp. 189ff.

34. See Saint Paul, "We live by faith, not by what is seen. We consider not the seen but the unseen" (Romans 8:25; 1 Corinthians 5:7, 4:18). See also van Buren's commentary on the influence of this Pauline eschatology on the early thinking of Martin Heidegger, *The Young Heidegger*, pp. 179ff.

35. We must be ready, Scripture tells us, "for the Son of Man is coming at an unexpected hour" (Matthew 24). See van Buren, *The Young Heidegger*, p. 190: "The Coming will arrive only in the Kairos, the moment, the 'fullness of time' (*BZ* 6). The time and content of this arrival are not objectively available in advance to be expected (*erwartet*), represented, and calculated, but rather are to be determined only out of the Kairos itself which will happen with 'suddenness.' . . . The situation of the parousio-kairological temporalizing of the believer/God relation is thus a futural Second Coming (*Wiederkunft*) that is textured by a having-been and that will be determined only out of the incalculable eye-opening moment of arrival."

36. Emmanuel Levinas, *Totality and Infinity*, p. 23. My use of this archaeology/teleology distinction is derived from Paul Ricoeur, *Freud and Philosophy: An Essay on Interpretation*, trans. Denis Savage (New Haven, Conn.: Yale University Press, 1970). Although Levinas does not acknowledge any direct debt to the Song of Songs in his reading of desire and love in *Totality and Infinity*, it is reasonable to suppose that he was influenced by Rabbi Hayyim de Volozhyn's comments on the Song in *Nefesh Hahayyim* (see full citation in note 1 above), a text which had a profoundly formative impact on Levinas as we know from his Talmudic commentaries.

37. Ibid., p. 23.

38. In his *Introduction to the Reading of Hegel* (ed. Allan Bloom, trans. James H.

Nichols, Jr. [New York: Basic Books, 1969]), Alexander Kojève describes the notion of desire-as-lack as follows: "The I of desire is an emptiness greedy for content; an emptiness that wants to be filled by what is full, to be filled by emptying this fulness, to put oneself—once it is filled—in place of this fulness, to occupy with its fulness the emptiness caused by overcoming the fulness that was not its own" (p. 38).

39. Levinas, *Totality and Infinity*, pp. 33–34. See my reading of Levinas's eschatological notion of desire in Richard Kearney and Ghislain Lafont, *Il Desiderio e Dio*. In this book, I also contrasted this Levinasian notion to the Hegelian-Kojévian reading of desire which I call "ontological-historical."

40. Ibid., p. 34.

41. Ibid. p. 35. Such desire is also, for Levinas, the possibility of freedom—freedom *from* the reign of hunger and fear, dominion and power; freedom *for* the desire of the absolute other whose trace is the face of this other before me.

42. Levinas, *De Dieu qui vient à l'idée*, p. 87.

43. Levinas, *Totality and Infinity*, p. 254.

44. Ibid., p. 255. See my chapter "Levinas and the Ethics of Imagining," in Richard Kearney, *Poetics of Modernity: Toward a Hermeneutic Imagination* (Atlantic Highlands, N.J.: Humanities Press, 1995), pp. 108–117; and also my dialogue with Levinas, "Ethics of the Infinite," in my *Dialogues with Contemporary Continental Thinkers*, pp. 47–70, reprinted in Kearney, *States of Mind*, pp. 177–199.

45. Emmanuel Levinas, *Entre nous* (Paris: Grasset, 1991), pp. 30–31.

46. Levinas, *Totality and Infinity*, p. 258.

47. Ibid.

48. Levinas, *Totality and Infinity*, p. 263.

49. Ibid., p. 265.

50. Ibid., p. 266.

51. Ibid.

52. Ibid., p. 272.

53. Ibid.

54. Ibid., pp. 276–277.

55. Ibid., p. 269.

56. Ibid., p. 272.

57. Ibid., p. 285. See how Levinas redefines this messianic structure of desire as "prayer" in *L'au-delà du verset*, p. 197: "On peut même se demander . . . si la prière, avant d'être le dire d'un dit, n'est pas une façon d'invoquer ou de rechercher ou de désirer, irréductible à toute intentionnalité apophantique ou doxique. . . .; on peut se demander si la prière n'est pas une façon de rechercher ce qui ne peut entrer dans aucune relation comme terme et où nous n'aurions donc à faire qu'à une quasi-référence. . . . Quasi-référence à un Dieu innommable. . . . On peut pousser l'audace jusqu'à demander si l'intentionnalité n'est pas déjà dérivée de la prière qui serait l'originaire penser-à-l'absent."

58. Ibid., p. 285.

59. John Caputo, "Hyperbolic Justice," in *Demythologizing Heidegger* (Bloomington: Indiana University Press, 1993), pp. 200–201.

60. Emmanuel Levinas, *Autrement qu'être*, p. 181. The passage in question reads: "Le sujet dans la responsabilité s'aliène dans le tréfonds de son identité d'une aliénation qui ne vide pas le Même de son identité, mais l'y astreint, d'une assignation irrécusable, s'y astreint comme personne où personne ne saurait le remplacer. L'unicité, hors

concept, psychisme comme grain de folie, le psychisme déjà psychose, non pas un Moi, mais moi sous assignation. Assignation à identité pour la réponse de la responsabilité dans l'impossibilité de se faire remplacer sans carence. A ce commandement tendu sans relâche, ne peut répondre que 'me voici' ou le pronom 'je' est à l'accusatif, décliné avant toute déclinaison, possédé par l'autre, malade, identitique. Me voici—dire de l'inspiration qui n'est ni le don de belles paroles, ni de chants. Astriction au *donner*, aux mains pleines, et, par conséquent, à la corporité" (pp. 180–181). The word "malade" carries a footnote which refers us to line 5:8 of the Song of Songs. In short, the allusion to the Song is indirect in the text itself (no full citation or quotation marks) and only acknowledged as such in the footnote.

61. Jacques Derrida, "En ce moment même dans cet ouvrage me voici," in *Psyché*, pp. 167ff. See also Derrida's tantalizing comments on the "desire of God" in the Pseudo-Dionysius in "Comment ne pas parler," also in *Psyché*, pp. 571ff.

62. Derrida, *Psyché*, pp. 168–169. Derrida comments as follows about the accusative nature of the desiring self in Levinas's reading: "Ce n'est pas le supposé signataire de l'ouvrage, E.L., qui dit 'Me Voici,' moi présentement. Il *cite* un 'me voici,' il thématise le non-thématisable. . . . Mais au-delà du *Cantique des Cantiques* . . . la citation de quiconque dirait 'me voici' doit marquer *cette* extradition où la responsabilité pour l'autre me livre à l'autre. Aucune marque grammaticale en tant que telle, aucune langue, aucun contexte ne suffiront à le déterminer. Cette citation-présente qui, en tant que citation, paraît effacer l'événement présent d'un 'me voici' irremplaçable, elle vient aussi *pour dire* que dans 'me voici' le Moi ne se présente plus comme un sujet présent à soi, se faisant présent à soi de soi-même (je-me): il est décliné, avant toute déclinaison, à l'accusatif' . . ." (ibid., p. 168).

63. Ibid., p. 169. Derrida elaborates on this point thus: "La négociation thématise ce qui ne se laise pas thématiser; et dans le trajet même de cette transaction, elle force la langue à contracter avec l'étranger, avec ce qu'elle ne peut que s'incorporer sans se l'assimiler. . . . La langue interdictrice est interdite mais elle continue à parler, elle n'en peut mais, elle ne peut plus que continuer étrangement à s'interrompre, interloquée par ce qui la traverse d'un seul pas, l'entraîne ensuite après lui tout en la laissant sur place. D'où la fonction essentielle d'une citation, sa mise en oeuvre singulière qui consiste, en citant l'irrécitable, à accuser la langue, à la citer tout entière à comparaître à *la fois* comme témoin et comme accusée dans ses limites" (ibid., p. 129).

64. Ibid., p. 169.

65. Derrida, *On the Name*, p. 80.

66. Jacques Derrida, *Specters of Marx*, pp. 167–170.

67. Derrida, *On the Name*, p. 36.

68. Ibid., pp. 35–36.

69. Ibid., p. 35. When Derrida speaks of atheism, we must, of course, take it with a pinch of fine salt, while still taking him at his word. In *On the Name* (p. 35), Derrida alerts us to the porous boundaries between theism and atheism. He notes, for example, that the apophasis of certain kinds of negative theology "at times so resembles a profession of atheism as to be mistaken for it." He goes on to observe that "like a certain mysticism, apophatic discourse has always been suspected of atheism" (citing the example of Angelus Silesius suspected by Leibniz). Derrida then introduces the rather startling idea that if apophasis inclines almost toward atheism, might it not be the case that, on the other hand, "the extreme and most consequent forms of declared atheism will have always testified to the most intense desire of God" (p. 36). On foot of this

arresting hypothesis, Derrida distinguishes between two kinds of desire *of God* (his italics): (1) the notion of desire at its most "insatiable" (therefore as lack seeking fulfillment) "according to the history and the event of its manifestation or the secret of its nonmanifestation" (presumably in the history of the revealed monotheistic "messianisms," for example) and (2) another voice of apophasis which seems foreign to every "anthropotheomorphic form of desire." Of this second desire—beyond desire—he writes: "But isn't it proper to desire to carry with it its own proper suspension, the death or the phantom of desire? To go toward the absolute other, isn't that the extreme tension of a desire that tries thereby to renounce its own proper momentum, its own movement of appropriation?" (p. 37). On the basis of this distinction, Derrida acknowledges the equivocal double genitive operative in the "desire *of* God"—"does it come from God in us, from God for us, from us for God?" (p. 37) And this, in turn, leads on to the crucial—and for Derrida ultimately unanswerable question—to *whom* is the discourse of the desire of God addressed? In other words, "if atheism, like apophatic theology, testifies to the desire of God, if it avows, confesses, or indirectly signifies, as in a symptom, the desire of God, in the presence of *whom* does it do this?" (p. 37; my italics). In short, "who speaks to whom?" (p. 37). It is perhaps telling that Derrida proceeds, having posed this impossible question, to analyze the role of testimony, revelation, confession, memory, and time in Dionysius and Augustine (who "haunts certain landscapes of apophatic mysticism," p. 40). See Derrida's remarks on Dionysius's theory of divine *eros* or "loving desire" in the *Divine Names* in note 75 below.

70. Derrida, *Given Time, I: Counterfeit Money*, trans. Peggy Kamuf (Chicago: University of Chicago Press, 1992), pp. 21–22.

71. Derrida, *Memoirs of the Blind*, p. 36.

72. Ibid., p. 37. Where Levinas finds himself in contradiction with himself on the question of the identity of the "other"—on the one hand pleading ignorance regarding the ethical origin of the other, on the other identifying it as God; on the one hand suggesting that the other is a singular and unique human other, on the other, that he/she is a trace of the divine absolute—Derrida turns this very undecidability into a deconstructive "aporia." For Derrida, desire of God *is* impossible for the simple reason that we can never tell if the desired one is God or not. Elsewhere—*Given Time*, p. 5—Derrida equates desire with a *desire to give* (that which one does not have) which is *impossible*. Hence desire becomes the desire of the impossible. And this resurfaces, later in the same text, as the desire to exit from the economy of the circle—that is, of "time as a circle" (p. 8). Once again, Derrida leaves us with an impossible question: "Why would one desire, along with the gift, if there is any, the exit? Why desire the gift and why desire to interrupt the circulation of the circle? Why wish to get out of it (*en sortir*)?" (p. 8).

73. Derrida, *Archive Fever: A Freudian Impression*, trans. Eric Prenowitz (Chicago: University of Chicago Press, 1996), p. 52.

74. John Caputo, *Prayers and Tears of Jacques Derrida*, pp. 364–365. " 'Pure presence' is, after all, what Derrida calls 'absolute evil'—absolute life, fully present life, the one that does not know death and does not want to hear about it" (*Specters of Marx*, p. 175).

75. See Derrida on Dionysius's tantalizing remarks on divine eros in "Comment ne pas parler," in *Psyché*, p. 571: "Ce Bien inspire toute une érotique, mais Deny nous prévient: il faut éviter de prendre le mot *erôs* sans en éclairer ici le sens, l'intention. Il faut toujours partir du sens intentionnel et non de la verbalité (*Noms Divins*, 708 b c,

pp. 104–105). '. . . qu'on n'imagine pas que nous allions contre l'Ecriture en vénérant ce vocable de désir amoureux (*erôs*)' (*ibid.*) . . . 'Il a même paru à certains de nos auteurs sacrés que 'désir amoureux' (*erôs*) est un terme plus digne de Dieu qu''amour charitable' (*agapè*). Car le divin Ignace a écrit: 'C'est l'objet de mon désir amoureux qu'ils ont mis en croix' (709 a b, p. 106). Les saints théologienes attribuent la même valeur, la même puissance d'unification et de rassemblement à *erôs* et à *agapé*, ce que la foule comprend mal, qui assigne le désir au corps, au partage, au morcellement (*ibid*). En Dieu, le désir est à la fois extatique, jaloux et condescendant (712 a et suiv.) Cette érotique conduit et reconduit donc au Bien, circulairement, c-à-d vers ce qui 'se situe fort au-delà de l'être considéré en soi et du non-être (716 d, p. 111).'"

76. Caputo, "Hyperbolic Justice," pp. 200–201.

77. Ibid., p. 3. See also the contrasting position of Jean-Luc Marion in "In the Name: How to Avoid Speaking of 'Negative Theology,'" in *God, the Gift, and Postmodernism*, pp. 20–42. Marion argues that negative theology is less onto-theological than Derrida supposes. Citing Dionysius's claim in *The Divine Names* (VII, I, 865c) that "what is praised multiply under multiple names is said to be anonymous and ineffable by the Scriptures," Marion suggests that this opens a "third way" beyond the simple affirmation and negation of names, a "beyond" where words assume a purely pragmatic function—"au-delà de tout nom et de toute dénégation de nom . . . la parole ne dit pas plus qu'elle ne nie—elle agit en se reportant à Celui qu'elle dé-nomme" (pp. 9–10). As such, the "hyper" (beyond) of negative theology "rétablit ni l'essence, ni la connaissance, mais les transgresse en vue d'une louange de ce qui précède et rend possible toute essence" (p. 10). Which is another way of saying that the "hyper" of essence is in fact an otherwise than essence or being (i.e., beyond onto-theology understood as a metaphysics of presence). And all that is thus considered beyond or other than being— as non-being and non-presence—operates, for Dionysius (and Marion)—according to the modality of desire: "s'il est permis d'ainsi parler, même le non-étant désire le bien qui se trouve au-dessus de tous les étants . . . même le non-étant participe du beau et du bien . . . tous les étants (. . .) et tous les non-étants se trouvent dans le beau et le bon sur un mode qui dépasse l'essence (*hyperousias*)" (*Divine Names*, IV, 3, 697a; IV, 7, 704b; IV, 10, 705d). Marion derives the following insight into the "desire of God" from this position: "L'horizon de l'être reste régional, parce qu'il laisse par définition hors de lui les non-étants. Or il est toujours possible de les prendre en considération, puisqu'ils se réfèrent au bien, même en n'étant pas, sur le mode du '*désir.*' Donc la première (et dernière) des dénominations de Dieu devra se tirer de l'horizon du bien, plutôt que de celui de l'être, étant entendu que même cette dé-nomination n'atteint pas Dieu en propre, ni au propre" (p. 15). Even Aquinas had this to say, as negative theologian, about the hyper-link between love-desire and God-goodness: "God, because he is infinite, cannot be captured in any way. . . . But he who loves more, because he desires more, will see God more perfectly and be more happy" (*Summa Theologiae* 1.129.6). See also Aquinas's discussion of desire and the formula associated with Dionysius: "*bonum est diffusivum sui.*" Marion develops this "God beyond being" (*Dieu sans l'être*) into a "theology of absence" which articulates itself as a "pragmatics of the word" which attests to the God-Good "beyond being" by an action of listening/attention and desire/ love (pp. 16, 22). But if the "third way" of de-nomination safeguards God "beyond every proper name," it also acknowledges the mystery of God's omnipresence in the world— "Dieu se connaît en toutes choses et aussi à part de toutes choses. Dieu se connaît par connaissance et aussi par inconnaissance" (*Divine Names* VII, 3, 872a). Thus while

respecting the invisibility and inaccessibility of God—according to the scriptural ordinance that no one can see the face of God (John 1:18; Exodus 32:23)—Marion accepts that we nonetheless need some kind of vision, even if (as Gregory of Nyssa realized) such "seeing is to be found in non-seeing" (*Vie de Moïse* II, 163). Even negative theology then has recourse to some kind of narrative imagination—albeit in the modality of *quasi* and *sicut*. So that when Paul acknowledges that God reveals himself "not only in [his] presence but much in his absence" (Philippians 2:12), he does not deny the necessity—and desirability—of *some kind of presence*, albeit a *quasi*-presence. But Marion himself stops short of embracing the full consequences of this position. Rather than looking to hermeneutic retrievals and reimaginings of biblical narratives and stories—the lives of prophets and apostles, of saints and martyrs (not to mention Abraham, Moses, Jacob, and Jesus)—Marion holds fast (1) to the *viae negativae* of the great mystical theologians (Dionysius, Athanasius, Basil, Gregory of Nyssa) and (2) to the mystical-phenomenological intuition of the "saturated phenomenon" whose very excess can be neither seen, known, spoken, or imagined, and whose very superabundance surpasses predication and nomination. It is perhaps here, indeed, that both Derrida's deconstruction and Marion's theology of absence-distance tend in their agreed repudiation of the "metaphysics of presence"—to underestimate the need for some kind of critical discernment—based on informed judgment, hermeneutic memory, narrative imagination, and rational discrimination. Their common reaction to the excesses of onto-theology might be said to entail its own form of excess—an excess of absence answering to the excess of presence. Thus while Marion demarcates his own position from the atheistic stance of Derrida's deconstruction—by stating that the donating intuition "[ne] ferait défaut auquel cas on pourrait bien rapprocher la théologie négative de l'athéisme ou la mettre en concurrence avec la déconstruction" (p. 25)—he nonetheless pushes the intuition of divine saturation to the point of sheer incomprehensibility and irrationalism—"l'excès d'intuition s'accomplit sous la figure de la stupeur, voire de la terreur que l'incompréhensibilité nous impose" (p. 26). For the theist Marion, no less than for the atheist Derrida, we are left with the dilemma of "holy madness," how to judge between true and false prophets, between good and evil ghosts, between holy and unholy messiahs.

78. Derrida, *Given Time*, pp. 21–22.

79. Caputo, *Prayers and Tears of Jacques Derrida*, p. 165. While Caputo concedes that "deconstruction and a certain religion have both been scared by the same (messianic) ghost," he seems to prefer Derrida's response to that of the revealed eschatological messianisms: "We cannot forget that the distinction between the messianic and the concrete messianisms is always a political distinction for Derrida, one that spells the *difference between war and peace*, the war that Christianity has waged relentlessly on Judaism, and all the wars among the determinate messianisms. That is perhaps the point of this distinction in the first place. For the history of Western politics, and of the relations between the West and the Middle East is and has been, from time immemorial, a history of wars waged in the name of the several messianisms, the incessant battle to take Mount Moriah. The *concrete messianisms have always meant war, while the meaning of the messianic is, or should be, shalom, pax.* . . . What room is there, in this Christian messianic eschatology, for Jews and Arabs, for Africans and immigrants, for *Gastarbeiter* and native populations?" (pp. 190–191; my italics). The choice between the messianic and messianism is clear for Caputo—peace or war.

80. John Caputo outlines the conundrum thus: "Derrida, 'who rightly passes for

an atheist,' is an atheist who has his own God, and who loves the name of God, loves that 'event,' and what 'takes place' or eventuates in that good name. He has no desire (it goes against *everything* that deconstruction is and desires), to prevent the event of that 'invention' " (p. 4). Indeed, deconstruction is nothing other than this desire of invention itself. "Getting ready for the 'invention' of the other, covenanting (*con-venire*) with its in-coming (*in-venire*), initialing a pact with the impossible, sticking to the promise of inalterable alterity, *tout autre*—that, says Derrida, 'is what I call deconstruction' (*Psy*, p. 53/RDR, p. 56). That is his passion" (*Prayers and Tears of Jacques Derrida*, p. 4). This insistence on the irreducible alterity and unpredictability of the Messiah may help explain why it is that the first to declare Jesus as Messiah are not his apostles (as one would expect) but *demons!* Jesus insists, tellingly, that they remain silent about his identity, as in Luke 4, for example: "In the synagogue there was a man who had the spirit of an unclean demon, and he cried out with a loud voice, 'Let us alone! What have you to do with us, Jesus of Nazareth? Have you come to destroy us? I know who you are, the Holy one of God.' But Jesus rebuked him, saying, 'Be silent and come out of him!' " (Luke 4:31–36). See also Luke 4:40–42: "Demons also came out of many, shouting: 'You are the Son of God!' But he rebuked them and would not allow them to speak, because they knew that he was the Messiah." How is it that holy and unholy spirits seem to recognize each other so immediately in this way? Are the Scriptures actually suggesting that the premature desire to identify and name the Messiah is in fact demonic? That reserve, discretion, and silence (or what Kierkegaard called the "indirect communication" of going "incognito") are more appropriate responses to the kerygma of the Messiah? See also Derrida, *Points . . . : Interviews, 1974–1994*, ed. Elisabeth Weber, trans. Peggy Kamuf and others (Stanford, Calif.: Stanford University Press, 1995), p. 41.

81. Derrida, *On the Name*, p. 74. This is why Derrida's religion is a "religion without religion" (*Given Time*, p. 49)—which means, in his own words, a religion "sans vision, sans vérité, sans révélation" ("On a Newly Arisen Apocalyptic Tone in Philosophy," in *Raising the Tone of Philosophy: Late Essays by Emmanuel Kant, Transformative Critique by Jacques Derrida*, ed. Peter Fenves [Baltimore: Johns Hopkins University Press, 1993], p. 167). As such, the "come" of deconstructive desire is a response to a plural and quasi-apocalyptic summons (*envois*) which addresses without message and without destination, without sender or decidable addressee, without last judgment, without any other eschatology than the tone of the "viens" (ibid.). Caputo reads this passage—correctly, I believe—as Derrida's way of distinguishing deconstruction's "apocalypse *sans* apocalypse" from any specific apocalypse of the Judeo-Christian-Islamic kind: "This apocalypse without any vision, verity or un-veiling, this apocalypse *sans* apocalypse, is not John's, which calls determinately and identifiably for Adon Yeshoua. . . . This apocalypse without apocalypse belongs to and opens up a messianic time without any messianisms, without Yeshoua or any other identifiable Messiah, Jewish, Christian, Islamic. . . . [As 'aleatory errance'] it moves by chance, not by a logic, not even a Heideggerian eschato-logic, whose *Spiel* is that the *Geschick*, gathering itself together in the unity of a *legein*, drives itself into an end-time, and then flips into another beginning" (*Prayers and Tears of Jacques Derrida*, pp. 99–100).

82. Ibid., p. 73.

83. Derrida, *Given Time*, p. 71.

84. John Caputo, *Prayers and Tears of Jacques Derrida*, p. 52.

85. In fairness, we should also take account here of Derrida's reference to "love" in

Sauf le nom (Paris: Galilée, 1993), p. 24, as the "infinite renunciation which in a certain way *gives itself back to the impossible.*"

86. *Who* is it I desire when I desire my God? *Who* comes when the other comes— unexpectedly and unpredictably like a thief in the night? Surely the first question for any vigilant and invigilating messiah is—"*Who* do you say that I am?" It is also worth recalling here that in the very passage where Saint Paul invokes the Lord coming like a thief in the night, he calls for sober and en-lightened vigilance: "But you, beloved, are not in darkness, for that day to surprise you like a thief; for you are children of light and children of the day; we are not of the night or of darkness. . . . So, let us keep awake and be sober" (1 Thessalonians 5).

87. Derrida, "Hospitality, Justice, and Responsibility" (UCD Round Table), in *Questioning Ethics.*

88. Ibid.

89. Derrida, "Foi et savoir: Les deux sources de la religion aux limites de la simple raison," in *La Religion,* ed. Jacques Derrida and Gianni Vattimo (Paris: Éditions du Seuil, 1996), p. 31.

90. Caputo, *Prayers and Tears of Jacques Derrida,* p. 73. One of the main reasons why Derrida insists—hyperbolically—that "*tout autre est tout autre*" is, Caputo argues, to safeguard the messianic from being reduced to any single face or faith, for that would imply a sectarian God who takes the side of one belief against others. (Caputo's think-ing here is remarkably similar to similar scruples expressed by Heidegger in his "scepti-cal" and "deconstructive" refusal to embrace a specifically Catholic, or indeed Chris-tian, worldview for fear it would limit our openness to what is still to come. See John van Buren, *Young Heidegger,* pp. 337–340.) That is why for deconstruction the Messiah has many faces and never actually comes. Deconstruction thus respects the "desire of God" by keeping desire constantly alive, primed for the incessant in-coming and in-vention of the other. But we might reply to Caputo here that if it is true that the Messiah may come at every instant, this does not mean that whatever/whoever comes in every instant is messianic. If we refuse to take sides or to judge—according to some sort of ethical criteria however approximative—that some others are less genuinely messianic than others, do we leave ourselves with any answer to those manic-psychotic visionaries who claim to hear the voice of God calling them to commit acts of cleansing sacrifice— David Koresh, Jim Jones, Peter Sutcliffe, Charles Manson? Or, more complex still, have we any answer to those official, eminently law-abiding inquisitors who executed heretics (Christ, Stephen, Giordano Bruno, Joan of Arc, Jean Huys) out of some mistaken obedience to what they believed was a messianic voice calling to them in the night? These are puzzling and troubling questions indeed, provoked and addressed (if not resolved) by the scrupulous work of thinkers like Caputo and Derrida himself, both of whom remain fully attentive to these radical problems. See especially Caputo's spirited and sophisticated responses to the charge that deconstruction lacks "criteria" to judge between just and unjust others, in *Modernity and Its Discontents* ed. James L. Marsh, John D. Caputo, and Merold Westphal (New York: Fordham University Press, 1992), pp. 18–22, 127–130, 178–194. In "Postscript" to *Poetics of Modernity* (1995) and "Epilogue" to the second edition of *Poetics of Imagining: Modern to Postmodern* (New York: Fordham University Press, 1998), I continue my hermeneutic exchange with deconstruction on this vexed issue of ethical criteria, judgment, and discernment. For making this issue a live and urgent one, I am indebted to the recent work of Caputo and Derrida.

91. Derrida, "Shibboleth: For Paul Celan," trans. J. Vilner, in *Word Traces*, pp. 102–103. One must recall here, however, that in his repeated efforts to show that "deconstruction is justice" (i.e., ethical), Derrida himself does tend to identify the messianic "other" who calls and comes as *victim* (see the chapter "Wears and Tears" in *Specters of Marx*) rather than just *any* other at all (e.g., oppressors and executioners). Caputo puts the dilemma thus: "The mistake is to think that deconstruction cannot oppose cruelty or oppression because then it could be 'excluding' or 'marginalizing' someone, viz. the oppressors. [That] the homicidal rapist, the plunderer, a violent military, all that is just the 'Other' and deconstruction recommends openness to the Other." The error here, according to Caputo, is to construe deconstruction in an excessively "formal" sense, thereby paying no attention to the "substantive merits" of what kind of power is in place (i.e., just or unjust, democratic or totalitarian). "Exclusion and marginalization," Caputo concludes, "are never merely formal ideas (but) always have to do with damaged lives and disasters. . . . People who produce victims are not the 'Other' to whom we owe everything" (*Against Ethics* [Bloomington: Indiana University Press, 1993], p. 119). But the problem for deconstruction is perhaps precisely that its very character *is* more "formal" than "substantive," as witnessed in Derrida's repeated denials that deconstruction is a program dealing with how we should behave or what we should do in our everyday world of "substantive" practices and decisions. (Indeed, it could be argued that Levinas is less "formal" than Derrida to the extent that he does identify the "Other" in specifically biblical allusions to "the widow, the orphan, the stranger"). It is true, of course, that Derrida holds that the "other" is always embedded in a specific language, history, or society as bearer of a "proper name" with his/her unique perspective of the "here, now, at this point," and so on. But surely it is not simply the singularity and uniqueness of every "other" (with his/her proper name and perspective) that helps us substantively distinguish between whether they are *good or evil*? (Hitler too was a unique, singular individual with a proper name and perspective.) Admittedly, Derrida could be said to be attempting to "deformalize" the question of justice somewhat in identifying the "other" as "refugee," "nomad," "exile," "emigré," "Jew"—in brief, as the displaced and disfranchised victim whose cry for justice may sometimes require the suspension or revision of the law. But these remain largely indeterminate characterizations (e.g., we are all potentially "nomads" to the extent that we become exiled from the logocentric fold), and we also encounter continuing problems of discernment in that several acts of slaughter have been carried out by individuals or groups that consider themselves victimized and dispossessed of their original rights (rightful homeland, rightful heritage, etc.)—Basques, Ulster Catholics and Protestants, Palestinians, ultra-Zionists, Tutus, Azeris, Serbs, Iraqis, Sudeten Germans, and so on. In an essay entitled "Hyperbolic Justice," Caputo aligns Derrida's deconstructive justice with the "myth of the smallest singularities . . . of the smallest hair on your head, of the least among us" (in *Demythologizing Heidegger*, pp. 200–201). But in so doing, Caputo is once again re-inscribing Derrida's open-ended deconstruction in a specifically biblical tradition of discernment—a line of re-inscription which ultimately leads Caputo to identify the Derridean "Other" not only with the "Jew [as] placeholder for all those who have no place," but more specifically with "Jesus the Jew" who gives justice to the "man with the withered hand" (*Prayers and Tears of Jacques Derrida*, pp. 230–231). "Flesh is the locus of obligation," insists Caputo in *Against Ethics* (p. 127). And one might add, *suffering* flesh, for Caputo confirms the claim that the flesh of the stranger that obliges us is always that of the victim, not the victimizer (p. 119). However,

even Caputo's more specified, substantiated, and deformalized version of deconstructive ethics is *still*, arguably, *too* hyperbolic—still not sufficiently prudent about the need for normative limits and narrative instantiations. I agree with Caputo's conclusions but have difficulties, at times, with his overly deconstructive means of getting there.

92. Caputo, *Prayers and Tears of Jacques Derrida*, p. 74.

93. Ibid., p. 102: "It is only when the 'come!' calls for something it cannot know or foresee that the come really has passion. Jacques' secret, if there is one, lies on a textual surface, inconspicuous by its superficiality, without a martyr to bear witness, without a revelation to unveil it, without a second coming or even a first. It is always to come."

94. Ibid., p. 169.

95. Critchley, *Very Little . . . Almost Nothing*, p. 80. See also the claim here by Joseph Campbell that "the monster comes through as a kind of God" whose "horrendous presence" explodes all our criteria of order and judgment and liquidates ethics. This is God as destroyer and horror-merchant. The full citation is as follows: "The monster comes through as a kind of God. . . . By a monster I mean some horrendous presence or apparition that explodes all of your standards for harmony, order and ethical conduct. . . . That's God in the role of destroyer. Such experiences go past ethical . . . judgments. Ethics is wiped out. . . . God is horrific" (*Power of Myth*, p. 222). One finds a similar invocation of mythic divinities who call and come in terror and darkness *irrespective of ethical distinctions between good and evil* in certain texts of the later Heidegger, e.g., when he even speaks of the "good of evil" or the "primal mythical force of might." See van Buren, *Young Heidegger*, pp. 371–377, 382–385, 392–394. Van Buren concludes with this troubling critical question: "so we can ask roughly what, according to the later Heidegger's preparatory sketches and drafts, is supposed to be coming in this second coming? Are we simply to call out: *Komm, Viens*, Come! Thy kingdom come, thy will be done?" (p. 392).

96. Derrida, *Specters of Marx*, p. 175: "Justice is desirable through and beyond right and law"; and he adds, elsewhere, "letting the other come is not inertia open to anything . . . deconstruction cannot wait." See "Psyche: Inventions of the Other," in *Acts of Literature/Jacques Derrida*, ed. Derek Attridge (New York: Routledge, 1992), and in *Reading de Man Reading*, ed. Wlad Godzich and Lindsay Waters (Minneapolis: University of Minnesota Press, 1989), p. 55. While acknowledging the element of "madness" involved in all attempts to judge and decide, when confronted with the impossible demand for justice, Derrida also acknowledges the need for prudence. This is the double bind of judgment when faced with the competing demands of justice and law (rights). Justice requires the law just as law demands justice (see Derrida, "Force of Law: The Mystical Foundations of Authority," in *Deconstruction and the Possibility of Justice*, ed. Drucilla Cornell, Michel Rosenfeld, and David Gray Carlson [New York: Routledge, 1992]; *Politique de l'amitié* [Paris: Galilée, 1995]; and Caputo's illuminating analysis "The Epoch of Judgment," in *Against Ethics* [1993]). See also, in this regard, Derrida's insistence in "Psyche: Inventions of the Other" that for the coming of the wholly other a "kind of resigned passivity for which everything comes down to the same is not suitable" [p. 55]). In his later writings, in the eighties and nineties, Derrida does recognize the need of deconstruction to curb the endless drift of deferral and deferment—especially when he acknowledges that, from an ethical point of view, "deconstruction cannot wait"; that the demand for justice is here and now, in each instant of judgment and decision. But while Derrida is aware of the dilemma of reconciling (a) the wholly other who surprises us with (b) the necessity for anticipatory horizons and

practical decisions, he hasn't yet, to my knowledge, gone far enough in spelling out what this kind of reconciliation actually entails. The difficulty of moderating madness with prudence still remains. The dilemma of how to judge between alterities, between something specifically "messianic" which brings peace and justice and not just "anything at all," appears (to me at any rate) to remain unresolved. Caputo's current work on a new metanoetics of meta-phronesis is a pioneering attempt to grapple with this fundamental ethical problem of deconstruction.

97. This is a hypothesis entertained, if not endorsed, by Caputo, *Prayers and Tears of Jacques Derrida*, p. 263: "All this talk in deconstruction about a messianic promise, about praying and weeping over something to come, about faith in something unforeseeable, does that not draw upon—even quite transparently—a Jewish archive? . . . Is deconstruction not the product of a Jewish mind?"

98. Ibid., p. 63. One could cite here, in support of Caputo's reading, the eschatological paradox of desire as *both* insatiate *and* overabundant, as *both* searching *and* saturated. See, for example, Psalm 78: "They ate and were filled. The Lord gave them what they wanted: they were not deprived of their desire," or again, Psalm 21: "You have given him his heart's desire." This could be said to correspond to the deconstructive paradox that the messianic is always deferred but is also a desire and demand for justice here and now, a justice that "cannot wait"!

99. Derrida, *Given Time*, p. 30: "It is a matter—desire beyond desire—of responding faithfully but also as rigorously as possible both to the injunction or the order of the gift ('give'/*donne*) *as well as* to the injunction or order of meaning (presence, science, knowledge). *Know* still what giving *wants to say, know how to give*, know what you want to say when you give, know what you intend to give, know how the gift annuls itself, commit yourself even if commitment is the destruction of the gift by the gift, give economy its chance."

100. Ibid., p. 30. Derrida makes a similar concession, I might add, when he acknowledges the need for infinite justice to be tempered by finite laws and approves Kant's recommendation to make hospitality conditional when it comes to the question of offering refugees political asylum in one's state. Thus while Kant argued for universal hospitality as the condition of perpetual peace—what Derrida calls *"unconditional or pure hospitality which does not seek to identify the newcomer, even if he is not a citizen"* (my italics)—Derrida acknowledges the practical wisdom of Kant's insistence on certain conditions of hospitality, e.g., that the visit of strangers be temporary, non-violent, and law-abiding. For Kant knew, observes Derrida, that *"without these conditions hospitality could turn into wild war and aggression"* ("Hospitality, Justice, and Responsibility," and also his essay *Cosmopolites de tous le pays, encore un effort!* [Paris: Galilée, 1996]); *Adieu à Emmanuel Levinas* [Paris: Galilée, 1997], pp. 69ff., 91ff.; and *De l'hospitalité/Anne Dufourmantelle invite Jacques Derrida à répondre* [Paris: Calmann-Lévy, 1997], especially 29ff.). In other words, if deconstruction—understood as impossible justice, gift, and hospitality—is indeed another name for "desire beyond desire," it too has its limits. It might also be noted here that the "other" who threatens war and aggression is not always the "outsider" seeking entry but may well be a projection of alien unconscious fears and fantasies *within ourselves* (e.g., scapegoating, witchhunting, ethnic cleansing, show trials, cold-war paranoia, UFOphobia, xenophobia, racism, and so on). See my development of this last point in my two related volumes *On Stories* and *Strangers, Gods, and Monsters*.

101. "It's not a question of one or the other," as Caputo rightly reminds us, "but of

inhabiting the distance between the two with as much grace and ambiance and hospitality as possible" (*Prayers and Tears of Jacques Derrida*, p. 173).

102. Derrida, "Hospitality, Justice, and Responsibility," pp. 65–83.

103. For this and other citations and ideas, I am indebted to Mark Patrick Hederman, *Manikon Eros* (Dublin: Veritas, 2000).

5. POSSIBILIZING GOD

1. 1 Corinthians 2:4; Romans 15:19; Timothy 1:7; Acts 4:33, 1:8, 8:10; Luke 1:35, 24:49, 9:1, 10:19, 24:28.

2. Cited and commented in Kearney, *Poétique du possible*, p. 252 n. 1.

3. This eschatological-Pauline vision of universal citizenship seems to have deeply influenced Immanuel Kant's theory of cosmopolitanism and more recently that of Julia Kristeva; see *Etrangers à nous-mêmes* (Paris: Fayard, 1988) and *Nations without Nationalism*, trans. Leon S. Roudiez (New York: Columbia University Press, 1993).

4. I am grateful to John Manoussakis for bringing this inscription to my attention. In the same monastery of the Khora in Istanbul, there is also an inscription of a portrait of Christ which reads *he khora ton zonton*, "The Container of the Living."

5. References to Aristotle and Aquinas. See excellent commentary on the distinction between Aristotle's potential and active intellect—from Alexander Aphrodisieus and the Arab commentators, Avicenna and Averroës, to Aquinas and Suarez—by Franz Brentano, "*Nous Poetikos*: Survey of Earlier Interpretations" and other essays from *Essays on Aristotle's De Anima*, ed. Martha C. Nussbaum and Amélie Oksenberg Rorty (Oxford: Clarendon Press, 1992), pp. 313–342.

6. For Hegel, possibility is the logical category of that which is actualizable (that is, non-self-contradictory) if not yet actual (see Hegel, *The Science of Logic* [Atlantic Highlands, N.J.: Humanities Press, 1989], p. 453).

7. On Henri Bergson, "Le possible et le réel" (1930), in *La Pensée et le mouvant* (Paris: Presses Universitaires de France, 1934): see my commentary in Kearney, *Poétique du possible*, pp. 34–35. On Alfred North Whitehead's notion of possibility and God, see, for example, *Dialogues of Alfred North Whitehead*, recorded by Lucien Price (New York: New American Library, 1964), pp. 134–135: "I wish I could convey this sense I have of the infinity of the possibilities that confront humanity—the limitless variations of choice, the possibility of novel and untried combinations, the happy turns of experiment, the endless horizons opening out. As long as we experiment, as long as we keep this possibility of progressiveness, we and our societies are alive. . . . It is the living principle in thought which keeps us alive." See Whitehead's related notion of "potential schemes" and "the extensive continuum which expresses the solidarity of all possible standpoints throughout the actual world" in *Process and Reality* (New York: Macmillan, 1929), pp. 66–67. For useful commentaries on Whitehead's concept of God, see John B. Cobb, "A Whiteheadian Doctrine of God," in *Process Philosophy and Christian Thought*, ed. Delwin Brown, Ralph E. James, Jr., and Gene Reeves (Indianapolis: Bobbs-Merrill, 1971), pp. 215–243; and Lewis Ford, "Creativity in a Future Key," in Robert C. Neville, ed., *New Essays in Metaphysics* (Albany: SUNY Press, 1987), pp. 179–197. I am grateful to my UCD colleague Timothy Mooney for bringing these passages in Whitehead to my attention and for instructing me on the various parallels between process thought and phenomenology in his splendid article "Deconstruction, Process, and Openness: Philosophy in Derrida, Husserl, and White-

head," in *Framing a Vision of the World*, ed. André Cloots and Santiago Sia (Leuven: Leuven University Press, 1999).

8. Cited in Kearney, *Poétique du possible*, p. 35.

9. See my detailed exploration of Husserl's notion of the possible in chapter 1 of Kearney, *Poetics of Imagining*, 2d ed., entitled "The Phenomenological Imagination," pp. 13–14, and in *Poétique du possible*, pp. 199–208. See also Jacques Derrida's innovative reading of Husserl's category of possibility as a Kantian Idea in his *Edmund Husserl's "Origin of Geometry": An Introduction*, trans. John P. Leavey, Jr. (Lincoln: University of Nebraska Press, 1989). The notion of "essential possibility" plays a particularly important role in Husserl's method as a realm of "free variation" leading to "eidetic intuition." In the realm of pure possibles, consciousness may prescind from merely empirical givens and explore, describe, and eventually intuit the "essence" of some thing or idea as the invariant totality that emerges from the freely varied horizon of real and ideal, empirical and fictional, possibilities.

10. Cited in *Poétique du possible*, p. 201.

11. See Paul Ricoeur, "La Liberté selon l'espérance," in *Le Conflit des interprétations* (Paris: Éditions du Seuil, 1969), p. 407

12. Ibid., pp. 408–409: "(Les postulats) désignent un ordre de choses à venir. . . . Les postulats parlent à leur façon d'un Dieu 'ressuscité des morts.' Mais leur façon est celle de la religion dans les limites de la simple raison; ils expriment l'implication existentielle minimale d'une visée pratique, d'une *Absichte*, qui ne peut se convertir en intuition intellectuelle. 'L'Extension'—*Erweiterung*—'l'accroissement'—*Zuwachs*—qu' ils expriment, n'est pas une extension du savoir et du connaître, mais une 'ouverture,' une *Eroffnung* . . . et cette ouverture est l'équivalent philosophique de l'espérance."

13. For a more detailed account of Kant's philosophical and religious analysis of human openness to a future Kingdom of possible ends, see my *Poétique du possible*, pp. 202–205. See also Ricoeur, "La Liberté selon l'espérance," pp. 410–414, where Ricoeur discusses Kant's postulates of freedom and immortality as philosophical analogies for the religious "expectation" (*Erwartung*) and hope in Resurrection.

14. Quoted in *Poétique du possible*, p. 205 n. 12.

15. Ibid., p. 204 n. 11.

16. From Derrida's *Husserl's "Origin of Geometry*," cited in *Poétique du possible*, p. 204. See also Jacques Derrida, "Comme si c'était possible," esp. p. 521 n. 27. See Derrida's admission of debt to Husserl on this subject, note 70 below. John Caputo offers this useful gloss: "an 'infinite' idea or intention [is] a regulative ideal, an 'idea in the Kantian sense,' to which no finite complex of intuitive content is ever fully adequate. For Husserl and Kant, 'God' is the very paradigm of such an idea, as an intention of an 'infinite being' which has no intuitive content at all and no hope at all of ever acquiring any" (introduction to *God, the Gift and Postmodernism*, p. 193).

17. *Poétique du possible*, p. 205; see also Derrida, "Comme si c'était possible," p. 519.

18. *Poétique du possible*, p. 207 n. 16.

19. Ibid., p. 207 n. 14, 15.

20. Husserl Manuscripts, E III, 4, and VIII, 1, and F 24. See my *Poétique du possible*, p. 21 n. 16.

21. On Husserl's remark to Edith Stein, see Jocelyn Benoist, "Husserl au-delà de l'onto-théologie?" *Les Études philosophiques* (October 1991). The full statement, cited by Benoist, reads: "La vie de l'homme n'est rien d'autre qu'un chemin vers Dieu. J'ai

essayé de parvenir au but sans l'aide de la théologie, ses preuves et sa méthode; en d'autres termes, j'ai voulu atteindre Dieu sans Dieu." Benoist goes on to argue that the God of Husserl's unpublished manuscripts is essentially a neo-Aristotelian God qua Telos. "Le Dieu des inédits, sous les traits aristotéliciens de l'entéléchie et du principe, ne réinstitue-t-il pas tout simplement ce qu'on appelle une onto-théologie?" (p. 436). For a more general account of the theological aspects and influences of Husserl's phenomenological project, see Dominique Janicaud's illuminating texts *Le Tournant théologique de la phénoménologie française* (Combas: L'Éclat, 1991), and *La Phénoménologie éclatée* (Paris: Éditions de l'Éclat, 1998).

22. See Louis Dupré's informative essay "Husserl's Thought on God," *Philosophy and Phenomenological Research* 29 (1969), and related articles on Husserl's "teleological" God by Xavier Tilliette, "Husserl et la notion de la nature," *Revue de métaphysique et de morale* 70 (1965): 257–269; Stephen Strasser, "Das Gottesproblem in der Spatsphilosophie Edmund Husserl," *Philosophisches Jahrbuch* (1967): 131ff.; and H. L. van Breda, "Husserl et le problème de Dieu," *Proceedings of the Tenth International Congress of Philosophy* (Amsterdam: North-Holland, 1949), pp. 1210–1212. Husserl's most charismatic designation of God is, Strasser concludes, as the supreme Eidos which "gives all the constituting activities unity, meaningful coherence and teleology." It is "no mundane being," as Husserl himself concedes, "but a final Absolute" (cf. Strasser). Louis Dupré, for his part, argues that Husserl's deity is an immanent pantheistic Telos rather than a transcendent and personal God. He suggests, moreover, that Husserl's philosophical God, like that of Kant and Descartes, usually serves as an ultimate solution to problems, ambiguities, and aporias that would otherwise remain unresolved. On Husserl's complex notion of the Absolute, see also R. O. Elveton, ed., *The Phenomenology of Husserl* (Chicago: Quadrangle Books, 1970), pp. 43, 182ff. The sheer diversity of interpretations of Husserl's God—as teleological, rationalist, deist, pantheist, Kantian, Aristotelian, Hegelian, Cartesian, and so on—testifies to a radical indeterminacy, ambiguity, and one might even say obliquity in Husserl's approach to God. It also betrays the fact that most of his declarations on the subject were made in unpublished manuscripts rather than in terms of clearly formulated arguments. This elusive treatment did not however prevent Husserl's phenomenological sketch of a divine teleology of the possible from exerting a deep influence on subsequent thinkers like Heidegger and Derrida (as outlined below).

23. For Sartre's analysis of possibility—and of "God" as the ultimate project of human possibility—qua ideal-but-impossible synthesis of being-for-itself-in-itself—see his conclusion to *Being and Nothingness* (New York: Philosophical Library, 1956). See also my commentaries on the metaphysical complexities and contradictions of Sartre's notion of the imaginary horizon of the possible in *Poétique du possible*, pp. 29–31 (especially notes 29–30), and *Poetics of Imagining*, 2d ed., ch. 3, pp. 80–94.

24. See Maurice Merleau-Ponty's comments on "essential possibility" and "world possibility" in *The Visible and the Invisible*; and my *Poétique du possible*, p. 30 n. 30 and p. 59 n. 7.

25. Nicolai Hartmann, *Möglichkeit und Wirklichkeit* (Berlin, 1939), ch. 31; see my analysis in *Poétique du possible*, pp. 205–206.

26. For Bergson and Whitehead on possibility, see note 7 above.

27. Ernst Bloch, *The Principle of Hope*, trans. Neville Plaice, Stephen Plaice, and Paul Knight (Oxford: Blackwell, 1986; French ed., Paris: Gallimard, 1976), p. 284.

28. On Sartre's treatment of imaginary possibility as a nihilating gesture of both

subjective freedom and pathological solipsism in *The Psychology of Imagination* (1940), see my analysis in *The Wake of Imagination*, ch. 5, and *The Poetics of Imagining*, 2d ed., ch. 3.

29. *Poétique du possible*, p. 243 n. 33.

30. Ibid., p. 243 n. 34.

31. Ibid., p. 243 n. 35.

32. Ibid., p. 245 n. 37.

33. Ibid., p. 245 n. 38.

34. Ibid., p. 245 n. 39.

35. Ibid., p.246 n. 40.

36. Ibid., p. 249 n. 51.

37. Ibid., p. 246 n. 41.

38. Ibid., p. 246 n. 42.

39. Ibid., p. 247 n. 44.

40. Ibid., p. 247 n. 45.

41. Ibid., p. 247 n. 46. See *The Principle of Hope* (French ed.), p. 281. Also, ibid., p. 299: "Le facteur subjectif représente ici la puissance inépuisée de changer le cours des choses, le facteur objectif est la potentialité inépuisée de la variabilité du monde.... La puissance subjective coïncide non seulement avec ce qui fait changer l'histoire de direction, mais aussi avec ce qui se réalise dans l'histoire, et elle se confondra d'autant plus avec ce qui se réalise que les hommes deviendront les producteurs conscients de leur histoire. La potentialité objective coïncide non seulement avec ce qui est modifiable, mais aussi avec ce qui est réalisable dans l'histoire et cela d'autant plus que le monde extérieur indépendant de l'homme deviendra davantage un monde en médiation avec lui."

42. Ibid., p. 248 n. 47.

43. Ernst Bloch, *The Philosophy of the Future* (New York: Herder, 1970), pp. 55–56. Bloch continues that for such traditional metaphysics, "being itself is understood as the identity of what has been. The origin only emerges archaically as arche; and the dialectical cosmology of disciplines is nothing less than the anamnetic anti-voyage back to the logical-ontology *ante-rem*" (ibid.).

44. *Poétique du possible*, p. 248 n. 49.

45. Ibid., p. 249 n. 52. For further explorations of the dialectical model of possibility as a sign of utopia or of the Messianic Kingdom, see my commentaries in *Poétique du possible*, pp. 243ff. n. 33–36, on such figures as Cornelius Castoriadis, Georg Lukács, and Herbert Marcuse (on utopia); and pp. 238–241 regarding Jürgen Moltmann and the theology of liberation (on Messianic hope).

46. In his introduction to *Being and Time* (trans. John Macquarrie and Edward Robinson [Oxford: Blackwell, 1962]), Heidegger states that for phenomenology, "possibility stands higher than actuality" (p. 63). Later in this text he refers to *Dasein*'s pre-awareness of its own death in *Angst* as a specific mood in which it "finds itself faced with the nothingness of the possible impossibility of its own existence" (*Being and Time*, H 266). This existential-human experience of "possible impossibility" may be usefully compared and contrasted with Derrida's notion of "impossible possibility" in "Comme si c'était possible" (1998), discussed below. For a detailed critical discussion of Heidegger's various concepts of possibility in *Being and Time* and subsequent texts, see my "Heidegger's Poetics of the Possible," in *Poetics of Modernity*, pp. 35–48.

47. See my *Poetics of Modernity*, p. 219 n. 34, on Edgar Lohner's contentious

translation of *Vermögen* in his version of the "Letter on Humanism" in Richard Zaner and Don Ihde, *Phenomenology and Existentialism* (New York: Capricorn Books, 1973), pp. 147–181.

48. On the significance of this "Turn," see William J. Richardson, *Heidegger: Through Phenomenology to Thought* (The Hague: Nijhoff, 1963).

49. See my more elaborate commentary on this key passage in "Heidegger's Poetics of the Possible," in *Poetics of Modernity*, pp. 44–48 and p. 220 n. 36; and in my "Heidegger, Le Possible et Dieu," in *Heidegger et la question de Dieu*, ed. Kearney and O'Leary, pp. 125–167. On the various theological interpretations of Husserl's and Heidegger's phenomenology, especially by figures like Marion, Levinas, and Henry in France, see Dominique Janicaud, *Le Tournant théologique de la phénoménologie française* (1991). See also my "Heidegger's Gods," in *Poetics of Modernity*, pp. 50–64; Jean-François Courtine, ed., *Phénoménologie et théologie* (Paris: Criterion, 1992), and George Kovacs, *The Question of God in Heidegger's Phenomenology* (Evanston, Ill.: Northwestern University Press, 1990).

50. Ibid., p. 220 n. 37.

51. Ibid., p. 45ff., my translation.

52. See Nicholas of Cusa, *Trialogus de Possest*, ed. Robert Steiger (Hamburg: Felix Meiner Verlag, 1973); and Peter J. Casarella, "Nicholas of Cusa and the Power of the Possible," *American Catholic Philosophical Journal* 64, no. 1 (1990): 7–35. Casarella makes some interesting comparisons between Cusanus's divine *possest* and Heidegger's power of the "loving possible."

53. Heidegger, "Letter on Humanism."

54. Martin Heidegger, *Der Spiegel* interview (1976), and *Beiträge zur Philosophie (Vom Ereignus)*, GA 65 (Frankfurt: Klostermann, 1994); on this Heidegger-Schelling connection, see George Seidel, "Heidegger's Last God and the Schelling Connection," pp. 91ff.

55. Martin Heidegger, *An Introduction to Metaphysics*, trans. Ralph Manheim (New York: Doubleday, 1961), p. 6ff. See also my analysis of this analogy of proper proportionality between ontology and theology in *Poétique du possible*, part 4, entitled "Le Chiasme herméneutique," pp. 211–256.

56. Martin Heidegger, " . . . Poetically Man Dwells . . . ," in *Poetry, Language, Thought* (New York: Harper and Row, 1971), p. 215.

57. This essay is published as a complementary text in Heidegger's *On Time and Being*, trans. Joan Stambaugh (Harper and Row: New York, 1972), p. 54.

58. Ibid., pp. 59–60.

59. Ibid., p. 8. See also my *Poetics of Modernity*, pp. 220–221 n. 41, on the crucial link between "possibility" and "Being understood as time which absences as it presences." For further analysis, see the chapter "Last Gods and Final Things" in my *Strangers, Gods, and Monsters*, and also the recent fascinating study by Hent de Vries, "Heidegger's Possibilism," in *Philosophy and the Turn to Religion* (Baltimore: Johns Hopkins University Press, 1999), pp. 279–296. Unfortunately, this analysis only came to my attention after I completed the present essay.

60. See here Heidegger's deconstructive reading of Kant's critical project in *Kant and the Problem of Metaphysics* (trans. James S. Churchill [Bloomington: Indiana University Press, 1962]) as it pertains to his understanding of possibility, p. 252: "Kant must have had an intimation of this collapse of the primacy of logic in metaphysics when, speaking of the fundamental characteristics of Being, 'possibility' (what-being)

and 'reality' (which Kant termed 'existence'), he said: 'so long as the definition of possibility, existence and necessity is sought solely in pure understanding, they cannot be explained save through an obvious tautology.'" But Heidegger does not ignore Kant's subsequent retreat to the logicist model: "And yet, in the second edition of the *Critique* did not Kant re-establish the supremacy of the understanding? And as a result did not metaphysics, with Hegel, come to be identified with 'logic' more radically than ever before?" (ibid.).

61. Derrida, "Comme si c'était possible" (henceforth referred to as "Comme si"). All translations are mine.

62. Ibid., p. 498. See also *Politiques de l'amitié* (Paris: Galilée, 1994) (translated under the title *Politics of Friendship*), p. 46: "Or la pensée du 'peut-être' engage peut-être la seule pensée *possible* de l'événement. De l'amitié à venir et de l'amitié pour l'avenir. Car pour aimer l'amitié, il ne suffit pas de savoir porter l'autre dans le deuil, il faut aimer l'avenir. Et il n'est pas de catégorie plus juste pour l'avenir que celle du *'peut-être.'* Telle pensée conjoint l'amitié, l'avenir et le peut-être pour s'ouvrir à la venue de ce qui vient, c'est-à-dire nécessairement sous le régime d'un *possible* dont la *possibilisation* doit gagner sur l'*impossible*. Car un possible qui serait seulement *possible* (*non impossible*), un *possible* sûrement et certainement *possible*, d'avance accessible, ce serait un mauvais *possible*, un *possible* sans avenir, un *possible* déjà mis de côté, si on peut dire, assuré sur la vie. Ce serait un programme ou une causalité, un développement, un déroulement sans événement. La *possibilisation de ce possible impossible* doit rester à la fois aussi indécidable et donc aussi décisive que l'avenir même."

63. Derrida, *Politiques de l'amitié*, p. 86.

64. "Comme si," p. 498.

65. Ibid., p. 515.

66. Ibid., p. 498.

67. Ibid., p. 498.

68. Ibid., p. 519.

69. Ibid., p. 516 (citing "Invention de l'autre," in *Psyché*, p. 59). It is useful to compare and contrast Derrida's position here with that of Whitehead; see Dean, "Deconstruction and Process Theology," and Griffin, "Postmodern Theology."

70. "Comme si," pp. 504–505.

71. Ibid., p. 520; also Derrida, *On Pardon* etc. (London: Routledge, 2001).

72. *Politics of Friendship*, p. 36

73. "Comme si," p. 505. Also see John D. Caputo and Michael J. Scanlon, "Apology for the Impossible: Religion and Postmodernism," and John D. Caputo, "Apostles of the Impossible: On God and the Gift in Marion and Derrida," in *God, the Gift, and Postmodernism*, pp. 1–19 and pp. 185–222. "For Derrida, the experience of the impossible represents the least bad definition of deconstruction . . . everything *interesting* for Derrida is impossible, not simply, logically or absolutely, impossible, but what he calls *the* impossible. . . . That is why Derrida can say he has spent his whole life 'inviting calling promising, hoping sighing dreaming.' Of the gift, of justice, of hospitality, of the incoming of the wholly other, of *the* impossible" (pp. 3–4). This leads Caputo to contrast "the impossible" to the "possible" in the form of a polar opposition or exclusion, for example, "experience is really experience when it is an experience of *the* impossible, not when it experiences the possible" (p. 191). But while there are indeed passages in Derrida which can suggest such a move, the more nuanced position outlined in "Comme si" shies away, I believe, from such a polar alternativism and speaks

instead in terms of a chiasm of "impossible possibility." Of course, if one intends the "possible" in the traditional metaphysical and logical senses of *potentia* and *possibilitas*, then Caputo is correct to oppose it to *"the* impossible"; but as will be clear from the above, I am speaking in this essay—as is Derrida when he speaks of the "perhaps" in "Comme si"—of a radically post-metaphysical notion of possibility as *posse*: at once the possibility *and* impossibility of God/alterity/transcendence/infinity/incoming event. That is why, eschatologically understood, the divine *posse* or "may-be" is *both* already here *and* always still to come (again), *both* incarnation *and* in-coming. In short, the God of eschatological possibility is simultaneously given *and* not given, possible *and* impossible—or to put it in denominational terms, Christian *and* Jewish. For Caputo's characteristically feisty, intriguing, and challenging discussion of Derrida's notion of the impossible, in comparison with Marion's concept of "saturation," see "Apostles of the Impossible," pp. 199–206.

74. See my essay "Khora or God?" in *From Aquinas to Derrida: John D. Caputo in Focus*, ed. Mark Dooley (forthcoming, 2002).

75. "Comme si," pp. 516–517.

76. Ibid.

77. Ibid., p. 519.

78. Ibid. This crucial passage reads in full as follows: "Mais comment est-il possible, demandera-t-on, que ce qui rend possible rende impossible cela même qu'il rend possible, donc, et introduise, mais comme sa chance, une chance non négative, un principe de ruine dans cela même qu'il promet ou promeut? Le *in-* de l'im-possible est sans doute radical, implacable, indéniable. Mais il n'est pas simplement négatif ou dialectique, il *introduit* au possible, il en est *aujourd'hui l'huissier*; il le fait venir, il le fait tourner selon une temporalité anachronique ou selon une filiation incroyable—qui est d'ailleurs, aussi bien, l'origine de la foi. Car il excède le savoir et conditionne l'adresse à l'autre, inscrit tout théorème dans l'espace et le temps d'un témoignage ('je te parle, crois moi'). Autrement dit, et c'est l'introduction à une aporie sans exemple, une aporie de la logique plutôt qu'une aporie sans exemple, une aporie de la logique plutôt qu'une aporie logique, voilà une impasse de l'indécidable par laquelle une décision ne peut pas ne pas passer. Toute responsabilité doit passer par cette aporie qui, loin de la paralyser, met en mouvement une nouvelle pensée du possible." At a practical level one might draw a parallel here with Leonardo da Vinci's "impossible machines"—from flying and diving apparatuses to a system of shafts and cogwheels for generating enormous heat to rival the sun—which were sketched in his unpublished notebooks but whose "possibility" remained a perpetual promise and spur to further creativity and inventiveness (see Owen Gingerich, "Leonardo da Vinci: Codex Leicester," *Museum of Science* [Boston] [winter 1997]).

79. "Comme si," pp. 518–519.

80. Ibid., p. 519.

81. Ibid., p. 517: "possibilité de l'impossible, impossibilité du possible, l'expérience en générale etc." See Derrida's admission of his debt to Husserl's notions of possibility/impossibility on p. 521 n. 27: "J'avais d'ailleurs, il y a bien longtemps, dans l'espace de la phénoménologie husserlienne, analysé de façon analogue une possibilité de forme apparemment négative, une im-possibilité, l'impossibilité de l'intuition pleine et immédiate, la 'possibilité essentielle de la non-intuition,' la 'possibilité de la crise' comme 'crise du logos.' Or cette possibilté de l'impossibilité, disais-je alors, n'est pas simplement négative: le piège devient aussi une chance: ' . . . cette possibilité (de la

crise) reste liée pour Husserl au mouvement même de la vérité et à la production de l'objectivité idéale: celle-ci a en effet un besoin essentiel de l'écriture" (*De la grammatologie* [Paris: Éditions du Minuit, 1967], p. 60; and also *Introduction à "L'Origine de la géométrie" de Husserl* [Paris: Presses Universitaires de France, 1962], p. 162, passim).

82. On this ambiguity, see Louis Dupré, "Husserl's Thought on God."

83. On this notion of God as "May-Be" and as "transfiguring posse," see my *Poétique du possible*, part 3; and my more recent "Transfiguring God," in the *Companion to Postmodern Theology*, ed. Graham Ward (Oxford: Blackwell, 2001).

CONCLUSION

1. Aristotle, *De Anima* 3.5, trans. R. D. Hicks (Buffalo, N.Y.: Prometheus Books, 1991); also Franz Brentano, "*Nous Poetikos*: Survey of Earlier Interpretations," pp. 313–315.

2. Aquinas, *De Unitate Intellectus contra Averroistas*; quoted in Brentano, "*Nous Poetikos*," pp. 319, 339. See also the fascinating commentary by L. A. Kosman, "What Does the Maker Mind Make?" in *Essays on Aristotle's De Anima*, ed. Nussbaum and Rorty, in particular the following passages, p. 344: "The maker mind makes everything. This suggestion has much to recommend it. It fits well with the description . . . [that] the *nous* in question is said to be what it is *toi panta poiein*—by virtue of making all things. . . . The notion that there is a mind which creates the world by thinking the ideas of all things has a rich history in Western philosophical thought, from the earlier of postclassical thinkers such as Albinus, through the Middle Ages, through Berkeley and Leibniz, and up to such modern philosophers as Fichte and Hegel."

3. Kosman, "What Does the Maker Mind Make?" p. 345.

4. Ibid., pp. 346–347. Kosman spells out this interpretation as follows, p. 347: "For here *nous* is being described as the active agency by which a person with the potentiality *for* understanding comes actually to have the power *of* understanding. . . . The maker mind makes both potential intellect and what is potentially thinkable in these senses of first potentiality . . . into what is actually *able* to think and what is actually think*able*").

5. Ibid.

6. Nicholas of Cusa (Cusanus), *Trialogus de Possest (On Actualized-Possibility)* in *Concise Introduction to the Philosophy of Nicholas of Cusa*.

7. Ibid., p. 79.

8. Nicholas of Cusa, *The Vision of God*, trans. Emma Gurney Salter (New York: E. P. Dutton, 1928), pp. 91 and 127–129.

9. Nicholas of Cusa, "Trialogus," p. 69.

10. Ibid.

11. Ibid., p.71.

12. Ibid., p. 81.

13. Ibid.

14. Ibid., p. 151. See Cusanus on God as "absolute potentiality" in *The Vision of God*, pp. 70–71: "absolute potentiality is infinity itself . . . where potential becoming is one with potential creating, where potentiality is one with act. . . . Thou God, who art Very Infinity, art that one Very God in whom I see all potential being to be actual being. For potency wholly freed from all potentiality limited to matter or to any passive

potentiality, is absolute being, for all that existeth in infinite being is itself infinite being pure and simple. Thus, infinite being, the potential being of all things is infinite being itself. . . . My God, Thou art all potential being."

15. Nicholas of Cusa, *Vision of God*, p. 43.

16. Nicholas of Cusa, "Trialogus," p. 71.

17. Schelling, SW VI, pp. 281ff., 287–293 (cited and with commentary by George Seidel, "Heidegger's Last God and the Schelling Connection," pp. 91ff.).

18. Ibid., p. 493. See Ian Leask's interesting commentary on Schelling's God as post-ontological in *Questions of Platonism* (London: Greenwich Exchange, 2000), pp. 91–92. "Schelling's 'unsaying' of Idealism does not only mean the primacy of being over Thought. By gesturing towards the very basis of any *conception* of Being, Schelling restates the ancient conviction that the highest point of all 'is' beyond Being, *Uberseindes*. For Schelling, God cannot be contained by any predicate—even Being. Eternal Freedom must, of necessity, be able both to *be* and to *be otherwise*; if it can be pinned down to a single predicate it is no longer free. . . . *Qua* absolute freedom, then, God is beyond both essence and being: 'God . . . in himself is not being but the pure freedom of being or not being and thus *over* being, as former thinkers have called him'" (*Werke*, vol. 12, p. 58); "God is outside of being, above being, but he is not only by himself free from being, that is, he is also a pure freedom to be or not to be, to accept being or not to accept it" (ibid., p. 33); "the Perfect spirit transcends every kind of being" (ibid., vol. 13, p. 256). Leask goes on to suggest that Schelling's obviation of the "idolatrous" dangers of both thought and being (including being-before-thought) as categories of God leads Schelling to a radical apophaticism which challenges onto-theology and the whole Scotist primacy of the *summum ens* over the God beyond being. "Whether or not we *can* think otherwise than Being," concludes Leask, "Schelling at least alerts us to the (negative) thought that, even accepting the limitations of thought about Being, God is no more contained by 'being' than Being is by Thought. What was apparently a closed issue—after the medieval reversal of the Areopagite's Platonic distinction—is burst open: Schelling gestures toward a god who is not the *Qui est*, not the god of philosophy, neither as an alter-ego nor a re-edition of the self. The question of the divine Good, beyond Being, is re-instated" (p. 92).

19. Heidegger, *Introduction to Metaphysics*, preface. See also my discussion of this hypothetical "analogy of proper proportionality" between Being and God in "Heidegger, Le Possible et Dieu," in *Heidegger et la question de Dieu*, ed. Kearney and O'Leary, and my *Poétique du possible*, ch. 11 and 12, pp. 219–251.

20. While the ontological notion of *Spiel* remains elusive in Heidegger's own work, it is developed by later phenomenologists such as Hans-Georg Gadamer, Eugen Fink, and Mikel Dufrenne. See my discussion of the central role of "ontological" play in these thinkers in *Poétique du possible*, pp. 260–267.

21. Cited and with commentary by Derrida in "Post-Scriptum," in *Derrida and Negative Theology*, ed. Coward and Foshay, pp. 313ff.

22. See the illuminating and scholarly analysis of the biblical and theological thematic of play by Hugo Rahner, *Der spielende Mensch* (Rhein: Verlag, 1949).

23. Jerome, *Commentarius in Zachariam*, II, 8, quoted by Rahner, *Der spielende Mensch*.

24. See *Poétique du possible*, p. 269 n. 25.

25. Hillesum, *An Interrupted Life*, p. 174.

26. Ibid., p. 176.

27. Here one would have to distinguish between notions of power (*potestas*) as eschatological *possest* rather than *potentia/possibilitas*, as *auctoritas* rather than *imperium*.

28. Hillesum, *An Interrupted Life*, pp. 192–193.

29. Meister Eckhart, *God Awaits You*, ed. Richard Chilson (Notre Dame, Ind.: Ave Maria Press, 1996), p. 36. The passage continues: "A pure heart is unencumbered, without worry, and not attached to things. It does not desire to have its own way, but is content to be immersed in God's loving will. A pure heart is forgetful of self." In this connection see also Hillesum, *An Interrupted Life*, p. 204: "Truly, my life is one long hearkening unto (*hineinhorchen*) my self and unto others, unto God. And if I say that I hearken, it is really God who hearkens inside me. The most essential and the deepest in me hearkening unto the most essential and deepest in the other. God to God." See also Hillesum on "soul," ibid., p. 229: "Sometimes it bursts into full flame within me. . . . And though I am sick and anemic and more or less bedridden, every minute seems so full and so precious. . . . 'I rejoice and exult time and again, oh God: I am grateful to You for having given me this life.' . . . A soul is forged out of fire and rock crystal."

30. *Poétique du possible*, p. 270 n. 27. My translation.

31. Ibid., p. 271.

32. Ibid., p. 272 n. 31. According to Augustine, the dance of transfiguration is a "mystic figure" of the second creation still to come (*De Civitate Dei* XVII, 14). As Hugo Rahner points out, however, Western theology, based on the metaphysics of substance-presence, was generally less inclined than Eastern theology toward the idioms of "play" and "dance" (*Der Spielende Mensch*, pp. 85ff.).

BIBLIOGRAPHY

Aquinas, Thomas. *De Unitate Intellectus contra Averroistas*. Translated by Beatrice H. Zedler. Milwaukee: Marquette University Press, 1968.

———. *Quaestiones de Anima*. Translated by James H. Robb. Milwaukee: Marquette University Press, 1984.

———. *Summa Theologiae*. New York: McGraw-Hill, 1981.

Aristotle. *De Anima*. Translated by R. D. Hicks. Buffalo, N.Y.: Prometheus Books, 1991.

Attridge, Derek. *Acts of Literature/Jacques Derrida*. New York: Routledge, 1992.

Augustine. *Confessions*. Translated by R. S. Pine-Coffin. New York: Penguin, 1961.

Barth, Karl. *Church Dogmatics*. Translated by G. W. Bromiley. Edinburgh: T. & T. Clark, 1960.

Bennington, Geoffrey, and Jacques Derrida. *Jacques Derrida: Circonfession/Derrida-base*. Paris: Éditions du Seuil, 1991. Translated into English by Geoffrey Bennington (Chicago: University of Chicago Press, 1993).

Benoist, Jocelyn. "Husserl au-delà de l'ontothéologie?" *Les Études philosophiques*. October 1991.

Benveniste, Emile. *Problems in General Linguistics*. Coral Gables, Fla.: University of Miami Press, 1971.

Bergson, Henri. "Le possible et le réel." In *La Pensée et le mouvant*. Paris: Presses Universitaires de France, 1934.

Bloch, Ernst. *The Philosophy of the Future*. Translated by John Cummings. New York: Herder and Herder, 1970.

———. *The Principle of Hope*. Translated by Neville Plaice, Stephen Plaice, and Paul Knight. Oxford: Basil Blackwell, 1986. French edition, *Le principe espérance* (Paris: Gallimard, 1976).

Boothby, Richard. *Death and Desire: Psychoanalytic Theory in Lacan's Return to Freud*. New York: Routledge, 1991.

Breda, L.H. van. "Husserl et le problème de Dieu." In *Proceedings of the Tenth International Congress of Philosophy*. Amsterdam: North-Holland, 1949.

Bretano, Franz. "*Nous Poetikos*: Survey of Earlier Interpretations." In *Essays on Aristotle's De Anima*, edited by Martha C. Nussbaum and Amélie Oksenberg Rorty. Oxford: Clarendon Press, 1992.

Breton, Stanislas. "'Je Suis (celui) qui Suis' (Ontologie et Métaphysique)." In *Libres Commentaires*. Paris: Éditions du Cerf, 1990.

———. "La quérelle des dénominations." In *Heidegger et la question de Dieu*, edited by Richard Kearney and Joseph S. O'Leary. Paris: Grasset, 1981.

Buber, Martin. *Moses: The Revelation and the Covenant*. New York: Harper, 1958.

161

Buber, Martin, and Franz Rosenzweig . *Scripture and Translation.* Translated by Lawrence Rosenwald and Everett Fox. Bloomington: Indiana University Press, 1994.

Campbell, Joseph. *The Power of Myth.* New York: Doubleday, 1988.

Caputo, John D. *Against Ethics: Contribution to a Poetics of Obligation with Constant Reference to Deconstruction.* Bloomington: Indiana University Press, 1993.

———. "Apostles of the Impossible: On God and the Gift in Marion and Derrida." In *God, the Gift, and Postmodernism,* edited by John D. Caputo and Michael J. Scanlon. Bloomington: Indiana University Press, 1999.

———. "Hyperbolic Justice." In *Demythologizing Heidegger.* Bloomington: Indiana University Press, 1993.

———. *The Mystical Element in Heidegger's Thought.* New York: Fordham University Press, 1982.

———.*The Prayers and Tears of Jacques Derrida: Religion without Religion.* Bloomington: Indiana University Press, 1997.

Caputo, John D., Mark Dooley, and Michael J. Scanlon, eds. *Questioning God.* Bloomington: Indiana University Press, 2001.

Caputo, John D., and Michael J. Scanlon. "Apology for the Impossible: Religion and Postmodernism." In *God, the Gift, and Postmodernism,* edited by John D. Caputo and Michael J. Scanlon. Bloomington: Indiana University Press, 1999.

Carroll, R. P. "On Steiner the Theologian." In *Reading George Steiner,* edited by Nathan A. Scott, Jr., and Ronald A. Sharp. Baltimore: John Hopkins University Press, 1994.

Casarella, Peter J. "Nicholas of Cusa and the Power of the Possible." *American Catholic Philosophical Journal* 64, no. 1 (1990): 7–35.

Childs, Brevard S. *Introduction to the Old Testament as Scripture.* Philadelphia: Fortress Press, 1979.

Clement (of Alexandria). *The Writings of Clement of Alexandria.* Translated by William Wilson. Edinburgh: T. & T. Clark, 1867.

Cobb, B. John. "A Whiteheadian Doctrine of God." In *Process Philosophy and Christian Thought,* edited by Delwin Brown, Ralph E. James, Jr., and Gene Reeves. Indianapolis: Bobbs-Merrill, 1971.

Coleridge, Samuel Taylor. *Biographia Literaria.* London: Dent, 1971.

Cornell, Drucilla, Michel Rosenfeld, and David Gray Carlson, eds. *Deconstruction and the Possibility of Justice.* New York: Routledge, 1992.

Courtine, Jean-François, ed. *Phénoménologie et théologie.* Paris: Criterion, 1992.

Coward, Harold, and Toby Foshay, eds. *Derrida and Negative Theology.* Albany: SUNY Press, 1992.

Critchley, Simon. *Very Little . . . Almost Nothing: Death, Philosophy, Literature.* London: Routledge, 1997.

Davies, Oliver. *Meister Eckhart: Mystical Theologian.* London: SPCK, 1991.

Dean, William. "Deconstruction and Process Theology." *Journal of Religion* 64 (1984): 1–19.

Derrida, Jacques. *Adieu à Emmanuel Levinas.* Paris: Galilée, 1997.

———. *Archive Fever: A Freudian Impression.* Translated by Eric Prenowitz. Chicago: University of Chicago Press, 1996.

———. "Comme si c'était possible, 'Within such Limits' . . ." *Revue internationale de philosophie* 3, no. 205 (1998): 497–529.

———. *Cosmopolites de tous le pays, encore un effort!* Paris: Galilée, 1997.

——. *De la grammatologie*. Paris: Éditions du Minuit, 1967.

——. *De l'hospitalité/Anne Dufourmantelle invite Jacques Derrida à répondre*. Paris: Calmann-Lévy, 1997.

——. *Edmund Husserl's "Origin of Geometry": An Introduction*. Translated by John P. Leavey, Jr. Lincoln: University of Nebraska Press, 1989.

——. "Foi et savoir: Les deux sources de la religion aux limites de la simple raison." In *La Religion*, edited by Jacques Derrida and Gianni Vattimo. Paris: Éditions du Seuil, 1996.

——. "Force of Law: The Mystical Foundations of Authority." In *Deconstruction and the Possibility of Justice*, edited by Drucilla Cornell, Michel Rosenfeld, and David Gray Carlson. New York: Routledge, 1992.

——. *The Gift of Death*. Translated by David Wills. Chicago: University of Chicago Press, 1995.

——. *Given Time, I: Counterfeit Money*. Translated by Peggy Kamuf. Chicago: University of Chicago Press, 1992.

——. "Hospitality, Justice, and Responsibility" (UCD Round Table), in *Questioning Ethics*, edited by Richard Kearney and Mark Dooley. London: Routledge, 1999.

——. "How to Avoid Speaking: Denials." In *Derrida and Negative Theology*, edited by Harold Coward and Toby Foshay. Albany: SUNY Press, 1992.

——. *Introduction à "L'Origine de la géométrie" de Husserl*. Paris: Presses Universitaires de France, 1962.

——. "Living On: Border Lives." In *Deconstruction and Criticism*, edited by Harold Bloom. London: Routledge, 1979.

——. *Memoirs of the Blind: The Self-Portrait and Other Ruins*. Translated by Pascale-Anne Brault and Michael Naas. Chicago: University of Chicago Press, 1993.

——. "Nombre de Oui." In *Psyché: Inventions de l'autre*. Paris: Galilée, 1987.

——. *Of Grammatology*. Translated by Gayatri C. Spivak. Baltimore: Johns Hopkins University Press, 1974.

——. "On a Newly Arisen Apocalyptic Tone in Philosophy." In *Raising the Tone of Philosophy: Late Essays by Emmanuel Kant, Transformative Critique by Jacques Derrida*, edited by Peter Fenves. Baltimore: Johns Hopkins University Press, 1993.

——. *On the Name*. Edited by Thomas Dutoit. Translated by David Wood, John P. Leavey, Jr., and Ian McLeod. Stanford, Calif.: Stanford University Press, 1995.

——. *Points . . . : Interviews, 1974–1994*. Edited by Elisabeth Weber. Translated by Peggy Kamuf and others. Stanford, Calif.: Stanford University Press, 1995.

——. *The Politics of Friendship*. Translated by George Collins. London: Verso, 1997.

——. *Politiques de l'amitié*. Paris: Galilée, 1994.

——. *The Post Card: From Socrates to Freud and Beyond*. Translated by Alan Bass. Chicago: University of Chicago Press, 1987.

——. "Post-Scriptum." In *Derrida and Negative Theology*, edited by Harold Coward and Toby Foshay. Albany: SUNY Press, 1992.

——. *Psyché: Inventions de l'autre*. Paris: Galilée, 1987.

——. "Psyche: Inventions of the Other." In *Acts of Literature/Jacques Derrida*, edited by Derek Attridge. New York: Routledge, 1992.

——. *Sauf le nom*. Paris: Galilée, 1993.

——. "Shibboleth for Paul Celan." In *Word Traces: Readings of Paul Celan*, edited by Aris Fioretos. Baltimore: Johns Hopkins University Press, 1994.

——. *Specters of Marx*. Translated by Peggy Kamuf. New York: Routledge, 1994.

——. "Théologie de la traduction." In *Qu'est-ce que Dieu?* Brussels: Publications des Facultés Universitaires Saint-Louis, 1985.

——. *The Truth in Painting.* Chicago: University of Chicago Press, 1987.

——. "Two Words for Joyce." In *Post-structuralist Joyce: Essays from the French*, edited by Derek Attridge and Daniel Ferrer. Cambridge: Cambridge University Press, 1984.

——. "Violence and Metaphysics." In *Writing and Difference*, translated by Alan Bass. New York: Routledge, 1981.

——. *Writing and Difference.* Translated by Alan Bass. New York: Routledge, 1981.

Desmond, William. *Being and the Between.* Albany: SUNY Press, 1995.

Le Dictionnaire de la Bible. Paris, 1912.

Dictionnaire encyclopédique de la Bible. Valence-sur-Rhône, 1973.

Le Dictionnaire théologique. Desclée, Belgium, 1963.

Dionysius, the Areopagite. "On the Divine Names." In *Pseudo-Dionysius: The Complete Works.* Translated by Colm Luibheid. London: SPCK, 1987.

Dooley, Mark. "The Becoming Possible of the Impossible: An Interview with Jacques Derrida by Mark Dooley." In *From Aquinas to Derrida: John D. Caputo in Focus.* Bloomington: Indiana University Press, 2001.

Dubarle, Dominique. *Dieu avec l'être: De Parménide à saint Thomas, essai d'ontologie théologale.* Paris: Beauchesne, 1986.

——. "La Nomination ontologique de Dieu." In *L'Ontologie de Thomas D'Aquin.* Paris: Éditions du Cerf, 1996.

Dupré, Louis. "Husserl's Thought on God." *Philosophy and Phenomenological Research* 29 (1969).

Dupuy, Bernard. "Heidegger et le Dieu inconnu." In *Heidegger et la question de Dieu*, edited by Richard Kearney and Joseph S. O'Leary. Paris: Grasset, 1980.

Elveton, R. O., ed. *The Phenomenology of Husserl.* Chicago: Quadrangle, 1970.

The Encyclopaedia Judaica. London: Macmillan, 1971–72.

Feraudy, Roselyne de. *L'Icône de la Transfiguration. Spiritualité orientale*, no. 23 (1978).

Ford, Lewis. "Creativity in a Future Key." In *New Essays in Metaphysics*, edited by Robert C. Neville. Albany: SUNY Press, 1987.

Fox, Michael. *The Song of Songs and the Ancient Egyptian Love Songs.* Madison: University of Wisconsin Press, 1985.

Fromm, Erich. *You Shall Be as Gods: A Radical Interpretation of the Old Testament and Its Tradition.* New York: Fawcett, 1966.

Gesché, Adolphe. "Apprendre de Dieu ce qu'il est." In *Qu'est-ce que Dieu?* Brussels: Publications des Facultés Universitaires Saint-Louis, 1985.

Gese, Hartmut, "Der Name Gottes." In *Alttestamentliche Studien.* Tubingen: J. C. B. Mohr, 1991.

Gilson, Étienne. *The Elements of Christian Philosophy.* New York: New American Library, 1960.

——. *The Spirit of Mediæval Philosophy.* Paris: Vrin, 1941.

Gingerich, Owen. "Leonardo Da Vici: Codex Leicester." In *Museum of Science* (Boston) (winter 1997).

Goncalves, Paul. "Vital Necrographies: Deconstruction, God, and Arche-Idolatry." *Scottish Journal of Religious Studies* 19, no. 1 (1999): 83–100.

Gratton, Peter, and John Manoussakis, eds. *Traversing the Imaginary.* Evanston, Ill.: Northwestern University Press, forthcoming.

Greeley, Andrew, and Jacob Neusner. *The Bible and Us: A Priest and a Rabbi Read Scripture Together.* New York: Warner Books, 1990.

Gregory of Nyssa. *Vie de Moïse.* 2d ed. Paris: Éditions du Cerf, 1955.

Greisch, Jean. *Le Cogito herméneutique.* Paris: Vrin, 2000.

——. "Penser la Bible: L'Herméneutique philosophique à l'école de l'exégèse biblique." *Revue biblique* 1 (January 2000).

Griffin, David Ray. "Postmodern Theology and A/Theology." In *Varieties of Postmodern Theology,* edited by David Ray Griffin, William A. Bearsdslee, and Joe Holland. Albany: SUNY Press, 1989.

Hartmann, Nicolai. *Möglichkeit und Wirklichkeit.* Berlin: de Gruyter, 1938.

Hederman, Mark Patrick. *Manikon Eros.* Dublin: Veritas, 2000.

Hegel, Georg Wilhelm Friedrich. *The Science of Logic.* Atlantic Highlands, N.J.: Humanities Press, 1989.

Heidegger, Martin. *Being and Time.* Translated by John Macquarrie and Edward Robinson. Oxford: Blackwell, 1962.

——. *Beiträge zur Philosophie: vom Ereignis.* GA 65. Frankfurt am Main: Klostermann, 1994.

——. *An Introduction to Metaphysics.* Translated by Ralph Manheim. New York: Doubleday, 1961.

——. *Kant and the Problem of Metaphysics.* Translated by James S. Churchill. Bloomington: Indiana University Press, 1962.

——. "Letter on Humanism." Translated by Edgar Lohner. In *Phenomenology and Existentialism,* by Richard Zaner and Don Ihde. New York: Capricorn Books, 1973.

——. *On Time and Being.* Translated by Joan Stambaugh. New York: Harper and Row, 1972.

——. " . . . Poetically Man Dwells. . . ." In *Poetry, Language, Thought.* New York: Harper and Row, 1971.

Herbert, A. "The Song of Songs." In *Peake's Commentary on the Bible,* edited by Matthew Black and H. H. Rowley. London: T. Nelson, 1962.

Hess, Moses. *Der Hebraische Gottesname* (1862). Jerusalem, 1954.

——. *Rome and Jerusalem.* Translated by Meyer Waxman. New York: Bloch, 1943.

Hillesum, Etty. *An Interrupted Life.* New York: Owl Books, 1996.

Husserl, Edmund. *Cartesian Meditations.* Translated by Dorion Cairns. The Hague: Nijhoff, 1960.

Janicaud, Dominique. *La Phénoménologie éclatée.* Paris: Éditions de l'Éclat, 1998.

——. *Le Tournant théologique de la phénoménologie française.* Combas: l'Éclat, 1991.

Jerome. *Commentaries in Zachariam.* In *Opera Exegetica.* Turnholti: Brepolis, 1959–70.

Jonas, Hans. "The Concept of God after Auschwitz: A Jewish Voice." In *Mortality and Morality: A Search for the Good after Auschwitz,* edited by Lawrence Vogel. Evanston, Ill.: Northwestern University Press, 1996.

Kearney, Richard. *Dialogues with Contemporary Continental Thinkers.* Manchester: Manchester University Press, 1984. Republished as *States of Mind: Dialogues with Contemporary Thinkers.* New York: New York University Press, 1995.

———."Eschatology of the Possible God." In *The Religious: Readings in Continental Philosophy*, edited by John D. Caputo. Oxford: Blackwell, 2001.

———. "The God Who May Be." In *Questioning God*, edited by John D. Caputo, Mark Dooley, and Michael J. Scanlon. Bloomington: Indiana University Press, 2001.

———."Heidegger, Le Possible et Dieu." In *Heidegger et la question de Dieu*, edited by Richard Kearney and Joseph S. O'Leary. Paris: Grasset, 1980.

———."Khora or God?" In *From Aquinas to Derrida: John D. Caputo in Focus*, edited by Mark Dooley. Forthcoming, 2002.

———. *On Stories*. London: Routledge, 2001.

———. *Poetics of Imagining: Modern to Post-modern*. New York: Fordham University Press, 1998.

———. *The Poetics of Modernity: Toward a Hermeneutic Imagination*. Atlantic Highlands, N.J.: Humanities Press, 1995.

———. *Poétique du possible: Phénoménologie herméneutique de la figuration*. Paris: Beauchesne, 1984.

———. *Strangers, Gods, and Monsters*. London: Routledge, 2002.

———. "Transfiguring God." In *Companion to Postmodern Theology*, edited by Graham Ward. Oxford: Blackwell, 2001.

———. *The Wake of Imagination*. London: Routledge, 1994.

Kearney, Richard, and Ghislain Lafont. *Il Desiderio e Dio*. Milan: San Paolo, 1997.

Kearney, Richard, and Joseph S. O'Leary, eds. *Heidegger et la question de Dieu*. Paris: Grasset, 1981.

Kearney, Richard, and Mark Dooley, eds. *Questioning Ethics: Contemporary Debates in Philosophy*. London: Routledge, 1998.

Kisiel, Theodore. *The Genesis of Heidegger's Being and Time*. Berkeley: University of California Press, 1993.

Kisiel, Theodore, and John van Buren, eds. *Reading Heidegger from the Start*. Albany: SUNY Press, 1994.

Kojève, Alexandre. *Introduction to the Reading of Hegel*. Edited by Allan Bloom. Translated by James H. Nichols, Jr. New York: Basic Books, 1969.

Kosman, L. A. "What Does the Maker Mind Make." In *Essays on Aristotle's De Anima*, edited by Martha C. Nussbaum and Amélie Oksenberg Rorty. Oxford: Clarendon Press, 1992.

Kovacs, George. *The Question of God in Heidegger's Phenomenology*. Evanston, Ill.: Northwestern University Press, 1990.

Kristeva, Julia. *Etrangers à nous-mêmes*. Paris: Fayard, 1988. Translated by Leon S. Roudiez under the title *Strangers to Ourselves* (London: Harvester Press, 1991).

———. *Nations without Nationalism*. Translated by Leon S. Roudiez. New York: Columbia University Press, 1993.

———. *Tales of Love*. Translated by Leon S. Roudiez. New York: Columbia University Press, 1987.

LaCocque, André. "The Revelation of Revelations." In *Thinking Biblically: Exegetical and Hermeneutical Studies*, by André LaCocque and Paul Ricoeur. Translated by David Pellauer. Chicago: University of Chicago Press, 1998.

———."The Shulamite." In *Thinking Biblically: Exegetical and Hermeneutical Studies*. Edited by Paul Ricoeur and André LaCocque. Translated by David Pellauer. Chicago: University of Chicago Press, 1998.

Leask, Ian. *Questions of Platonism*. London: Greenwich Exchange, 2000.

Levinas, Emmanuel. *L'au-delà du verset*. Paris: Éditions du Minuit, 1982.

———. *Autrement qu'être; ou, Au-delà de l'essence*. The Hague: Nijhoff, 1974. Translated by Alphonso Lingis under the title *Otherwise Than Being, or Beyond Essence* (Pittsburgh: Duquesne University Press, 1998).

———. *Beyond the Verse: Talmudic Readings and Lectures*. Translated by Gary D. Mole. London: Athlone Press, 1994.

———. *De Dieu qui vient à l'idée*. Paris: Vrin, 1982.

———. *Entre nous: Essais sur le penser-à-l'autre*. Paris: Grasset, 1991.

———. *Le Temps et l'autre*. Paris: Fata Morgana, 1979.

———. *Totality and Infinity: An Essay on Exteriority*. Translated by Alphonso Lingis. Pittsburgh: Duquesne University Press, 1969.

Madec, Goulven. *Le Dieu D'Augustin*. Paris: Éditions du Cerf, 1998.

Magliola, Robert. *On Deconstructing Life-Worlds: Buddhism, Christianity, Culture*. Atlanta: Scholars Press, 1997.

Maimonides. *The Guide of the Perplexed*. Translated by Shlomo Pines. Chicago: University of Chicago Press, 1963.

Manoussakis, John. "I-M-Possible: Contrapunctus et Augmentationem" In *Traversing the Imaginary*, edited by John Manoussakis and Peter Gratton. Evanston, Ill.: Northwestern University Press, forthcoming.

———. "From Exodus to Eschaton: On the God Who May Be." *Modern Theology*, October 2001.

Marcel, Gabriel. *Coleridge et Schelling*. Paris: Aubier-Montaigne, 1971.

Marion, Jean-Luc. *Etant donné: Essai d'une phénoménologie de la donation*. Paris: Presses Universitaires de France, 1997.

———. *God without Being*. Translated by Thomas A. Carlson. Chicago: University of Chicago Press, 1991.

———. *L'Idole et la distance*. Paris: Grasset, 1977.

———. "L'Idole et l'icône." *Revue de métaphysique et de morale*, no. 4 (1979): 433–445.

———. "In the Name: How to Avoid Speaking of Negative Theology." In *God, the Gift, and Postmodernism*, edited by John D. Caputo and Michael J. Scanlon. Bloomington: Indiana University Press, 1999.

———. "The Saturated Phenomenon." In *Phenomenology and the "Theological Turn,"* by Dominique Janicaud et al. New York: Fordham University Press, 2000.

Marsh, James L., John D. Caputo, and Merold Westphal, eds. *Modernity and Its Discontents*. New York: Fordham University Press, 1992.

Meister Eckhart. *God Awaits You*. Edited by Richard Chilson. Notre Dame, Ind.: Ave Maria Press, 1996.

———. *Meister Eckhart: A Modern Translation*. By Raymond Bernard Blakney. New York: Harper, 1941.

Melville, Herman. *Moby Dick*. New York: Modern Library, 1930.

Merleau-Ponty, Maurice. *The Phenomenology of Perception*. Translated by Colin Smith. New York: Routledge, 1962.

———. *The Visible and the Invisible*. Edited by Claude Lefort. Translated by Alphonso Lingis. Evanston, Ill.: Northwestern University Press, 1968.

Merton, Thomas. *No Man Is an Island*, Kent: Burns and Oates, 1997.

Mooney, Timothy. "Deconstruction, Process, and Openness: Philosophy in Derrida, Husserl, and Whitehead." In *Framing a Vision of the World*, edited by André Cloots and Santiago Sia. Leuven: Leuven University Press, 1999.

Muller, John P., and William J. Richardson. *Lacan and Language*. New York: International Universities Press, 1982.

Nicholas of Cusa. *Trialogus de Possest*. In *A Concise Introduction to the Philosophy of Nicholas of Cusa*, by Jasper Hopkins. Minneapolis: University of Minnesota Press, 1980.

———. *Trialogus de Possest*, edited by Robert Steiger. Hamburg: Felix Meiner Verlag, 1973.

———. *The Vision of God*. Translated by Emma Gurney Salter. New York: E. P. Dutton, 1928.

O'Leary, Joseph S. *Questioning Back: The Overcoming of Metaphysics in Christian Tradition*. Minneapolis: Winston Press, 1985.

———. *Religious Pluralism and Christian Truth*. Edinburgh: Edinburgh University Press, 1996.

———. *La Vérité chrétienne à l'âge du pluralisme religieux*. Paris: Éditions du Cerf, 1994.

O'Rourke, Fran. *Pseudo-Dionysius and the Metaphysics of Aquinas*. Leiden: Brill, 1992.

Price, Lucien, ed. *Dialogues of Alfred Whitehead*. New York: New American Library, 1964.

Procopius of Gaza. *Commentary on Genesis*. Patrologiæ Cursus Completus: Series Græca, edited by J.-P. Migne, vol. 87. Paris, 1851.

Quignard, Pascal. *Le Sexe et l' effroi*. Paris: Gallimard, 1994.

Rad, Gerhard von. *Old Testament Theology*. Translated by D. M. G. Stalker. New York: Harper, 1962.

Rahner, Hugo. *Der spielende Mensch*. Rhein: Verlag, 1949.

Rashi. *The Torah: With Rashi's Commentary*. Translated by Rabbi Yisrael Isser Zvi Herczeg. The Sapirstein Edition, 4th ed. New York: Mesorah Publications, 1997.

Richardson, William J. *Heidegger: Through Phenomenology to Thought*. The Hague: Nijhoff, 1963.

———. "In the Name of the Father: The Law." In *Questioning Ethics*, edited by Richard Kearney and Mark Dooley. New York: Routledge, 1998.

Ricoeur, Paul. *Autrement*. Paris: Presses Universitaires de France, 1997.

———. "D'un testament à l'autre: Essai d'herméneutique biblique." In *La Mémoire et le temps: Mélanges offerts à Pierre Bonnard*. Edited by Daniel Marguerat and Jean Zumstein. Geneva: Labor et Fides, 1991.

———. *Freud and Philosophy: An Essay on Interpretation*. Translated by Denis Savage. New Haven, Conn.: Yale University Press, 1970.

———. "From Interpretation to Translation." In *Thinking Biblically: Exegetical and Hermeneutic Studies*, by André LaCocque and Paul Ricoeur. Translated by David Pellauer. Chicago: University of Chicago Press, 1998.

———. "Heidegger et la question du sujet." In *Le Conflit des interprétations*. Paris: Éditions du Seuil, 1969.

———. *Lectures on Ideology and Utopia*. Edited by George H. Taylor. New York: Columbia University Press, 1986.

———. "La Liberté selon l'espérance." In *Le Conflit des interprétations*. Paris: Éditions du Seuil, 1969.

———. "The Nuptial Metaphor." In *Thinking Biblically: Exegetical and Hermeneutic Studies*, by André LaCocque and Paul Ricoeur. Translated by David Pellauer. Chicago: University of Chicago Press, 1998.

———. "Paul Ricoeur: Un parcours philosophique" (interview with François Ewald). *Magazine littéraire* 390 (2000): 20–27.

Rosenzweig, Franz. "The Eternal: Mendelssohn and the Name of God." In *Scripture and Translation*, by Martin Buber and Franz Rosenzweig. Translated by Lawrence Rosenwald and Everett Fox. Bloomington: Indiana University Press, 1994.

Sartre, Jean-Paul. *Being and Nothingness*. Translated by Hazel E. Barnes. New York: Philosophical Library, 1956.

———. *The Psychology of Imagination*. New York: Citadel Press, 1972.

Schelling, Friedrich. *Of Human Freedom*. Translated by James Gutmann. Chicago: Open Court, 1936.

Seidel, George. "Heidegger's Last God and the Schelling Connection." *Laval théologique et philosophique* 55, no. I (1999): 85–98.

Sidiropoulos, Christos. "L'Homme Jesus et le principe trinitaire." Ph.D. thesis, University of Strasbourg, 1978.

Strasser, Stephen. "Das Gottesproblem in der Spätsphilosophie Edmund Husserl." *Philosophisches Jahrbuch* (1967).

Taylor, Charles. *A Catholic Modernity?* Dayton: University of Dayton Press, 1996.

Tertullian. *Adversus Prazean*. Patrologiæ Cursus Completus: Series Latina, edited by J.-P. Migne, vol. 2. Paris, 1878.

Tilliette, X. "Husserl et la notion de la nature." *Revue de métaphysique et de morale* 70 (1965).

Van Buren, John. *The Young Heidegger: Rumor of the Hidden King*. Bloomington: Indiana University Press, 1994.

Vogel, Lawrence, ed. *Mortality and Morality: A Search for the Good after Auschwitz*. Evanston, Ill.: Northwestern University Press, 1996.

Volozhyn, Rabbi Hayyhim de. *Nefesh Hahayyim*. Translated into French as *L'Ame de la vie*. Paris: Verdier, 1986.

Vries, Hent de. *Philosophy and the Turn to Religion*. Baltimore: Johns Hopkins University Press, 1999.

Waters, Lindsay, and Wlad Godzich, eds. *Reading de Man Reading*. Minneapolis: University of Minnesota Press, 1989.

Whitehead, Alfred. *Dialogues of Alfred North Whitehead*, recorded by Lucien Price. New York: New American Library, 1964.

———. *Process and Reality*. New York: Free Press, 1978.

Wills, Garry. *Saint Augustine*. New York: Viking, 1999.

Zimmerli, Walter. *I Am Yahweh*. Atlanta: John Knox, 1982.

Zizek, Slavoj. *On Belief*. London: Routledge, 2001.

———. *The Ticklish Subject*. London: Verso, 1999.

Zumbrunn, Emilie. "L'exégèse augustinienne de 'Ego sum qui sum' et la 'Métaphysique de l'Exode.' " In *Dieu et l'être*. Centre d'Études des Religions du Livre. Paris: Études Augustiniennes, 1978.

INDEX

Index

Richard Kearney is a professor of philosophy at Boston College and University College Dublin. He is the author of numerous books on modern philosophy and culture, as well as two novels and a volume of poetry. His books have been translated into many European languages. In recent years he has been engaged in debates on ethics, aesthetics, and religion with such continental philosophers as Ricoeur, Derrida, Kristeva, Levinas, and Caputo.